STRATEGY, LAW, AND ETHICS FOR BUSINESS DECISIONS

CHRISTINE LADWIG
SOUTHEAST MISSOURI STATE UNIVERSITY

GEORGE SIEDEL
UNIVERSITY OF MICHIGAN

WEST
ACADEMIC
PUBLISHING

© 2020 LEG, Inc. d/b/a West Academic
    444 Cedar Street, Suite 700
    St. Paul, MN 55101
    1-877-888-1330

West, West Academic Publishing, and West Academic are trademarks of West Publishing Corporation, used under license.

Printed in the United States of America

ISBN: 978-1-64242-610-6

Acknowledgments

This book is the product of the shared advice, experience, and wisdom of the students, business leaders, entrepreneurs, and professionals with whom we have worked over the years. We have learned from them that the decision making concepts covered in this book are valuable in all types of organizations and in all cultures.

We thank the outstanding researchers whose work has improved business decision making theory and practice over the years. This book includes citations to their publications. In an era of powerful search engines, detailed citations are unnecessary. Instead, brief citations like the ones in this book provide enough information to enable you to easily locate the sources. Although the book includes many citations to primary legal sources, discussions of the law in this book are not intended and should not be construed as legal advice.

We acknowledge and thank the publishers of earlier books that relate to the Three Pillar model. Chapters 4 and 5 have been adapted and updated from George Siedel's book *Using the Law for Competitive Advantage* (Jossey-Bass) and Chapters 8 and 9 are adapted from his book *Negotiating for Success: Essential Strategies and Skills* (Van Rye Publishing, LLC).

Many thanks to Helena Haapio, International Contract Counsel for Lexpert Ltd. in Helsinki, Finland, and a leader in the Proactive Law Movement in Europe. Parts of Chapter 8 are adapted from two publications that she coauthored with George Siedel: a book titled *A Short Guide to Contract Risk* (Gower 2013) and the article "Using Proactive Law for Competitive Advantage" in the *American Business Law Journal*.

Thank you to Van Rye Publishing, LLC, for providing outstanding editorial services in the preparation of this book and the earlier trade publication from which it has been adapted, *The Three Pillar Model for Business Decisions: Strategy, Law & Ethics*.

Thanks to Glenn P. Ladwig, patent attorney and partner at Saliwanchik, Lloyd & Eisenschenck, for his suggestions and contributions to Chapter 7.

Thank you to reviewers Susan Marsnik (University of St. Thomas) and Adam Sulkowski (Babson College) for sharing their advice and expertise. The Association of Law Teachers has honored Professor Marsnik with a lifetime achievement award for her contributions to legal education. Professor Sulkowski is an award-winning scholar who is especially well-known for his research on law and sustainability.

We also very much appreciate the support and assistance of Sarah Bowser Agan, Acquisitions Editor, and the West Academic Publications team: Laura Holle, Carol Logie, Greg Olson and Rebecca Schneider.

Introduction

This is a book about competition. We live in a global economy that is driven by fierce competition for business and career success. For those of you with drive and a competitive spirit, the goal in writing this book is to help you succeed. This requires that you understand the three pillars that are the foundation of business decisions: strategy, law and ethics. Understanding these pillars is also valuable when you make any type of personal or leadership decision.

This book takes you through four steps that enable you to use the Three Pillar model for business decisions:

Step One: Become a legally savvy leader. This does not require memorization of legal rules. Instead, you should understand how the law works in practice. Various surveys have identified the key legal areas that every business leader should understand: product liability, employment law, government regulation, intellectual property, contracts, and dispute resolution. This book provides briefings on each area and shows how they impact your key stakeholders: customers, employees, government, and investors.

Step Two: Become an effective risk manager for the strategies you develop. After your briefings on the law, you are now ready to focus on the Law Pillar. The Law Pillar emphasizes risk management. This book explains how to manage the legal risks that constitute the main threat to your business success. For example, the chapter on product liability describes how to make strategic new product decisions, how to isolate product risks by creating subsidiaries, and how to design new products to minimize the risk of being sued for selling a defective product.

Step Three: Align the Strategy Pillar with the Law and Ethics Pillars to create value. This step applies an understanding of how each element contributes to effective, holistic decisions. Many leaders think that there is an inherent tension between the Strategy Pillar, with its value creation orientation, and the Law Pillar, with its risk management orientation. This book explains how you can overcome this tension and align the two pillars by focusing on the interests of each of your stakeholders. For example, by focusing on customer interests, a process designed to prevent product liability can be transformed into a powerful product development tool.

Step Four: Develop an ethical organization. Understanding the Ethics Pillar of decision making enables you to play a leadership role in developing compliance and values standards for your organization. This role requires that you "walk the talk" by using a principled process for making ethical decisions. As discussed in Chapter 3, by combining the Ethics Pillar with the Law Pillar and the Strategy Pillar, you can become a responsible corporate citizen while at the same time creating value for your shareholders and other stakeholders.

According to a quote attributed to J. Irwin Miller, former CEO of Cummins, Inc., "A healthy branch cannot survive on a rotten trunk." We hope that this book will enable you to grow a healthy branch—your business—while also nourishing the healthy trunk that symbolizes the environment in which business operates.

About the Authors

Christine Ladwig is an associate professor of business law at Harrison College of Business and Computing, Southeast Missouri State University. She has received undergraduate and graduate degrees in the life and physical sciences, including a Ph.D. in Biology (The George Washington University), and degrees in law and accounting, including a joint J.D.-M.Acc. (Southern Illinois University), and a LL.M. in Intellectual Property Law (Albany Law School). She currently maintains three active licenses to practice law in the states of California, Illinois, and Missouri.

Professor Ladwig has received finalist awards in business law teaching competitions, and has published numerous refereed journal articles, case studies, conference proceedings, and a textbook chapter. She has also received several national awards recognizing outstanding, distinguished, or meritorious paper submissions. She is a co-founder and current Editor-in-Chief of the *Journal of Business Law and Ethics Pedagogy* (JBLEP), a peer-reviewed national journal focusing on educational exercises and methodology in business law and ethics.

George Siedel is the Williamson Family Professor of Business Administration and the Thurnau Professor of Business Law at the Ross School of Business, University of Michigan. He completed his graduate studies at the University of Michigan and Cambridge University. He has served as a visiting professor at Stanford University and Harvard University and as a Visiting Scholar at University of California, Berkeley. As a Fulbright Scholar, he held a Distinguished Chair in the Humanities and Social Sciences.

Professor Siedel has received several research and teaching awards, including the Maurer Award, the Ralph Bunche Award, the Hoeber Award, and the Executive Program Professor of the Year Award from an international consortium of thirty-six leading universities. In 2018, he received the Distinguished Career Achievement Award from the Academy of Legal Studies in Business.

The Organization of This Book

This book uses a Three Pillar model that reflects three critically-important aspects of decision making: formulating a *Strategy*, understanding the applicable *Law*, and applying *Ethics*. In Chapters 1–3, we introduce the Three Pillar model. These chapters show you how to create value when making business decisions by combining strategy, law, and ethics.

The remaining chapters show you how to apply the model when dealing with specific stakeholders and risks. Surveys of business leaders have identified the key stakeholders affected when you make business decisions, as well as the top risks affecting companies. In this book, we align the stakeholders with business risks and ethics so that you can adopt a legally-savvy and ethically-sound management style and ultimately create value for stakeholders.

According to survey data, the four key business stakeholders are:

1. Customers
2. Employees
3. Government
4. Investors

Other surveys have concluded that the top risks affecting companies are:

1. Tort Law (including Product Liability)
2. Employment Law
3. Regulatory Law
4. Intellectual Property Law
5. Contracts
6. Dispute Resolution

This book links the four key stakeholders to the first four risks. This structure enables you to become legally savvy about these risks while at the same time understanding how to manage them and create value for your stakeholders. For example, Chapter 4 links the first stakeholder (your customers) to the first risk (tort and product liability law—a major risk for business). That chapter, titled "Transform Product Liability into Product Innovation," includes these elements:

- **Legal briefing:** The features of tort and product liability law that every business decision-maker should understand to become legally savvy

- **Risk management:** Business strategies and solutions to minimize product liability

- **Interest-based value creation:** Aligning the Strategy Pillar with the Law Pillar to create value for stakeholders

- **Three Pillars cases:** Summaries and excerpts from court cases with discussion questions you can use to test your understanding of the material in the chapter

- **Key takeaways:** An executive summary of the chapter

- **Three Pillars decisions:** Scenarios that enable you to practice using the Three Pillars (Strategy, Law, and Ethics) when making business decisions

Chapters 5 through 7 link the other three key stakeholders—employees, government, and investors—with areas of the law that are especially relevant to them:

- Chapter 5: Use Employment Law to Attract and Retain the Best Business Talent

- Chapter 6: Use Government Regulation to Develop New Business Models

- Chapter 7: Use Your Intellectual Property to Create Shareholder Value

Chapters 8 and 9 address the final two significant business risks identified by surveys of business leaders: contract and dispute resolution processes. Understanding these processes is especially important because they affect all stakeholders.

- Chapter 8: Develop Contracts That Create Value for Both Sides

- Chapter 9: Use Dispute Resolution Processes for Value Creation

Like Chapter 4, Chapters 5–9 include these features: a legal briefing, risk management to minimize your liability, interest-based value creation, court cases, key takeaways, and decision making scenarios. In some cases, the interest-based value creation perspective even provides ideas for new business models based on opportunities the law creates. An example is Chapter 4's coverage of the

Regulatory Gap Strategy, which has been used by companies like Southwest Airlines and Uber.

The ultimate goal of this book is to enable you to make ethically-responsible decisions that minimize your legal risks while creating value for your business and its stakeholders. Our hope is that your ability to use the Three Pillar model when making business decisions will also add value when making decisions in other areas of your life—even when ordering a pizza, as described in the opening of Chapter 1.

Summary of Contents

Table of Contents

Table of Cases

STRATEGY, LAW, AND ETHICS
FOR BUSINESS DECISIONS

CHAPTER 1

Meet the Three Pillar Model (Strategy, Law, Ethics)

EVERYDAY DECISIONS AND THE THREE PILLARS

While your friend is driving to your apartment, you develop a sudden craving for pizza and place an order with a nearby restaurant. You then text your friend and ask her to pick up the pizza on the way to your apartment.

US President Barack Obama decides, in his words, "to make the killing or capture of Osama bin Laden the top priority of our war against al Qaeda." He then authorizes the operation that results in bin Laden's death.

What does your personal decision to buy a pizza have in common with the President's leadership decision?

Both scenarios illustrate the Three Pillars that provide the foundation for decisions in business, leadership, and everyday life: strategy, law, and ethics. This book focuses on the Three Pillars as they relate to business decisions. But these pillars are also important when making a variety of decisions beyond business, ranging from your personal decision to order a pizza to the President's decision to authorize the bin Laden operation.

Let's start with the pizza example. You probably did not complete a Three Pillar analysis when deciding to ask your friend to pick up your dinner. But had you done so, your focus might have been only on the Strategy Pillar. In the language of strategy, your decision focused on "formulating" and "implementing" a strategy. You formulated your strategic goal—acquiring a pizza—and developed an implementation plan that involved ordering the pizza and texting your friend to ask her to pick it up. In all likelihood, you did not consider the legal and ethical implications of your strategy. But your failure to consider the Law and Ethics

Pillars does not mean they were absent. And this failure might have dramatic consequences for you, your friend, and others.

Consider the case of *Kubert v. Best*, decided in 2013 by an appellate court in New Jersey. The case resulted from an accident on September 21, 2009. A husband and wife were riding a motorcycle when a pickup truck heading in the opposite direction crossed the centerline and struck them. The husband and wife were severely injured, and their left legs had to be amputated. Immediately before the accident, a friend sent a text message to the truck driver, and he responded by texting a reply. The husband and wife sued both the driver and his friend. They settled with the driver, and the case proceeded against the friend who sent the message.

The court noted that under New Jersey law, it is illegal to drive while using a cell phone that is not hands-free, and a driver who injures someone using a handheld cell phone is subject to a possible prison sentence. But this case's resolution did not turn on criminal law or the driver's involvement. Instead, the issue was whether someone who sends a text to a driver can be held liable for damages. The court decided that "the sender of a text message can potentially be liable if an accident is caused by texting . . . if the sender knew or had special reason to know that the recipient would view the text while driving and thus be distracted." Despite this potential liability, the court decided that the friend who sent the text was not liable in this case because there was no proof that she "knew or had special reason to know that the driver would read the message while driving. . . ."

As this case illustrates, when you are considering the strategic decision (the Strategy Pillar) of whether and how to obtain a pizza, you should also consider whether your decision is legal (the Law Pillar). In this situation, the Law Pillar of decision making requires you to consider liability for damages. This pillar also involves decision making under uncertainty. For example, if you aren't in New Jersey, how likely is it that the country or state where you are located will apply a rule similar to the New Jersey rule? And even if you are in New Jersey, do the facts in your case fall within the rule? In other words, how likely is it that a jury would decide that you knew or had a special reason to know that your friend would read the text while driving?

If you are risk-averse, you probably would decide to change your strategic implementation plan by, say, asking the restaurant to deliver the pizza or making the pizza yourself. But even if you proceed as originally planned despite the legal risk, you must still consider the third pillar—the Ethics Pillar. Is it ethical to place your friend (and others) at risk by texting her while she is driving? Considering the Ethics Pillar is important even when you are absolutely certain that your decisions are legal.

Let's now move from this personal decision to leadership decision making—President Obama's decision to authorize the operation that led to bin Laden's death. The President and his advisors initially focused on the Strategy Pillar as they formulated the strategy to capture or kill bin Laden. They also developed an implementation plan—the raid on bin Laden's compound.

With a strategy in place, the President then focused on the Law Pillar. His strategy, like virtually any other personal, business, or leadership strategy, raised several legal questions. Three questions were especially important: did the President have the legal right to "authorize a lethal mission, to delay telling Congress until afterward, and to bury a wartime enemy [bin Laden] at sea"?[1]

According to an account in *The New York Times*,[2] a few days before the raid, a top-secret team of four lawyers provided the President with legal advice relating to these questions. As with most legal advice, the law was not entirely clear. And like other political or business leaders, the President had to decide whether to proceed under conditions of legal uncertainty. In addition, even if the law clearly supported the strategy, the President still had to consider the Ethics Pillar: what were the ethical ramifications of authorizing a mission to kill bin Laden?

As these examples illustrate, the Three Pillar model provides the framework for everyday decisions as simple as ordering a pizza and leadership decisions as complex as the bin Laden raid. This model is especially important in making business decisions, which are the focus of this book. Business decision-makers who overemphasize the Strategy Pillar to the detriment of the Law and Ethics Pillars risk destroying their companies and careers.

ORIGINS OF THE THREE PILLAR MODEL

The Three Pillar model has foundations in naturalistic, philosophical, and sociological theories. In "How Relationality Shapes Business Ethics," Timothy L. Fort (Everleigh Chair in Business Ethics in the Business Law and Ethics Department at Indiana University's Kelley School of Business) provides an insightful analysis of the Three Pillar model's origins. The end result of his analysis is a framework that enables business leaders to take "into account all the forces that are a natural part of human life" when making decisions. These forces are based on "legal, economic, and ecologizing (integrity-based) values."[3]

Emphasizing a corporate social responsibility perspective but arriving at a conclusion similar to Fort's model, Archie B. Carroll (a professor emeritus at the

University of Georgia's Terry College of Business) and Mark S. Schwartz (a business law and ethics professor at York University) developed a three-domain model that builds on earlier work by Carroll. In their model, the three overlapping domains are economic, legal, and ethical.

Their concept of the economic domain covers activities designed to have a positive economic impact on a business, specifically "(i) the maximization of profits and/or (ii) the maximization of share value." They divide the legal domain into three categories: compliance, avoidance of civil litigation, and anticipation of changes in legislation. The ethical domain "refers to the ethical responsibilities of business as expected by the general population and relevant stakeholders."[4]

TRANSLATING THEORY INTO PRACTICE: THE HARVARD MODEL

The clearest practical perspective on the Three Pillar model comes from the Harvard Business School (HBS). Years ago, HBS designed a module called "Leadership, Values and Decision Making" that was taught to all students entering the school's MBA program. Although the module appeared to successfully address the intersection of economic, legal, and ethical issues that shape business decisions, faculty members at Harvard "examined the need to teach more about business law" in light of the globalization of business and increased use of technology.[5] The faculty eventually voted to expand the module into an entire course that all MBA students would be required to take. Following input from many stakeholders (students, alumni, advisory boards, etc.), the course was offered for the first time in 2004 under the name "Leadership and Corporate Accountability" (LCA).

Professor Lynn Sharp Paine was one of the key leaders in developing the course. Paine, the John G. McLean Professor at Harvard Business School, holds a law degree from Harvard and a doctorate in moral philosophy from Oxford. Although she has earned international renown for high-quality research, Paine emphasizes the practical focus when she describes the course: "We are training future practitioners. . . . We focus not on rare events or abstract issues in moral philosophy, but on decisions that students will have to make in their careers."[6]

LCA focuses on three key elements—economics, law, and ethics—that form the foundation for decision making in business. As described in the 2011 online version of the course syllabus, a business leader's responsibilities "fall into three broad categories: economic, legal, and ethical. Economic responsibilities relate to resource allocation and wealth creation; legal responsibilities flow from formal laws and regulations; and ethical responsibilities have to do with basic principles and standards of conduct."[7]

The HBS course mirrors the theoretical work by Fort, Carroll, and Schwartz: "Using the tripartite framework of economics, law, and ethics, we will consider decisions that involve responsibilities to each of the company's core constituencies—investors, customers, employees, suppliers, and the public." These constituencies are also called stakeholders—that is, those who have an interest (a "stake") in the business.

Like other courses at HBS, LCA is not static and continues to evolve to reflect new issues and cases. The online syllabus illustrates the types of issues addressed in the course that relate to the four constituencies. These issues include fiduciary duties, insider trading, conflicts of interest, product liability, fraud, the employment-at-will doctrine, labor law, discrimination, environmental responsibility, privacy, and property rights.

The course is especially challenging and important because it takes students beyond the basics covered in introductory courses on finance, marketing, operations, and so on into what the syllabus calls the "grey areas" of business. These real-world grey areas are shaped by the economics, law, and ethics triad that is a staple of everyday business decision making. The overlap of the three perspectives is depicted by a diagram from a course overview that students receive at the beginning of LCA.

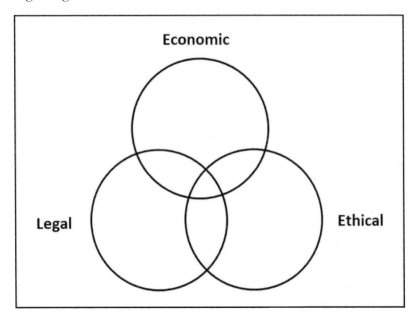

As the course overview notes, "The basic idea is that outstanding managers develop plans of action that fall in the 'sweet spot' at the intersection of their economic, legal, and ethical responsibilities."[8] The course guide for instructors elaborates on what is also described as the "zone of sustainability":[9]

> Actions and strategies that fall inside this zone tend to be acceptable to the firm's constituencies and thus repeatable over time, while those that lie outside typically invite negative repercussions from injured, wronged, or otherwise disappointed parties. Actions outside the zone may even lead to the firm's failure, especially if pursued at length.

The three dimensions of the Harvard model can also be depicted in the form of a decision tree adapted from a diagram developed by Constance Bagley, a senior research fellow at Yale School of Management who previously held business law appointments at Harvard Business School and the Stanford Graduate School of Business. Originally appearing in "The Ethical Leader's Decision Tree,"[10] the tree is reproduced in an article Bagley coauthored with Mark Roellig and Gianmarco Massameno.[11]

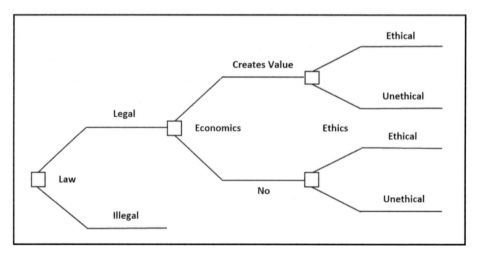

The ideal decision making path would follow the Legal, Creates Value, and Ethical branches, although in some cases, another path might be justified. For example, business leaders might decide to take an action that benefits society even if it doesn't create economic value for shareholders. But this decision may raise legal concerns that will be addressed later in this chapter.

Bagley's decision tree intends to help answer the question: "What's the right thing to do?" Keeping that objective in mind, consider the following case involving Apple, Inc. and the US Government. What's the right thing for Apple to do in these circumstances? The company and federal officials have very different views of the best option to select. This situation illustrates the difficulty companies may encounter in their actions—or lack of actions, as in this circumstance—when economics, law, and ethics are intertwined along the decision making path.

STRATEGY	
LAW	***Three Pillars Case: One Bad Apple***
ETHICS	

In 2016, the US Federal Bureau of Investigation (FBI) sought the assistance of Apple, Inc. to access the iPhone data of terrorist Syed Rizwan Farook. In this Motion to Compel, the Department of Justice (DOJ) argues why the company should cooperate with the FBI's request. This case poses an ethical dilemma for Apple as it tries to balance the interests of all the stakeholders involved.

CASE 5:16-CM-00010-SP: IN THE MATTER OF THE SEARCH OF AN APPLE IPHONE SEIZED DURING THE EXECUTION OF A SEARCH WARRANT ON A BLACK LEXUS IS300 CALIFORNIA LICENSE PLATE 35KGD203

ATTORNEYS FOR THE APPLICANT, UNITED STATES OF AMERICA. Rather than assist the effort to fully investigate a terrorist attack by obeying this court's order of February 16, 2016, Apple has responded by publicly repudiating that order. Apple has attempted to design and market its products to allow technology, rather than the law, to control access to data which has been found by this Court to be warranted for an important investigation. Before Syed Rizwan Farook and his wife Tafsheen Malik shot and killed 14 people and injured 22 others at the Inland Regional Center in San Bernardino, Farook's employer issued him an iPhone. The Federal Bureau of Investigation ("FBI") recovered that iPhone during the investigation into the massacre. . . . The phone may contain critical communications and data prior to and around the time of the shooting that, thus far: (1) has not been accessed; (2) may reside solely on the phone; and (3) cannot be accessed by any other means known to either the government or Apple. The FBI obtained a warrant to search the iPhone, and the owner of the iPhone, Farook's employer, also gave the FBI its consent . . . Because the iPhone was locked, the government subsequently sought Apple's help in its efforts to execute the lawfully issued search warrant. Apple refused.

The Order does not, as Apple's public statement alleges, require Apple to create or provide a "back door" to every iPhone; it does not provide "hackers and criminals" access to iPhones; it does not require Apple to "hack [its] own users" or to "decrypt" its own phones; it does not give the government "the power to reach into anyone's device" without a warrant or court authorization; and it does not compromise the security of personal information. . . . In the past, Apple has consistently complied with a significant number of orders . . . to facilitate the execution of search warrants on Apple devices running earlier versions of iOS. . . . Based on Apple's recent public statement . . . Apple's current refusal to comply with the Court's Order, despite the technical feasibility of doing so, instead appears to be based on its concern for its business model and public brand marketing strategy. Accordingly, the government now brings this motion to compel.

THREE PILLARS CASE QUESTIONS

(1)   Assuming Apple's refusal was legal (the case ended before this was determined because the FBI was able to access the iPhone through another source), do you think Apple's decision would create value for the company and shareholders? For iPhone users? Why?

(2)   Assuming again that Apple's refusal to help the FBI was legal, is this decision ethical? How do you make this determination?

(3)   Apple asserted in its public statement that its help to open Farook's phone would make information and data on all iPhones vulnerable. If true, would this be a valid reason for Apple to refuse to cooperate with the government? The government was later able to gain access to the phone through help from a third party. Does the government now have an ethical obligation to share that access information with Apple?

(4)   What do you believe the government means when they say Apple is refusing to comply because of "concern for its business model and public brand marketing strategy"? If true, is this a valid reason for Apple's noncompliance?

EXPANDING THE HARVARD MODEL

The Harvard model and the decision tree provide a valuable framework for making business decisions. However, by expanding the economics perspective, the model also becomes useful in making decisions beyond the business sphere.

While economics is a key discipline relating to the business goal of value creation, other disciplines and functions also contribute to business success. Business school courses are based on three disciplines in addition to economics—law, psychology, and statistics. The landmark Carnegie study of business education, for instance, recommended that business schools place "heavy weight on preparation in the four foundation areas—quantitative methods, economics, law and public policy, and psychology-sociology," with two required three-credit courses on regulation and law.[12]

Business success depends on key functions that draw on these disciplines. As noted in the opening sentence of a *Harvard Business Review* article on business functions: "Business units come and go, but finance, HR, IT, marketing, legal, and R&D are forever."[13]

The departmental organization of business schools often mirrors key business functions. For example, at the University of Michigan's Ross School of Business the economics discipline is represented by a Business Economics area, while other academic areas reflect the seven key business functions that are present in virtually every major company: (1) Accounting, (2) Business Law, (3) Finance, (4) Management & Organizations, (5) Marketing, (6) Strategy, and (7) Technology and Operations.

Departments at the University of Pennsylvania's Wharton School are organized along the same lines, except that Strategy is included in the Management Department and there are three additional departments—two industry-related (Health Care Management and Real Estate) and one discipline-related (Statistics).

The "Big Seven" functions represented in both company and business school organizational structures are critical to the success of businesses of all sizes. The most important issues facing an entrepreneur starting a business, for example, relate to accounting, financing, legal, marketing, operations, staffing, and strategic concerns.

Strategy is the most likely candidate among the seven functions to replace economics. Defined broadly, strategy involves establishing and achieving goals. In a business setting, strategy focuses on the goal of value creation for shareholders, which brings into play all functions and disciplines, including economics.

Strategy is also an attractive candidate because it is important in all organizations, even nonprofits that are not concerned with generating profits for shareholders. And on a personal level, your strategic ability to establish and achieve goals is key to your success, however you choose to define it. So by replacing economics with strategy, the Three Pillar model (strategy, law, ethics) becomes a framework that is more appropriate for all forms of business, leadership, and personal decision making.

THE THREE PILLAR MODEL AND BUSINESS DECISIONS

Although the Three Pillar model (strategy, law, ethics) can be applied within all organizations (public or private, business or nonprofit) and also when making personal decisions as simple as ordering a pizza, this book focuses on using the model to make business decisions. The key questions that business decision-makers should address are:

1. Strategy Pillar: What is our value creation goal, and how do we intend to achieve it? (*Note: After a strategic plan has been formulated, the remaining two pillars can be considered in either order.*)

2. Law Pillar: How can we manage the legal risks associated with our strategy?

3. Ethics Pillar: Is our proposed strategic decision ethical?

We now examine each of the pillars as they relate to business before turning in Chapter 2 to some of the major challenges in using the Three Pillar model—such as the significant gap between the Strategy Pillar and the Law Pillar.

The Strategy Pillar

According to Pulitzer Prize-winning historian Alfred Chandler, "Strategy is the determination of the basic long-term goals of an enterprise, and the adoption of courses of action and the allocation of resources necessary for carrying out these goals."[14] This definition states the twin aspects of business strategy (as well as other types of strategy): formulating goals and planning for implementation. The late Yogi Berra, a baseball legend, summarized the risk in not having a strategic plan: "If you don't know where you are going, you might wind up someplace else."

The goal in business is often framed in terms of value creation. Harvard professor Michael Porter summarizes the two key issues that form the basis of strategic choice as (1) the attractiveness of industries and (2) the competitive position within an industry.

Industry attractiveness, according to Porter, is determined by "five competitive forces: the entry of new competitors, the threat of substitutes, the bargaining power of buyers, the bargaining power of suppliers, and the rivalry among the existing competitors." Competitive position within an industry is based on value creation and "superior value stems from offering lower prices than competitors for equivalent benefits or providing unique benefits that more than offset a higher price."[15]

Business leaders often frame their goals in terms of value creation for shareholders. The so-called "shareholder primacy" theory asserts that shareholders should have top priority over other corporate stakeholders. This theory has been criticized because, in emphasizing shareholder profits, it allegedly encourages short-term thinking. The legal foundations of this theory are analyzed later, in Chapter 2.

The Law Pillar

According to *Black's Law Dictionary*, law represents "A system of principles and rules of human conduct. . . ." In a business setting, law represents the "rules of the game," the framework for business operations and decision making. As a manager in an executive course at the University of Michigan put it, law provides the architecture in which business is conducted.

Whereas law has always been a key element in business success, its importance accelerated in the last half of the twentieth century. Chayes, Greenwald, and Wing, in a *Harvard Business Review* article published in 1983,[16] referred to the "growth in the scope, nature, and complexity of government regulation" and the "equally rapid rise in consumer, shareholder, employee, and competitor litigation" in concluding that managers need "to include legal advice as an essential element of business planning and decision making."

More recently, the global dimension of business has enhanced the role of law in business decision making. The first question an investor should raise when considering an investment in another country is this: "Does this country have a rule of law or, instead, will the company be subject to the arbitrary whims of government officials?"

This question became especially important after market systems developed in former Communist countries. As George Melloan observed, writing in the *Wall Street Journal*, a market system cannot be established in an emerging economy "without first creating a legal system that protects the right of all individuals to hold, buy or sell property and without corresponding legal protections for the contracts through which those transactions are conducted."[17]

Once you decide that your target country follows the rule of law, you must then understand what the law requires. As Carolyn Hotchkiss (Professor Emeritus and former Dean at Babson College) has observed:

> Law provides the ground rules for international trade and investment in goods, services and technology. An understanding of the ground rules for that trade and investment allows managers to compete successfully

in the most competitive global markets. A working understanding of the international legal environment allows managers to make judgments about the political and business risk of doing business in countries around the world.[18]

Echoing this observation, Jere Morehead, President of the University of Georgia (and Meigs Professor of Legal Studies in the Terry College of Business), has emphasized the importance of international business law courses in business schools.[19] And a survey of business leaders presented at a conference on the Internationalization of US Education in the twenty-first Century concluded that the two most important international skills that companies seek in their professional staff and line managers are an appreciation for cross-cultural differences and an understanding of legal/government requirements.[20]

Surveys of senior executives highlight the importance of the Law Pillar. For example, sessions on law ranked third (behind only Organization Behavior and Finance) in terms of value according to more than nine hundred senior managers attending general, industry, and functional executive programs at the University of Michigan.[21]

This high ranking of law is not surprising given the considerable amount of time business leaders spend on legal issues. Although studies over the years have concluded that leaders spend a high percentage of their time on legal matters, prominent management scholar Henry Mintzberg published the most telling research in his *Harvard Business Review* classic "The Manager's Job: Folklore and Fact."[22] In this article, Mintzberg describes the four roles that managers play as decision-makers: entrepreneur, resource allocator, disturbance handler, and negotiator.

Mintzberg concludes that managers act as *entrepreneurs* when trying to improve the business and adapt it to a changing environment. They act as *resource allocators* in making budgeting decisions, authorizing projects, and designing the organizational structure. Both of these roles are replete with legal issues relating to new product development, marketing plans, department reorganization, mergers and acquisitions, and so on.

Law becomes even more important when managers play their other two roles. Mintzberg notes that as *disturbance handlers*, managers must respond involuntarily when "pressures of a situation are too severe to be ignored—a strike looms, a major customer has gone bankrupt, or a supplier reneges on a contract. . . ."

The manager's role as a *negotiator* is equally important. In Mintzberg's words, "Managers spend considerable time in negotiations: the president of the football team works out a contract with the holdout superstar; the corporation president leads the company's contingent to negotiate a new strike issue; the foreman argues a grievance problem to its conclusion with the shop steward." These negotiations are filled with legal issues because, to cite a familiar adage, negotiation takes place within the shadow of the law.

In addition to these four roles that require them to become legal decision-makers, managers are legal communicators. They must be prepared to discuss legal matters with all company stakeholders—notably investors (and their representatives, the Board of Directors), creditors, customers, employees, suppliers, and government regulators.

Managers' decisional and communication roles increase as they move up the ranks. It is no surprise that they spend considerable time with their lawyers. As the CEO of United States Steel Corporation put it, "The CEO and the GC [General Counsel] must have the kind of relationship in which they're able to practically finish each other's sentences."[23]

The Law Pillar's importance extends beyond its impact on managers in large companies. For example, entrepreneurs starting a business must make decisions regarding

- the legal form of their business,
- government regulations that govern how they develop and market their products and services,
- liability risks in manufacturing and selling their products,
- protection of their intellectual property,
- the nature of their contracts with customers and suppliers,
- legal considerations relating to financing the business, and
- the law that governs hiring employees.

It is no surprise that legendary entrepreneur David Packard, cofounder of Hewlett-Packard, concluded that business law and management accounting were the most valuable courses he took at Stanford's Graduate School of Business.[24]

The Ethics Pillar

In broad terms, ethics focuses on determining whether conduct is right or wrong and "prescribes what humans ought to do in terms of rights, obligations, benefits to society, fairness, or specific virtues."[25] According to the *Stanford Encyclopedia of Philosophy*, when applied to business, ethics is a discipline that focuses on the "moral features of commercial activity."

The Ethics Pillar is especially important because unethical conduct by one company can harm a broad swath of stakeholders, as illustrated by the emissions scandal involving Volkswagen (VW) that erupted in late 2015. At the time, VW was the world's leader in car sales. Shortly after United States government regulators announced that VW had cheated on air pollution tests, VW CEO Martin Winterkorn stated that he was "deeply sorry that we have broken the trust of our customers and the public." The head of VW in the United States put it more bluntly: "Our company was dishonest [with the regulators]. . . . We have totally screwed up."[26]

In addition to its obvious impact on the company, the scandal had a ripple effect on many stakeholders. The following Reuters headlines, printed in the months following Winterkorn's announcement, reveal the impact not only on VW's leaders and shareholders but also on Germany, the local community, government regulators, employees, the diesel industry, suppliers, and customers.

- Shareholders: "VW Shares Plunge on Emissions Scandal"

- Germany: "Volkswagen Scandal Threatens 'Made in Germany' Image"

- Community: "Diesel Scandal Casts Gloom Over VW's Home Town"

- Regulators: "VW Scandal Exposes Cozy Ties Between Industry and Berlin"

- Company Leaders: "Former VW Boss Investigated for Fraud"

- Employees: "VW Halts Hiring at Financing Arm After Emissions Scandal"

- Industry: "VW Rivals Risk Bigger Blow as Emissions Scandal Hits Diesel"

- Suppliers: "Car Parts Maker Says VW Suppliers Should Not Pay for Scandal"

- Customers: "Volkswagen Diesel Owners in US Face Lost Value and Limbo"

Not mentioned in these headlines is the potential health hazard to the public resulting from the company's violation of environmental regulations. The United

States government alleged that VW violated the Clean Air Act. The company faced potential fines of over $90 billion, which did not include fines from non-US regulators or damages from lawsuits filed by customers.

An editorial in the *Financial Times* titled "Bankers Not Only Ones Pushing Ethical Boundaries" discussed problems in the banking industry in recent years, such as guilty pleas and settlements by banks charged with rigging foreign exchange and LIBOR rates.[27] (These cases involved Barclays, Citicorp, Deutsche Bank, JP Morgan Chase, the Royal Bank of Scotland, and other banks that paid billions of dollars in fines and settlements.) The editorial then observed that in other industries "companies around the world are pushing ethical boundaries," citing a $2 billion accounting scandal at Toshiba and General Motors' $900 million settlement with United States regulators for covering up its faulty ignition switches that resulted in more than one hundred deaths.

The examples in the editorial dramatically illustrate the consequences of improper conduct, but the headline referring to "pushing ethical boundaries" illustrates a popular misconception that the problems fall entirely within the realm of the Ethics Pillar. All of the cases mentioned in the editorial, along with the VW scandal, involved violations of the law and illustrate the need for business leaders to understand both the Law Pillar and the Ethics Pillar. Writing in *The New York Times*, Robert Prentice (Ed & Molly Smith Professor of Business Law at the McCombs School of Business, University of Texas) observed that scandals such as Enron, WorldCom, and ImClone involved serious ethical lapses, but they also occurred "because their participants had an insufficient knowledge of, appreciation for and, yes, fear of the law."[28]

The fear of the law that Prentice mentions is justified, considering legal penalties that have both civil and criminal dimensions. Claims against BP for the Deepwater Horizon oil spill illustrate both types of consequences. BP agreed to settle government claims for $18.7 billion. This settlement did not include an earlier $4 billion paid to settle a criminal investigation, an estimated $10.3 billion to settle several civil cases, and an undetermined amount the company would need to settle future civil cases (around three thousand such cases).[29]

But it is not enough for a company to understand and comply with the Law Pillar alone, and that is where the Ethics Pillar becomes important. The late author Rushworth Kidder, in his book *How Good People Make Tough Choices*, suggests that "decision making is driven by our core values, morals and integrity" and involves decisions that are either a clear choice between "right" and "wrong" or determinations that are more nuanced because the decision-maker is caught between a "right" and another "right."

Companies and their leaders make decisions that fall into the clear choice category all the time; for example, it has been argued that VW knew that its programming of vehicles to "fool" the emissions tests was a "wrong," yet it took this action anyway—possibly because the company lacked an appreciation for or fear of the law, as described by Prentice.[30]

Much more difficult for companies are decisions that are clearly legal but ethically questionable. Is it acceptable to test unknown products on animals with the goal of protecting humans who will use those products in the future? Is it ethical for a pharmaceutical company to set high prices on a patented drug to increase profits and cover the cost of drug development, even if that reduces affordability for some of the people who need it? Kidder believes that without legal compliance, you can "never arrive at a genuinely ethical mindset. But neither will you get there by compliance alone." The toughest choices are choosing between options that are all on the "right" side of the law.

This difficulty of achieving a "genuinely ethical mindset" is illustrated in the following case—*POM Wonderful LLC v. Coca-Cola Company*—where the juice maker POM Wonderful brought suit against soft drink manufacturer and competitor Coca-Cola for misleading labeling. With questionable strategies being applied by both companies, many ethical considerations are raised by this litigation.

STRATEGY	
LAW	***Three Pillars Case: It's Not the Real Thing***
ETHICS	

Citation: *POM Wonderful LLC v. Coca-Cola Co.*, 166 F.Supp.3d 1085 (C.D. Cal. 2016)

Juice products, especially those containing pomegranate juice, have become popular among consumers who believe these products have associated health benefits. POM Wonderful, a manufacturer whose product lines include juice, juice blends, teas, concentrates, and extracts, brought a claim against competitor Coca-Cola for false/misleading advertising related to one of the latter's beverages. POM also made similar unsuccessful claims against other competitors, including Ocean Spray Cranberries, Inc. (in 2010) and Tropicana Products, Inc. (in 2011). In this decision by the US District Court of Central California, Judge Otero finds that POM Wonderful might have had "unclean hands" in its infringement action. This case illustrates—with regard to the companies on both sides of the issue—that although a strategy may be legal, it's important to consider the ethics of strategic decisions.

ORDER GRANTING IN PART AND DENYING IN PART PLAINTIFF'S MOTION FOR PARTIAL SUMMARY JUDGMENT [DOCKET NO. 498]

HONORABLE S. JAMES OTERO, UNITED STATES DISTRICT JUDGE

POM initiated the instant action against Coca-Cola on September 22, 2008, asserting three causes of action associated with Coca-Cola's sales of "Minute Maid® Enhanced Pomegranate Blueberry Flavored 100% Juice Blend" ("the Juice"). . . . POM's . . . claim centers on allegations that Coca-Cola has made false and/or misleading statements as to the pomegranate and blueberry juice content in the Juice product. POM alleges that consumers will believe the main ingredients in Coca-Cola's Juice product are pomegranate and blueberry juice, when in fact pomegranate juice ranks third and blueberry juice ranks fifth, by volume.

. . . POM further alleges that it has "invested millions of dollars in researching the nutritional qualities and health benefits of pomegranate juice, an investment that continues to this day," and further alleges that "[a] key element of P[OM's] marketing campaign has been its concentration on the health benefits associated with pomegranates and pomegranate juice. . . ." According to POM, this "investment of millions of dollars to research and promote the nutritional qualities and health benefits associated with pomegranate juice" enabled POM to "largely create the burgeoning market for genuine pomegranate juice that exists today."

. . . POM identifies Coca-Cola . . . as one of several "[u]nscrupulous competitors [that] have set out to cash in on [POM's] success" and to profit from the fact that, "[d]ue to POM's marketing efforts and funding of research, . . . many consumers now associate pomegranate juice with certain nutritional qualities and health benefits." POM claims that Coca-Cola's Juice label contains many misleading elements not required by federal or state regulation, by, for example, naming the Juice "Pomegranate Blueberry" and juxtaposing this brand name with a picture of a pomegranate and other fruits when in fact the Juice is primarily composed of cheaper apple and grape juices. As a result, POM alleges that Coca-Cola "wrongfully misleads and deceives consumers, and tricks them into believing that they are getting a similar product [to POM's] (i.e., all natural pomegranate blueberry juice with all of its associated health benefits) for a lower price, when in fact they are getting a very different product primarily containing apple juice and grape juice."

Coca-Cola filed its Answer . . . on September 30, 2009, in which it asserts a number of affirmative defenses. At issue in the instant Motion is the thirty-forth affirmative defense, in which Coca-Cola alleges that "P[OM]'s claims against

[Coca-Cola] are barred, in whole or in part, due to unclean hands." In support of this affirmative defense, Coca-Cola offers the following:

> Plaintiff has engaged in naming, labeling, marketing and advertising conduct designed to deceive consumers about its products. For instance, Plaintiff describes its Pomegranate Blueberry juice product as Pomegranate Blueberry 100% Juice, yet at the time it filed its Complaint, Plaintiff's product contained other ingredients, including plum, pineapple, apple, and blackberry juices from concentrates and natural flavors. In addition, Plaintiff's name, label, advertisements, website, and promotions of Plaintiff's pomegranate juice products—including its 100% pomegranate juice product and its 100% juice blend products, such as its Pomegranate Blueberry 100% Juice product—are designed to give consumers the false impression that these juices are fresh-squeezed, and not "from concentrate." In addition, Plaintiff alleges that it "largely created the burgeoning market for genuine pomegranate juice," by educating the public about health claims through its advertisements and/or promotions. Many of Plaintiff's health claims are not supported by any substantial scientific evidence. Indeed, by Plaintiff's own admission, many of its advertising claims constitute mere "puffery." Thus, Plaintiff is seeking to capitalize in this case on the fruits of its own misconduct in the form of misleading labeling and advertising.

Thus, Coca-Cola's unclean hands defense alleges three distinct forms of misconduct: (1) that POM's juice product contained ingredients other than pomegranate and blueberry notwithstanding being labeled "Pomegranate Blueberry 100% Juice" ("ingredient claim"); (2) that POM gave the false impression that its juices were "fresh-squeezed" rather than "from concentrate" ("'from concentrate' claim"); and (3) that POM's health claims about its pomegranate products are "not supported by any substantial scientific evidence" ("health advertisement claim").

... Coca-Cola first argues that a finding by the Federal Trade Commission ("FTC") that POM violated the Federal Trade Commission Act ("FTC Act") by making false and misleading claims about the health benefits of several of POM's pomegranate products is sufficient, standing alone, to demonstrate that POM engaged in inequitable conduct.... On January 10, 2013, the FTC issued an opinion ("FTC Opinion") in which it found that POM and its officers violated Sections 5(a) and 12 of the FTC Act by disseminating advertising and promotional materials representing that consumption of certain doses of pomegranate juice products treats, prevent, or reduces the risk of heart disease, prostate cancer, or erectile dysfunction ("ED") without having a reasonable basis to substantiate these claims. . . . Coca-Cola contends that these "are precisely the type of statutory violations that renders a party's hands unclean," and POM "should not be permitted to recover on the theory that, but for Coca-Cola's sales of the Juice, P[OM]'s fraud would have been even more successful than it was."

. . . Coca-Cola seeks to offer at trial evidence that POM engaged in inequitable conduct by advertising the results of studies regarding the purported health benefits of pomegranate consumption when POM knew that these and related studies reached inconclusive, statistically insignificant, or even negative results. For example, Coca-Cola points to advertisements by POM claiming that pomegranate and pomegranate juice consumption (1) reduces the risk of heart disease; (2) prevents men from "dying of prostate cancer"; and (3) improved erections in men. Coca-Cola has also supplied evidence that studies relied on and referenced in these advertisements (1) reached inconclusive results; (2) were undermined by other research that POM forestalled; (3) relied on improper premises, methods, and indicators; (4) were known by POM employees to be statistically insignificant; and (5) were determined by independent authorities, including the United States government, at an early stage to be unsubstantiated. This evidence tends to show that POM knowingly relied upon inconclusive, discredited, or simply false studies in its health advertisements to consumers, and is sufficient to create a genuine issue whether POM engaged in inequitable conduct.

. . . [T]he Court finds that Coca-Cola has introduced evidence sufficient to create a genuine issue as to whether POM's conduct is inequitable. . . . Thus, the Court DENIES POM's Motion as to pertains to Coca-Cola's health advertisement claim.

IT IS SO ORDERED.

THREE PILLARS CASE QUESTIONS

(1)   Describe the concern that POM Wonderful has with the Coca-Cola product. If this claim of misleading labeling proves to be false, would Coca-Cola's conduct still be unethical?

(2)   What is the defense of "unclean hands" (https://en.wikipedia.org/wiki/Clean_hands)? Describe the basis of Coca-Cola's unclean hands defense against POM Wonderful. When an unclean hands defense is successful, then any judgment against

the defendant is typically reduced or eliminated. What do you think is the legal principle behind the unclean hands defense?

(3)   This is not the first time that POM Wonderful has brought the same allegation of deceptive labeling against a competitor. In a number of the previous cases, California juries found that the competitor labels were not misleading, and the defendants prevailed. In another case, the defendant company was found liable. Additionally, POM has itself been cited by the FTC for false and misleading advertising claims/labels. Some analysts have suggested that POM brings these suits to antagonize competing food and beverage industry manufacturers and distract from its own transgressions. If true, is this a viable strategy to promote the company?

(4)   Imagine that POM Wonderful sues small and startup companies for mislabeling, even though the company knows that it will likely lose the case. Why do you think POM would adopt such a strategy? Is the strategy ethical?

(5)   In March 2016, a jury found that POM Wonderful did not prove by a preponderance of the evidence that the label on Coca-Cola's juice product misled a substantial portion of consumers. Instead of engaging in litigation with competitors or making unsubstantiated claims about its own products, what is a legal and ethical strategy that POM Wonderful can apply to compete against other juice products on the market?

––––––––

The decision making process becomes more focused, effective, and advantageous when managers strategize within the dimensions of law and ethics. In Chapter 2, we look at some challenges with aligning the three pillars and at the relative importance of each pillar—strategy, law, and ethics—in the model's application to decision making.

KEY TAKEAWAYS

This book focuses on the three pillars that provide the foundation for decisions in business, leadership, and everyday life: strategy, law, and ethics. In order to make sound, responsible business decisions, you should consider the following:

1. **The Strategy Pillar.** You should contemplate the questions: *what is our value creation goal, and how do we intend to achieve it?* In order to research the law and evaluate the ethics of accomplishing your business goal, you must first develop a strategy that outlines your objectives. A well-designed strategy is ground zero for moving forward.

2. **The Law Pillar.** In a business setting, law represents the "rules of the game"—the framework for business operations and decision

making. Once you have decided on a strategy to accomplish your goal, the next step is to evaluate the legality of your design. What you discover in your due diligence investigation of legal concerns will allow you to refine and adjust your strategy, ultimately creating value for your business within a legal framework.

3.   **The Ethics Pillar.** Some businesses believe that as long as they abide by the law, they do not need to be concerned with ethics. However, a business that keeps ethics at the forefront of its decision making will benefit from the ability to recruit and retain top employees and customers, and it will create value that will attract investors and maintain a respectable, highly-regarded profile in the business community.

STRATEGY
LAW   ***Three Pillars Decision: Last Trip to Disney World***
ETHICS

In this analysis, a major recreation industry player needs to carefully consider some of the questionable benefits of its popularity with the public.

According to the *Wall Street Journal* (WSJ), the famous amusement park Walt Disney World (WDW) is a relished location for families of the dearly departed to spread the ashes of cremated friends and relatives. The WSJ describes the smuggling in of cremated human remains ("cremains") in pill bottles or plastic bags and the depositing of them in favorite park locations: *Pirates of the Caribbean, It's a Small World*, and—most popular by far—the *Haunted Mansion*. When such an incident occurs, it interrupts ride operations and involves an environmentally safe cleanup by Disney employees using vacuums with high-efficiency filters.

VALUE GOAL: Respectfully diminish and/or prevent the depositing of human cremains within attractions at WDW Park.

STRATEGY: Develop and implement a plan to reduce/prevent the depositing of cremains at WDW Park.

LAW: Research the law related to the depositing of cremated human remains in public and private places in the state of Florida, where WDW is located. How does this research affect or alter the strategy you developed?&

ETHICS: Apply ethics to your strategy by working through these four steps of ethical decision making: (1) describe the ethical dilemma, (2) identify the stakeholders involved, (3) analyze options (including how each group of stakeholders will be affected), and (4) make a decision based on your analysis.

After examining ethical issues associated with the strategy, determine whether any modifications should be made.

℞*Check for law research materials in the Appendix: Legal Resources for Business Decisions*

STRATEGY LAW ETHICS	***Three Pillars Decision: Reservations of the Heart***

In the situation described below, the hospitality industry wrestles with a decision that could save lives but also may result in significant civil liability if not properly implemented and monitored.

"Each year, more than 250,000 Americans die from sudden cardiac arrest."[31] A technological advance—the "automated external defibrillator" or "AED"—has been promoted as a life-saving device that may be used by non-medical personnel to treat a person whose heart has stopped beating. The AED device "guides the user through the process by audible or visual prompts without requiring any discretion or judgment."[32] According to the American Heart Association, use of the AED could potentially save at least twenty thousand lives annually.

Some state governments require AED placement in health and fitness centers, schools, swimming pools, daycare centers, dental offices, and places of public assembly.[33] There are, however, locations that have resisted the addition of AEDs, such as hotels and resort centers. Hotel operators have expressed concerns about being sued for logistical failures: failing to have enough units, failing to place units in the proper locations, and failing to properly maintain units. Their fears may not be unfounded; according to the US Food and Drug Administration, there have been forty-five thousand reports of AED devices failing or malfunctioning (primarily due to lack of proper maintenance) since 2005 and eighty-eight manufacturer recalls.[34] However, advocates of adding AEDs to all public locations argue that, with the widespread adoption of the devices, hotels that fail to add the life-saving technology will likely experience greater liability risk for *not* installing this option.

VALUE GOAL: To add the potential life-saving technology of AEDs within the hospitality industry.

STRATEGY: Select a US state and develop a strategy to add AEDs to hotels within that state.

LAW: Research the AED law of the state you selected. How does this research affect or alter the strategy you developed? Refine your strategy to align with the law.℞

ETHICS: Hotels may incur liability whether they decide to add AEDs or continue to resist this option. Because of this dichotomy, apply ethics to your strategy of adding AEDs to hotels and be sure to include the option of doing nothing (no addition of AEDs). In your analysis, work through these four steps of ethical decision making: (1) describe the ethical dilemma, (2) identify the stakeholders involved, (3) analyze options (including how each group of stakeholders will be affected), and (4) make a decision based on your analysis. After examining ethical issues associated with both strategies, determine what the best course of action would be: (1) Add AEDs or (2) Do not add AEDs.

&*Check for law research materials in the Appendix: Legal Resources for Business Decisions*

STRATEGY	
LAW	***Three Pillars Decision: "Fair and Square" Strategy***
ETHICS	

The scenario described below is a cautionary tale for companies that try to compete by employing strategies that fail to incorporate the pillars of Law and Ethics into their decision making.

In 2012, California consumer Cynthia Spann filed a class-action lawsuit against retail giant J.C. Penney, alleging that the company tricked her into thinking she was getting good deals on falsely advertised "sale" merchandise. Spann claimed in her complaint that:

> [d]uring at least the last four years, J.C. Penney has misrepresented the existence, nature and amount of price discounts by purporting to offer specific dollar discounts from expressly referenced former retail prices, which are misrepresented as "original" retail prices. These purported discounts are false, however, because the referenced former retail prices are fabricated and do not represent J.C. Penney's true "original" prices.[35]

Spann's experience focused on being induced to spend more than $200 on items with fake discounts, which she would not have otherwise spent if she knew the truth behind the merchandise pricing. Customer complaints suggest the strategy used by the retailer involved artificially inflating prices, then deceiving the buyer by taking what appeared to be deep discounts off those prices.

Also in the year 2012, J.C. Penney supposedly halted the fake sales scheme in favor of CEO Ron Johnson's "Fair and Square" strategy, which offered items at "everyday low prices." The approach failed miserably, however—loyal shoppers accustomed to the heavy discounting of sales were confused by the simplified pricing. According to a J.C. Penney spokesperson, "while our prices continue to represent a tremendous value every day, we now understand that customers are motivated by promotions and prefer to receive discounts through sales and coupons applied at the register."[36]

In 2013, J.C. Penney ousted CEO Johnson and apparently went back to its standard pricing practice, which included what had been characterized as "fake prices." Penney's isn't the only company engaged in this deception; retailers Jos. A. Bank and Kohl's have also been sued for listing prices that were allegedly "misleading, inaccurate and deceptive marketing."[37]

VALUE GOAL: Provide a pricing strategy that both satisfies consumers and protects profits.

STRATEGY: Develop and implement a plan to effectively address consumer pricing expectations.

LAW: Access the Federal Trade Commission's (FTC) "Advertising FAQ's: A Guide for Small Business" and determine how the FTC determines if an ad is deceptive. Compare these rules to your strategy and make any adjustments to be sure your plans comport with the law.☜

ETHICS: Apply ethics to your strategy by working through these four steps of ethical decision making: (1) describe the ethical dilemma, (2) identify the stakeholders involved, (3) analyze options (including how each group of stakeholders will be affected), and (4) make a decision based on your analysis. After examining ethical issues associated with the strategy, determine whether any modifications should be made.

☜*Check for law research materials in the Appendix: Legal Resources for Business Decisions*

STRATEGY LAW ETHICS	***Three Pillars Decision: "Nor Any Drop to Drink. . ."***[38]

This decision making scenario examines formulating an ethical strategy when danger is an unavoidable element of business operations.

In 2007, twenty-nine-year-old Dave Buschow died of thirst during a wilderness survival course exercise in Utah. Although Dave's guides who accompanied him had emergency water supplies available, they withheld that resource because the focus of the twenty-eight-day program was to push "past those false limits your mind has set for your body."[39] Participants in the course could drink water only from natural sources on the land and couldn't carry anything to drink with them. After walking for approximately ten hours in one-hundred-degree heat, Dave collapsed and could not be revived. The medical examiner cited the cause of death as dehydration and an electrolyte imbalance. Administrators at the course's school—Boulder Outdoor Survival School (BOSS)—maintained that Dave signed liability waivers and expressly assumed the risk of serious injury or death prior to participating. They also indicated that they believed Dave failed to read the course materials, may have withheld health information, and may have also eaten too much prior to beginning the course.[40]

VALUE GOAL: To provide challenging, rigorous survival training while maintaining safety for participants.

STRATEGY: Develop a strategy for a survival-training program that tests the mental and physical limits of participants but also provides protection against serious injury or death.

LAW: Research the law related to engaging in high-risk activities, liability waivers, and negligence. What is the legal responsibility for providers of a risky survival course such as the one designed by BOSS? How does this research affect or alter the strategy you developed? If necessary, refine your strategy to align with the law.෨

ETHICS: There is a concern in this case about finding a balance between the intent of the program and the safety of participants. In examining this situation, apply ethics to your strategy by working through these four steps of ethical decision making: (1) describe the ethical dilemma, (2) identify the stakeholders involved, (3) analyze options (including how each group of stakeholders will be affected), and (4) make a decision based on your analysis. After examining ethical issues associated with the strategy, determine whether any modifications should be made.

෨*Check for law research materials in the Appendix: Legal Resources for Business Decisions*

---

1   Savage, "How 4 Federal Lawyers Paved the Way to Kill Osama bin Laden," *The New York Times*, October 28, 2015.

2   *Id.*

3   *Journal of Business Ethics*, September 1997.

4   "Corporate Social Responsibility: A Three-Domain Approach," *Business Ethics Quarterly*, October 2003.

5   "An Education in Ethics," *Harvard Magazine*, September–October 2006.

6   Datar, Garvin, and Cullen, *Rethinking the MBA* (2010).

7   Leadership and Corporate Accountability, Course Syllabus, http://www.hbs.edu/rethinking-the-mba/docs/harvard-business-school-leadership-and-corporate-accountability-2011-course-syllabus.pdf.

8   "The Basic LCA Framework," Harvard Business School N9-315-060.

[9] "Instructor's Guide to Leadership and Corporate Accountability," Harvard Business School 5-307-032.

[10] *Harvard Business Review*, February 2003.

[11] "Who Let the Lawyers Out?: Reconstructing the Role of the Chief Legal Officer and the Corporate Client in a Globalizing World," *University of Pennsylvania Journal of Business Law*, forthcoming.

[12] Pierson, *The Education of American Businessmen* (1959).

[13] Leinwand and Mainardi, "Rethinking the Function of Business Functions," February 2013.

[14] *Strategy and Structure* (1962).

[15] *Competitive Advantage* (1985).

[16] "Managing Your Lawyers," January–February 1983.

[17] "Coase Was Clear: Laws Can Cure or Kill," October 21, 1991.

[18] *International Law for Business* (1994).

[19] "Making International Law an Integral Part of the International Business Program," *The Journal of Legal Studies Education*, December 1994.

[20] "2014 US Business Needs for Employees with International Expertise," https://www.wm.edu/offices/revescenter/globalengagement/internationalization/papers%20and%20presentations/davidsonkediaexec.pdf.

[21] Siedel, "Six Forces and the Legal Environment of Business," *American Business Law Journal*, Summer 2000.

[22] March–April 1990.

[23] Harrison, "Champions of Change," *InsideCounsel*, November 1, 2014.

[24] *AMBA Executive*, September 1997.

[25] "Volkswagen Diesel Scandal," *Chicago Tribune*, September 22, 2015.

[26] Masters, "Bankers Not Only Ones Pushing Ethical Boundaries," September 25, 2015.

[27] "Lessons Learned in Business School," August 20, 2002.

[28] Gilbert and Kent, "BP Agrees to Pay $18.7 Billion to Settle Deepwater Horizon Oil Spill Claims," *Wall Street Journal*, July 2, 2015.

[29] https://www.linkedin.com/pulse/volkswagen-scandal-ethical-issue-craig-vansandt/.

[30] http://www.ncsl.org/research/health/laws-on-cardiac-arrest-and-defibrillators-aeds.aspx.

[31] *Id.*

[32] *Id.*

[33] *Id.*

[34] *Cynthia E. Spann v. J.C. Penney Corp. Inc. et al.*, case number 8:12-cv-00215.

[35] https://www.reddit.com/r/pricing/comments/1bl3e8/jc_penneys_failed_attempt_at_fair_and_square/.

[36] http://business.time.com/2013/01/30/j-c-penney-brings-back-sales-but-whats-the-deal-with-those-suggested-prices/.

[37] https://www.poetryfoundation.org/poems/43997/the-rime-of-the-ancient-mariner-text-of-1834.

[38] http://www.nbcnews.com/id/18443746/ns/us_news-life/t/man-dies-taking-survival-test-under-guides-care/#.XN1zSC_MwWo.

[39] https://www.denverpost.com/2007/05/02/buschow-death-who-is-to-blame/.

CHAPTER 2

The Key Chasm: Closing the Gap Between Strategy and Law

EXISTING MODEL GAPS

Chapter 1 describes the Harvard model and its expansion into a model that can be used by all organizations. The following diagram depicts the expanded version of the Harvard model in which economics is replaced by strategy:

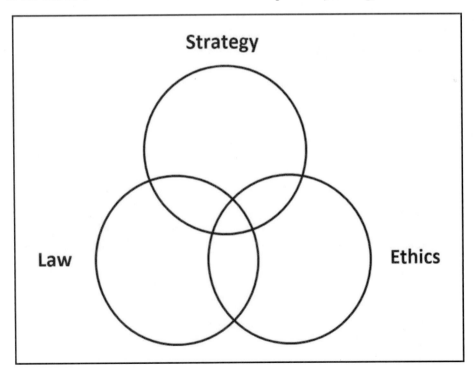

This revised model—with its sweet spot in the middle—might be more aspirational than descriptive of the overlap among the Three Pillars. True, the overlap between the Strategy Pillar and the Ethics Pillar has increased in recent years, especially as more companies embrace corporate social responsibility. For example, in discussing what they call the "intertwined nature of business and ethical interests,"[1] Bagley et al. note that former Johnson & Johnson CEO Ralph Larson was asked whether he wanted the company "to maximize shareholder value or be a good corporate citizen." He answered, "Yes."

Law and ethics are even more intertwined than strategy and ethics. Legal doctrines such as fraud, unconscionability, good faith, and fiduciary duty provide solid guidelines for ethical conduct. Ben W. Heineman, former senior vice president of General Electric Company, succinctly noted two key decision making questions: "Is it legal?" and "Is it right?"[2] Furthermore, company "codes of conduct" often blend law and ethics.

Unlike the overlap between strategy and ethics and the overlap between law and ethics, strategy and law are often engaged in parallel play with the result that, in practice, the model often looks like this:

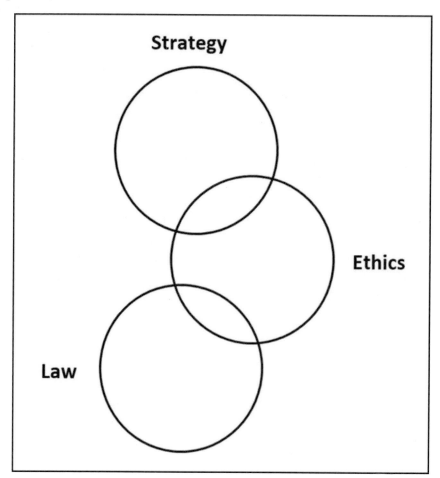

For example, the multitude of strategy concepts and frameworks that have developed over the years provide little explicit mention of law. A notable exception is a PESTLE analysis, which scans the external environment of business through the lens of six factors: **P**olitical, **E**conomic, **S**ocial, **T**echnological, **L**egal, and **E**nvironmental. The legal factor in this analysis focuses on the legal concerns that impact business operations and decision making.

Other models implicitly recognize the importance of the Law Pillar. For example, Professor Constance Bagley (a senior research fellow at Yale School of Management), in her book *Winning Legally* (2005), and Richard Shell (the Thomas Gerrity Professor in the Legal Studies and Business Ethics Department at Wharton), in his book *Make the Rules or Your Rivals Will* (2004), analyze how the law affects each of Michael Porter's five forces that were mentioned in Chapter 1.

But in practice, it is difficult for business leaders to bridge the gap between law and strategy. This difficulty arises from the mysterious nature of the Law Pillar, which is the product of the complexity of law and misconceptions about the role of lawyers. The next two sections explore these two factors—complexity and misconceptions—in greater detail. The section that follows them will then describe how businesses can create a sweet spot by closing the gap between the Strategy Pillar and the Law Pillar. While Harvard calls this sweet spot the "zone of sustainability," for reasons described later, a more precise name is the "zone of sustainable competitive advantage."

COMPLEXITY OF LAW

Managers often feel frustrated when making law-related business decisions. This frustration results in large part from not understanding the branches that form the basic structure of the Law Pillar and the many fields emanating from those branches. The main branches are represented by the following simplified roadmap of the law.

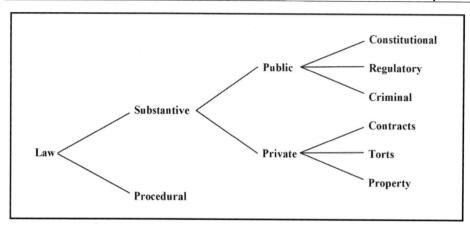

The labels for the roadmap's two main branches, substantive law and procedural law, are descriptive. Substantive law refers to the substance of the law—the legal rules that govern business operations and decision making. Procedural law refers to the procedures used to enforce substantive law. For example, procedural law deals with how cases are filed and appealed and the rules of evidence that are used during trials.

Substantive law is primarily a concern of business decision-makers, whereas procedural law is a main concern of lawyers. But in recent years, business leaders have also become interested in procedural law—in the guise of alternative dispute resolution (ADR). Business leaders' interest in ADR arose in the latter half of the twentieth century when they began to question why they outsourced their disputes to the court system, often at great cost in time and money. Chapter 9 of this book includes a review of ADR concepts and management tools.

Substantive law branches into public law and private law. Public law includes areas of law where the government plays a key role. The constitutional law branch focuses on the basic legal principles that govern society and the organization of government into executive, legislative, and judicial functions. Regulatory law—an area of law that is especially important to business and is covered in Chapter 6—encompasses the work of governmental agencies that exercise all three functions. Criminal law involves cases brought by a public official asserting that a defendant has committed a crime.

Private law includes areas of law that involve, for the most part, individuals and private entities. (Private law is also called civil law, but "civil" has other meanings in the law. For example, it is used to distinguish criminal from noncriminal cases and to distinguish common law systems that originated in England from civil systems that originated in continental Europe.) There are three main categories of private law. Contract law (covered in Chapter 8) deals with creating and enforcing legal agreements. Tort law (Chapter 4) involves a wrongful act that injures a person or property. Property law (Chapter 7) focuses on the right to own and use property.

Six of the endpoints in the roadmap—constitutional, criminal, contracts, torts, property, and procedure—are the core subjects that students study in law schools worldwide. A law student's brain is molded to think in these categories. As a result, when you pose a question to a lawyer, the answer will usually consider one or more of these six main branches along with many related fields. Wikipedia, for instance, lists more than one hundred areas of law study and practice.[3] The complexity of a lawyer's advice is often amplified when the business is engaged in global transactions.

Employment law illustrates the branches of law that managers must consider when making business decisions. Employment law touches everyone in business, from entrepreneurs hiring their first employees to CEOs managing large corporations. This area of law, which brings into play all of the main branches of public and private law, includes collective bargaining agreements, discrimination, employee benefits, health and safety, hiring and firing, work hours, and pay.

MISCONCEPTIONS ABOUT THE ROLE OF LAWYERS

In addition to its complexity, the Law Pillar is mysterious because of misconceptions about the role of lawyers. Media headlines contribute to confusion when they focus on contentious civil and criminal trials that have the potential to destroy companies and careers.

The media-created perception that lawyers are mainly litigators is especially misleading because the number of cases that go to trial has dropped dramatically in recent years. In the mid-twentieth century (1962), more than 11 percent of federal civil cases reached trial; by 2002, that number dropped to less than 2 percent.[4]

The real day-to-day legal issues are often overlooked in the media because they are buried in articles that focus on business transactions, not conflict. And there are many of these articles. A study by Lee Reed (Emeritus Professor of Legal Studies and former holder of the Scherer Chair at the University of Georgia's Terry College of Business) concluded that during a randomly-selected month almost half of the articles on the front pages of Sections A and B and the editorial page of the *Wall Street Journal* focused on a legal issue or on law-related subject matter.[5]

To effectively use legal advice, managers should understand that a lawyer's role in business involves much more than litigation. From a big-picture perspective, lawyers serve two functions that are critical to business success.

First, they serve an advisory role. Virtually every important business decision includes legal questions and requires legal advice. Second, they serve an implementation role that has two branches. If a business decision results in litigation, lawyers manage the litigation process and advise the managers who are responsible for making settlement decisions. If the business decision requires transactional work, they assist managers with the transaction—creating a joint venture, meeting regulatory requirements, acquiring real estate, creating a contract, completing a merger, developing a pension plan, and so on.

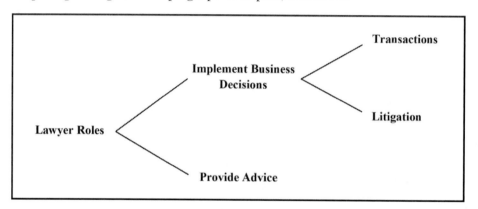

When providing advice and assisting business leaders with their transactional and litigation decisions, lawyers often view managing risk as their *raison d'être*. According to Ronald Gilson (Marc and Eva Stern Professor of Law and Business at Columbia University): "When my question—what does a business lawyer really do—is put to business lawyers, the familiar response is that they 'protect' their clients, that they get their clients the 'best' deal."[6] The president of Booz Allen Hamilton has observed that his lawyer "is the person who is charged with protecting the corporation and making sure risks are understood and managed appropriately."[7]

Understanding legal risk management is especially important to business leaders because legal risk is the most important category of business risk. This is reflected in the Travelers Business Risk Index developed from a survey of more than twelve hundred business risk managers representing ten industries. The managers were questioned about their greatest risk concerns among several categories, including financial, operational, and legal risk. Only two categories— "Legal Liability" and "Medical Cost Inflation"—were among the top ten risks in every industry. Another category of legal risk, "Complying with Laws," was in the top ten list for nine of the ten industries.[8]

An Accenture survey of C-suite executives (CEOs, CFOs, etc.) spread across seven industry groups in Asia Pacific, Europe, Latin America, and North America concluded that "Legal Risks" constitute the top external pressure faced by business, well ahead of the second and third risks—"Business Risks" and "Regulatory Requirements."[9]

Other studies describe the specific types of risks that concern business. A Norton Rose Fulbright survey of litigation trends in twenty-six countries listed the most common types of litigation, including the percentage of companies affected by each type of litigation.[10]

- Contracts (38%)

- Labor/Employment (37%)

- Regulatory/Investigations (18%)

- Personal Injury and Product Liability (15% and 11%, respectively)

- Intellectual Property/Patents (13%)

- Dispute Resolution Process—i.e., Class Actions (10%)

Another survey, by AlixPartners, concluded that the top three categories of litigation are Contract, Employment, and Intellectual Property/Patent. The respondents were compliance and legal officers from companies representing more than twenty industries. Eight percent of the respondents reported that they had "been involved in a 'bet the company' lawsuit during the prior 12 months." Half of these "bet the company" lawsuits were contract disputes and 38 percent involved intellectual property.[11]

Yet another study, a global survey by Berwin Leighton Paisner, concluded that 80 percent of respondents (C-suite executives from a variety of sectors) "expected their business to experience material losses as a result of legal risks."[12] According to this survey, the top three legal risk priorities are (in order of priority) legislation/regulation, dispute management, and contractual risk.

Regulation also tops the list of concerns in two other surveys. An EY survey of Chief Operating Officers and heads of investment operations in the Americas and Europe concluded that their top challenge (by a wide margin) is compliance with regulatory requirements.[13] And a PwC Annual Global CEO Survey concluded that "Over-regulation remains the top concern for business. . . ."[14] According to Robert Bird (the Eversource Energy Chair in Business Ethics in the

Business Law Department at the University of Connecticut School of Business) and Janine Hiller (a business law professor who is the Sorenson Professor in Finance at Virginia Tech's Pamplin School of Business), "A blossoming risk management industry has driven the need for positions in contract and regulatory risk management."[15]

One implication of these surveys and studies is that legal risk has a major impact on a company's bottom line. As noted by Henry Lowenstein (former Dean at California State University at Bakersfield and currently a business law professor at Coastal Carolina University, where he holds the Baxley Professorship), "As a practical matter for businesses today, the legal expense line is now a significant factor on company balance sheets."[16]

When working with lawyers on the legal issues that dominate business risk management, business leaders should understand whom the lawyer represents and the lawyer's duty to provide independent professional judgment, along with related attorney-client privilege concerns. As noted in an ACC/Georgetown study on the role of general counsel, lawyers face a continuing challenge in maintaining "professional independence and recognizing the organization as a client, as opposed to the CEO or other members of the C-suite. . . ."[17]

The independence issue becomes complicated in a global economy because an in-house lawyer's duty of independence varies from country to country, with repercussions on attorney-client privilege. But even when independence is not legally required, obtaining and understanding independent professional advice is especially important to business leaders. Providing this advice often requires managerial courage from the lawyers. As defined by the ACC/Georgetown study, "Managerial courage is about the willingness and ability to speak up and represent the organization and act in its best interest, even when it feels uncomfortable or may reflect poorly on colleagues."[18]

The combination of a risk management focus and independence often causes tension between lawyers and business decision-makers. Mangers sometimes refer to the law department as the "department of sales prevention." Other managers refer to the law function as the "department of no," in contrast to IT and other "departments of now" that need legal information as quickly as possible.[19] Despite this tension, the lawyers' focus on risk management enables business leaders to balance an unbridled emphasis on shareholder value creation represented by the Strategy Pillar with managing risks represented by the Law Pillar.

Although a balance between reward and risk is necessary, the Strategy Pillar and the Law Pillar often operate on separate tracks that do not intersect. In the next section, we examine how the gap between these two key elements in business decision making can be closed in a manner that enhances the opportunity for business success.

CLOSING THE GAP BETWEEN STRATEGY AND LAW

The gap between the Strategy Pillar and the Law Pillar is reminiscent of the "mind the gap" recording that one hears when traveling on the London Underground and elsewhere. While minding the gap—that is, understanding that the gap exists—is important, deciding what action to take after you are warned of the gap is essential. This section focuses on *how* to mind the gap.

How large is this gap? The Berwin Leighton survey mentioned earlier concluded that most board-level respondents felt that their firms do not use "legal-risk reports to inform strategic, risk-based business decisions."[20] But the strategy-law gap is not all bad news for companies such as Microsoft that are able to close the gap successfully. According to a Microsoft attorney, "the business strategy is developed in close cooperation with Legal and Corporate Affairs—it's not a business strategy and then the legal strategy, it's a common strategy. . . ."[21]

By closing the gap, companies using the Microsoft approach have an opportunity to create competitive advantage over their rivals. According to University of Connecticut Professor Robert Bird, when this happens, the competitive advantage can be sustainable. In other words, the sweet spot in decision making that Harvard calls the zone of sustainability might be more accurately described as the zone of sustainable competitive advantage.[22]

Bird's conclusion is based on a legal analysis using a resource attribute framework developed by strategy professor Jay Barney. One takeaway from this analysis is that law's complexity is a factor in creating a resource that, in Barney's language, is imperfectly imitable by competitors. In other words, managers who are able to penetrate the veil of complexity and mystery that surrounds the law have an opportunity to create a sustainable competitive advantage.

Bird and coauthor David Orozco (a business law professor and the Dean's Emerging Scholar at Florida State University's College of Business) describe various pathways of corporate legal strategy in an article in the *MIT Sloan Management Review*.[23] They emphasize the need for "a fundamental change from managing risk to creating business opportunities" that requires business leaders to "possess legal astuteness and regard the law as a key enabler of value creation."

The next section discusses how you can become legally savvy (that is, legally astute). We then turn to how you can use your understanding of the law to close the gap between the Strategy Pillar and the Law Pillar through a reframing process.

Becoming a Legally Savvy Business Leader

Savvy business leaders have a practical understanding of the realities of law and business. Many people in business lack the legal savvy necessary to bridge the gap between managing risk and creating value. For example, the aforementioned Berwin Leighton survey concluded that only 25 percent of the directors and CEOs surveyed had a clear understanding of legal risk.[24]

The need to become legally savvy is obviously important for business leaders tasked with establishing a company's strategic direction. But middle managers who implement strategy also play an important role in legal decision making. A Corporate Executive Board Legal Leadership Council survey concluded that middle managers make 75 percent of legal decisions and that almost "80% of corporate employees made a decision or completed an activity with a significant legal implication in the past year."[25]

These middle-management decisions involved, for example, signing contracts, developing new products, creating intellectual property, interacting with government officials, entering a new market, creating marketing materials, establishing product safety standards, and executing an acquisition agreement. Less than one-third of these middle managers consulted the legal department when making their decisions. In other words, most of them relied on their own knowledge of the law when making business decisions that were rife with legal concerns.

How does someone become a legally savvy business leader? Three common options are (1) learn on the job, (2) attend law school, or (3) take business law courses in business school. Learning on the job is challenging and risky because, without a foundational understanding of legal concepts and frameworks, it is difficult for a manager to decide when to seek legal advice and how to communicate effectively with a lawyer. These difficulties might account for the large number of aforementioned "bet the company" lawsuits that are in progress. Even when company survival is not at stake, litigation is an expensive and time-consuming learning process.

Law schools and business schools are typically the best option to become legally savvy.[26] The law school option not only provides valuable knowledge about details of the law, but other benefits that are especially useful in a business career, such as developing critical thinking and communication skills, the ability to think logically, understanding how to prevent and resolve business disputes, an ability to evaluate global legal trends that impact business, and understanding a business leader's legal responsibilities.

The problem with the law school route for becoming legally savvy is that the time (in the United States three years of graduate study) and expense can exceed the benefits for someone who does not intend to practice law. So, the option of taking business law courses while pursuing a business degree is the most cost-effective approach. Recognizing the importance of these courses, the AACSB (the accrediting body for business schools) has adopted an international accreditation standard that states an expectation that business school degree programs will cover the legal context of organizations. As Jeffrey Garten (former dean of the Yale School of Management) has noted: "All students ... should gain a fundamental understanding of business law."[27]

On a general level, this "fundamental understanding" includes the study of the interaction between business and society. A leading book on undergraduate education, for instance, concluded that business law courses, more than any other business school area of study, "help prepare students for the complexity of roles demanded by the modern business enterprise."[28] On a specific level, the "fundamental understanding" includes the most important legal concerns that managers must understand, as listed in the surveys described earlier: contracts, employment law, government regulation, tort law, intellectual property, and the legal process.

But just as important as these areas of law are the skills that enable you to make decisions in a legally savvy manner. In addition to the general legal skills that result from the study of law (such as critical thinking skills, understanding how to prevent and resolve business disputes, and an ability to evaluate global legal trends that impact business), business law courses provide graduates with seven management skills that are essential to success in business.

1.   The ability to recognize the legal issues that arise on a daily basis in business. In her book *Winning Legally* (2005), Professor Bagley noted that businesses swim "in a sea of law." A director at Royal Dutch Shell confirmed this perspective with this story:

> Two young fish swim along and happen to meet an older fish swimming the other way, who nods at them and says, "Morning, boys. How's the water?" The two young fish swim on for a bit, until, eventually, one of them looks over at the other and goes, "What the hell is water?" Like

water, law is around us—everywhere. It affects everything a company does. But somehow you can't see it, at least not on the surface.[29]

Business graduates should have the ability to recognize the legal issues that lurk beneath the surface of the legal sea in which they swim.

2.   The ability to decide which legal issues require you to seek professional advice. Having a lawyer at your elbow to provide advice on the myriad legal issues you face daily is not feasible in terms of time and expense. You must address most of these issues on your own, in effect acting as your own lawyer. But you also must be able to decide which issues are serious enough to require legal counsel so that you can make sound business decisions and avoid litigation, especially the "bet the company" litigation that so many companies face today.

3.   The ability to communicate effectively with lawyers when you seek their advice. Effective communication begins when you place legal issues in perspective using the legal roadmap depicted earlier. Communication also requires a fundamental understanding of the main branches in the roadmap, because they reflect the key legal concerns that companies today face.

4.   The ability to evaluate the advice an attorney provides. The responsibility for deciding when and how to take legal risks when making business decisions falls on you, not your attorney. In exercising this responsibility, you often must balance legal advice with recommendations from others in the business. For example, when the media contacts you after someone has been injured by your product, your attorney might suggest that you not comment—or at least not apologize—while your public relations advisor might recommend that you do both. The decision is yours.

5.   The ability to implement the legal decisions that you make. Using the same example, you must decide what to say and how to say it when meeting with the media.

6.   The ability to discuss legal issues with stakeholders. As a business leader—whether an entrepreneur operating a start-up or the head of a major corporation—you are (in effect, if not in title) the "Chief Legal Communicator" when discussing legal concerns with company shareholders, employees, customers, government regulators, suppliers, and other stakeholders.

7.   The ability to exercise leadership in emphasizing legal responsibilities to everyone in your organization. Many of the costly decision making blunders that the media loosely calls "ethical lapses" are in fact violations of the law. You must ensure that all employees understand their legal responsibilities.

Reframing the Strategy Pillar and the Law Pillar: A Trip to the Balcony

Becoming a legally-savvy business leader is necessary but not sufficient for business success. The problem is that, even if you understand the law, the Strategy Pillar and the Law Pillar often operate as separate silos when key business questions are framed in terms of either shareholder value or risk management—either reward or risk.

At best, this parallel play is unfortunate because you will miss opportunities to create value through synergies between strategy and law. At worst, the silo mentality is destructive when it creates a conflict between the Strategy Pillar and the Law Pillar—for example, when a risk-averse approach results in an overly legalistic contract that destroys a business opportunity. In the words of former PepsiCo CEO Indra Nooyi when commenting on the combination of a perfect contract with a flawed business deal, "We cannot afford this separation of church and state."[30]

An important cause of this silo mentality is what decision researchers call frame blindness. Mental frames are often useful because they enable us to simplify and organize complexity so that we can make rational decisions. But simplification can come at a cost. When we view the world through a particular window—from the perspective of the Strategy Pillar or the Legal Pillar, for example—we see only part of the landscape. Narrowing the scope of our vision causes us to become susceptible to frame blindness—think of it as the blind spot on the side-view mirrors of your car. By failing to consider the big picture, we often miss the best options when making decisions.[31]

For example, one of this book's authors (Siedel) gives students an exercise in which they play the role of a business leader who must decide whether to accept a settlement offer from the opposing side in a lawsuit. Almost all of the students exhibit frame blindness by concentrating on the legal issues raised in the case. In so doing, they overlook strategic concerns such as the possibility of creating a joint venture with the other side.

Closing the gap between strategy and law requires reducing frame blindness by reframing the shareholder value orientation that characterizes the Strategy Pillar and the risk management orientation that dominates the Law Pillar. A major challenge that inhibits reframing is what Max Bazerman and Don Moore call the "fixed-pie assumption" that is often made during negotiations.[32]

Bazerman and Moore observe that this assumption is a fundamental bias that distorts negotiators' behavior as they fight over what they think is a fixed pie: "When negotiating over an issue, they [negotiators] assume that their interests necessarily and directly conflict with the other party's interests." By identifying interests that are not in conflict, business decision-makers (like negotiators) have an opportunity to expand the pie so that it benefits the company and its stakeholders.[33]

Management decisions within the Law Pillar can be especially susceptible to fixed-pie thinking because litigation is typically a zero-sum game where one side wins and the other side loses. But the fixed-pie assumption also impacts decisions within the Strategy Pillar when decision-makers assume that a gain for some stakeholders must necessarily result in a loss for shareholders.

Avoiding fixed-pie thinking requires a big-picture mindset. In his book *Getting Past No* (1993), William Ury uses the phrase "going to the balcony" as a metaphor to describe the mental detachment often necessary to create this mindset. From the balcony, business leaders have the opportunity to gain a broad perspective that allows them to see the entire playing field without the blind spots that hinder decision making when they are closer to the action.

As a leader your view from the balcony enables you to realize that the playing field of business includes many key stakeholders (in addition to shareholders) who impact your business success. Which stakeholders have the greatest effect on a company's economic value? A McKinsey survey that posed this question produced responses from 1,396 executives worldwide. Responders were allowed to select multiple responses from a list of stakeholders. Three-quarters of the executives felt that customers had the greatest effect on economic value. The other main categories were government/regulators (53 percent), employees (49 percent), and investors (28 percent).[34]

In the early twentieth century, a view from the balcony would have been greatly beneficial to workers in the radium industry, where strategy frame blindness was partially to blame for the tragic deaths of early radium workers. The exposure of young women to the deadly radioactive glow-in-the-dark paint, used to illuminate clocks and dials, was directly attributed to the strategies of US Radium Corporation and other companies of the time. Because selling the luminous products was a very lucrative business, company executives ignored signs of illness among their staff and repeatedly refused to stop or alter production. As a result of this exclusion of the interests of other stakeholders and a failure to take precautions in protecting their workforce, many radium factories closed in the late-1920s.

STRATEGY

LAW   ***Three Pillars Case: Luminous Legacy***

ETHICS

"The approach of death is swift, and the law moves slowly," news reporter Lemuel Parton wrote while describing the situation of Grace Fryer and other victims of radium poisoning (later known as the "Radium Girls") as they awaited a result to their lawsuit. Newspaper headlines of May 1928 announced: "FIVE MARTYRS TO RADIUM, DYING OF SLOW POISON, FIGHTING FOR LAST REWARD." This case focuses on what happens when companies decide to disregard the right and ethical choice to protect their employees in favor of the viability of the organization.

The recipe for glow-in-the-dark paint was created by inventor William J. Hammer in the early 1900s after he received a sample of radium salts from scientists Pierre and Marie Curie. Hammer's discovery was used by the US Radium Corporation to produce a luminous trade-secret paint known as *Undark*, which was originally used to light the wristwatches and instrument panels used by military soldiers during the First World War. The glowing paint was also marketed for non-military uses, such as house numbers, switch plates, and doll eyes.

US Radium employed hundreds of mostly young women in its factory located in Orange, New Jersey during the period from about 1917 to 1926. These employees, earning about five cents per item, would paint the tiny brushstrokes of radium-contaminated paint onto the company's products and were encouraged to "lip-dip" by placing the camel-hair brush in their mouths to keep the tip's fine point. The women would be covered in radioactive dust after the day's work and were nicknamed "ghost girls" because they glowed in the dark as they walked home at night.

In 1922, one of US Radium's former employees, Grace Fryer, was concerned when she began losing teeth for no discernible reason; an x-ray of her jaw demonstrated a honeycombed pattern of bone decay. Simultaneously, many women presented the same types of ailments, and their health providers suspected that theses ailments were related to employment with US Radium, where they all had painted products with the glowing paint. It was discovered that owners and managers at US Radium had taken extensive precautions to protect themselves from radiation while at the same time encouraging employee contact with the substance and insisting it was safe. "Rosy cheeks" were the only side effect of swallowing the pigment, supervisors told workers. Women who worked with *Undark* were so comfortable that they would paint their nails and teeth with it.

In 1925, Grace Fryer was examined by a specialist who declared her to be in perfect health, which was confirmed by a colleague who was present during the review. It turns out that the specialist and witness were both on the US Radium payroll. In 1927, Fryer and several other affected women filed suit against US Radium for damages, and the case was later settled for a fraction of the monies requested. During the court battle, US Radium accused many of the women of suffering from syphilis, and the company promoted this as the source of their disease symptoms. By 1927, more than fifty women had died due to poisoning developed while working at US Radium.[35] Grace Fryer passed away on October 27, 1933, at age thirty-five; the medical examiner listed her cause of death as "radium sarcoma, industrial poisoning." Reports claim that the victims were so contaminated that radioactivity can still be detected today by Geiger-counters at their gravesites.[36]

THREE PILLARS CASE QUESTIONS

(1)   It was proposed that US Radium's actions were a result of being "in the dark" about the effects of radium, which at the time was being added to everything from lipstick to chocolate. If this description is accurate, would the company's conduct in this case be excusable or understandable? Why?

(2)   One of the watch dial companies realized that workers were being affected by the paint after several died from radium poisoning. After paying out $90,000 in medical expenses, the company changed its qualifications for filing workers' compensation claims from five years to three years to limit costs. Although this action was legal, was this an ethical decision?

(3)   The tremendous costs associated with lawsuits from injured and dying radium workers was at least partially responsible for the closing of several manufacturing sites, despite demand for the products continuing for many years. If you were the CEO of US Radium Corporation, how could you have reframed corporate strategy to provide for greater company success and worker protection?

———————

Viewing the business playing field from the balcony enables you to reframe your fixed-pie thinking by considering the interests of all stakeholders affected by your decisions, not only the interests of shareholders. Just as the most successful negotiators have the ability to look at deals from the opposing side's perspective, you should examine your value creation and risk management decisions from the perspective of all stakeholders, such as those identified in the McKinsey survey: customers, government, and employees.

What are these stakeholder interests? How can you link these interests to company interests to create a larger pie that benefits all parties? By addressing these questions, you can move beyond the shareholder value focus of the Strategy Pillar and the value protection focus of the Law Pillar to a joint interest-based mindset. This mindset creates an overlap of the Strategy Pillar and the Law Pillar that has the potential to benefit all stakeholders while creating competitive advantage for your company.

However, an interest-based approach faces an important legal challenge: does the law require business leaders to make decisions that give "primacy" to shareholders by maximizing the value they receive before considering the interests of other stakeholders? If the answer to this question is "yes," then an interest-based model that considers benefits to employees, customers, and other stakeholders is legally suspect.

The Michigan Supreme Court discussed this question in an iconic case, *Dodge v. Ford Motor Co.* (1919). Two shareholders of the Ford Motor Company, Horace and John Dodge (who owned 10 percent of the stock) claimed that the company should pay shareholders a dividend beyond the regular dividend of 60 percent per year. Among other things, they wanted the court to order the company to pay shareholders 75 percent of the accumulated cash surplus of over $50 million.

Henry Ford dominated the company, holding 58 percent of the company's stock. He wanted to plow most of the profits back into the company so that he could expand the business and (as he was quoted by the court) "employ still more men; to spread the benefits of this industrial system to the greatest possible number, to help them build up their lives and their homes." During the trial, Ford elaborated on these goals when answering questions posed by the Dodge brothers' lawyer, Elliott Stevenson. Here is an excerpt from the trial transcript, which begins with the lawyer asking Ford about a newspaper interview in which Ford apologized for making an "awful profit" on car sales:[37]

> *Stevenson*: I will ask you again, do you still think those profits were "awful profits?"
>
> *Ford*: Well, I guess I do, yes.
>
> *Stevenson*: And for that reason you were not satisfied to continue to make such "awful profits?"
>
> *Ford*: We don't seem to be able to keep the profits down.

Stevenson: [A]re you trying to keep them down? What is the Ford Motor Company organized for except profits, will you tell me, Mr. Ford?

Ford: Organized to do as much good as we can, everywhere, for everybody concerned.

Stevenson: What is the purpose of the company?

Ford: To do as much as possible for everybody concerned. . . . To make money and use it, give employment, and send out the car where the people can use it. . . . [A]nd incidentally to make money.

Stevenson: Incidentally make money?

Ford: Yes, sir.

Stevenson: But your controlling feature, so far as your policy. . . is to employ a great army of men at high wages, to reduce the selling price of your car, so that a lot of people can buy it at a cheap price, and give everybody a car that wants one?

Ford: If you give all that, the money will fall into your hands; you can't get out of it.

This case raises questions about the legal purpose of a corporation. Deciding the case in favor of the Dodge brothers (on grounds that withholding the dividends was a breach of duty to shareholders), the court's comments could be construed as a rallying cry for advocates of shareholder primacy: "A business corporation is organized and carried on primarily for the profit of the stockholders."

The court's statement aligns with the views of Nobel Prize-winning economist Milton Friedman and other proponents of shareholder primacy, including those who believe that the *Dodge* court's opinion states a legal requirement. These proponents overlook the fact that the statement is not law because the court was merely stating an opinion (called *dicta*) that was not essential to its decision. As Professor Lynn Stout observed, other sources of law do not require maximizing shareholder wealth. To the contrary, "A large majority of state codes contain so-called other-constituency provisions that explicitly authorize corporate boards to consider the interests of not just shareholders, but also employees, customers, creditors, and the community, in making business decisions."[38]

Despite state codes that do not require an exclusive shareholder focus, over the last several decades shareholder primacy has been the mantra of business leaders. In 2019, however, top US CEOs participating in the Business Roundtable declared a commitment to "all stakeholders"—including "workers, consumers, the cities and towns in which their companies operated, and society as a whole."[39] In their declaration, Chairman Jamie Dimon, the CEO of JPMorgan Chase, hoped that this stance will "help to set a new standard for corporate leadership."

This change aligns well with sustainability pioneer John Elkington's "Triple Bottom Line"—economic prosperity, environmental quality, and social justice—which he first developed over twenty years ago.[40] Elkington, who commented on the 2019 declaration, believes that businesses will embrace these values as simply a global, natural evolution of people's growing awareness and concern. Corrupt business practices, child labor, theft of intellectual property, low employee wages, sexual harassment, placing profit ahead of human welfare—eliminating these negative aspects of international business operations is an essential and valuable focus for twenty-first-century wealth creation and sustainability. Early evidence of change, according to Elkington, will come in the language used by companies and the vocabulary used by business people. Terms like "lean production, social capital, sustainability, stakeholders, value migration" all signal that consideration of the broader landscape is afoot.[41]

As echoed by author Rick Wartzman from the Drucker Institute, "Words matter. The words of the [Business] Roundtable—a Who's Who of those at the helm of the largest U.S. corporations, from Abbott to Zebra Technologies—matter a lot. In the end, though, it is the actions of Roundtable members that will matter the most."[42]

As Wartzman indicated, when language changes, it is hoped that actions follow. The challenges in balancing the interests of multiple stakeholders is illustrated in the following case—*Shlensky v. Wrigley*—where the majority shareholder and officer of the Chicago Cubs baseball team led a company decision to forego nighttime lighting at the ballpark. Although the court determined that the decision was free of illegality, there is a definite question of whether the interests of all stakeholders were contemplated.

STRATEGY LAW ETHICS	***Three Pillars Case: Take Me out to the "Night" Game***

Citation: *Shlensky v. Wrigley*, 95 Ill. App. 2d 173 (Ill. App. Ct. 1st Dist. 1968)

In the mid-1960s, William Shlensky, a minority shareholder of the company that owned the Chicago Cubs baseball team, brought a lawsuit against the majority shareholder and president Phillip K. Wrigley and other defendants in an attempt to force the club to install nighttime lighting at Wrigley Field. This case illustrates the struggle of companies to balance the interests of various stakeholders in business decision making. Here are excerpts from the decision of Justice Sullivan of the Illinois Appellate Court.

SULLIVAN, Justice.

This is an appeal from a dismissal of plaintiff's amended complaint on motion of the defendants. The action was a stockholders' derivative suit against the directors for negligence and mismanagement. . . . Plaintiff sought damages and an order that defendants cause the installation of lights in Wrigley Field and the scheduling of night baseball games.

. . . The Cubs, in the years 1961–65, sustained operating losses from its direct baseball operations. Plaintiff attributes those losses to inadequate attendance at Cubs' home games. He concludes that if the directors continue to refuse to install lights at Wrigley Field and schedule night baseball games, the Cubs will continue to sustain comparable losses and its financial condition will continue to deteriorate.

. . . Plaintiff alleges that the funds for the installation of lights can be readily obtained through financing and the cost of installation would be far more than offset and recaptured by increased revenues and incomes resulting from the increased attendance.

Plaintiff further alleges that defendant Wrigley has refused to install lights, not because of interest in the welfare of the corporation but because of his personal opinions 'that baseball is a 'daytime sport' and that the installation of lights and night baseball games will have a deteriorating effect upon the surrounding neighborhood.'

. . . It is charged that the directors are acting for a reason or reasons contrary and wholly unrelated to the business interests of the corporation; that such arbitrary and capricious acts constitute mismanagement and waste of corporate assets, and that the directors have been negligent in failing to exercise reasonable care and prudence in the management of the corporate affairs.

. . . Plaintiff argues that the allegations . . . set forth a cause of action under the principles set out in *Dodge v. Ford Motor Co.,* 204 Mich. 459, 170 N.W. 668. In that case plaintiff, owner of about 10% of the outstanding stock, brought suit against the directors seeking payment of additional dividends and the enjoining of further business expansion. From the authority relied upon in that case it is clear that the court felt that there must be fraud or a breach of that good faith which directors are bound to exercise toward the stockholders in order to justify the courts entering into the internal affairs of corporations. This is made clear when the court refused to interfere with the directors' decision to expand the business. The following appears on page 684 of 170 N.W.:

. . . The judges are not business experts. It is recognized that plans must often be made for a long future, for expected competition, for a continuing as well as an immediately profitable venture. . . . We are not satisfied that the alleged motives of the directors, in so far as they are reflected in the conduct of business, menace the interests of the shareholders.'

Plaintiff in the instant case argues that the directors are acting for reasons unrelated to the financial interest and welfare of the Cubs. However, we are not satisfied that the motives assigned to Philip K. Wrigley, and through him to the other directors, are contrary to the best interests of the corporation and the stockholders. For example, it appears to us that the effect on the surrounding neighborhood might well be considered by a director who was considering the patrons who would or would not attend the games if the park were in a poor neighborhood. Furthermore, the long run interest of the corporation in its property value at Wrigley Field might demand all efforts to keep the neighborhood from deteriorating. By these thoughts we do not mean to say that we have decided that the decision of the directors was a correct one. That is beyond our jurisdiction and ability. We are merely saying that the decision is one properly before directors and the motives alleged in the amended complaint showed no fraud, illegality or conflict of interest in their making of that decision.

. . . Affirmed.

DEMPSEY, P.J., and SCHWARTZ, J., concur.

THREE PILLARS CASE QUESTIONS

(1)   Justice Sullivan states that Shlensky's filing was a "stockholders' derivative suit." Define the purpose of this type of litigation through research at The Free Dictionary's Free Legal Dictionary: https://legadictionary.thefreedictionary.com/stockholder%27s+derivative+suit. If Shlensky had prevailed, would he be entitled to the damages awarded (see "Suing a Corporation as a Corporate Shareholder," at https://www.legalmatch.com/law-library/article/suing-a-corporation-as-a-corporate-shareholder.html)?

(2)   Read about the Business Judgment Rule (BJR) for company directors and officers at The Free Legal Dictionary: https://legal-dictionary.thefreedictionary.com/Business+Judgment+Rule. Did the BJR protect the decision made by the Ford Motor Company to forego issuing dividends? Did the BJR protect Wrigley's decision to prevent installation of nighttime lighting at the Cubs' stadium? Explain.

(3) The court in *Shlensky* determined that the decision of the Cubs' directors was legal. What statements made by the court could support the banning of nighttime lighting at the stadium as an ethical decision?

(4) On August 8, 1988, nighttime lighting was used for the first time at Wrigley Field. A *Chicago Tribune* article recounts how addition of the lighting was contemplated in 1982 but was delayed by legislation and the interests of residents surrounding the ballpark, who wanted to keep the stadium in the dark. Based on this knowledge, did Phillip Wrigley and the Cubs company directors make the right decision to forego nighttime lighting in the 1960s? Why? Would it make a difference if the decision was only based on Wrigley's opinion that baseball was a "daytime" sport?

(5) One of Shlensky's arguments in the case was that the decision to avoid nighttime lighting was "wholly unrelated to the business interests of the corporation." Do you agree with this reasoning? Explain your answer.

(6) Is there a strategy that the directors could implement that would act as a compromise between the stakeholder interests in this case? Discuss.

So, the bottom line is that the law does not prevent a trip to the balcony to consider the interests of stakeholders beyond shareholders. As we will explain in the next chapter, this interest-based approach, in addition to linking the Strategy Pillar to the Law Pillar, enables you to establish values that can guide decisions within the Ethics Pillar as well.

KEY TAKEAWAYS

The Three Pillars are inter-related and should overlap in the decision making process. However, because of a considerable gap between the Strategy and Law Pillars, it is incumbent upon business decision makers to gain a better understanding of how law relates to strategy. This may be accomplished in part by:

1. **Awareness of the Gap.** Once you recognize the importance of law to business decision making, you can bridge the law-strategy gap by increasing your understanding of legal and ethical concepts that relate to strategy.

2. **Finding Balance.** In business, there are many stakeholders and issues to consider in decision making. Closing the gap may be as straightforward as adjusting minor planning details once legal knowledge is applied, or improving communication with legal advisors when designing new strategies.

3.   A Joint-Interest Mindset. A focus on making money in business is important; after all, the very definition of a "business" is "any activity or enterprise entered into for profit."[43] Yet successful businesses can move beyond the *profit-above-all-else* mindset by creating value for all stakeholders when they focus on the application of legal and ethical principles to business strategies.

STRATEGY LAW ETHICS	*Three Pillars Decision: "You've got a fast car . . . "*[44]

The sharing economy is a good example of where industries need to consider the many interests of the various stakeholders involved.

Most everyone is familiar with ride-sharing services such as Uber and Lyft, which feature unregulated drivers offering rides in their personal vehicles. The advent of these companies was a definite disruptor of the taxi industry, where cab drivers are facing longer days, declining wages, and ultimately—many believe—extinction.

Recently, another potential threat has materialized on the transportation horizon in the form of *car sharing*. Vehicle rental companies have been gearing up to fight the current trend toward individuals renting their personal vehicles to individuals (peers). Proponents of the peer-to-peer car rentals, such as those provided by the company Turo, claim that profits are high and that the benefits flow in both directions. Individuals can rent vehicles that car rental companies don't stock—like the Tesla Model X—and owners can pay their car loans off quickly. This "Airbnb for cars" is rapidly becoming a major concern for the $30-billion-dollar per year car rental industry.

VALUE GOAL: To design a service that takes advantage of the increasing trend in car-sharing.

STRATEGY: Develop a strategy that would allow a car-sharing service to operate in the states of New York and California, where rental fees are among the highest in the nation.

LAW: Research the laws of New York and California with regard to car-sharing. Do these provisions affect or alter the strategy you developed? If necessary, refine your strategy to align with the law.&

ETHICS: Apply ethics to your strategy by working through these four steps of ethical decision making: (1) describe the ethical dilemma, (2) identify the stakeholders involved, (3) analyze options (including how each group of stakeholders will be affected), and (4) make a decision based on your analysis. After examining ethical issues associated with the strategy, determine whether any modifications should be made.

Check for law research materials in the Appendix: Legal Resources for Business Decisions

STRATEGY LAW ETHICS	***Three Pillars Decision: McFacts v. McFiction***

Hot coffee in this next decision places McDonald's Corporation in a hot mess with regard to its strategy for trying to satisfy some customers at the expense of others.

Chances are, you have heard of (and maybe even discussed) the McDonald's hot coffee lawsuit. Yet not many know the real story behind the case of *Stella Liebeck v. McDonald's Restaurants.* On the day when seventy-nine-year-old Mrs. Liebeck spilled coffee on herself, resulting in serious burns requiring an eight-day hospitalization, McDonald's was serving their java brews at a temperature between 180 and 190 degrees Fahrenheit—thirty to forty degrees above most other restaurants. Coffee served within that temperature range causes third-degree burns within 3 to 7 seconds. The Shriner's Burn Institute in Cincinnati had warned McDonald's that coffee served above 130 degrees was "dangerously hot."[45]

In the decade before Mrs. Liebeck's accident, more than seven hundred people claimed scalding injuries by McDonald's hot coffee, yet the company never lowered the temperature.[46] McDonald's knew the temperature of its coffee could cause serious injury but continued to serve it that way because it believed the coffee "tasted better" at that temperature.[47] The company agreed at trial that its coffee was "not fit for human consumption" and could offer no explanation as to why they did not warn customers about the danger.[48]

VALUE GOAL: To provide a viable hot coffee product to consumers that reduces the risk of injury.

STRATEGY: Develop a strategy that provides hot coffee to consumers and minimizes the risk of scalding/burn injury.

LAW: Are there any laws related to the temperature of coffee products served to consumers? Also examine the following *Journal of Food Science* (67(7):2774–2777 July 2006) article: "At What Temperatures Do Consumers Like to Drink Coffee?"[49] Does this research affect or alter the strategy you developed? If necessary, refine your strategy to align with the law and consumer safety.*

ETHICS: There is a significant ethical concern with McDonald's attitude toward these consumer injuries. Overseeing Judge Robert Scott called the company's behavior in this case, "callous."[50] In examining this situation, apply ethics to your strategy by working through these four steps of ethical decision making: (1) describe the ethical dilemma, (2) identify the stakeholders involved, (3) analyze options (including how each group of stakeholders will be affected), and (4) make a decision based on your analysis. After examining ethical issues associated with the strategy, determine whether any modifications should be made.

&*Check for law research materials in the Appendix: Legal Resources for Business Decisions*

STRATEGY	
LAW	***Three Pillars Decision: TripAdvising in Jamaica***
ETHICS	

Social media has created significant benefits—as well as significant drawbacks—for companies with a strong dependence on the Internet for their business success. This decision examines the required extent of company responsibility in protecting consumers.

According to the *Detroit Free Press*, scores of female travelers have been writing complaints on the travel site TripAdvisor, warning of sexual harassment by male workers at Jamaican vacation resorts. Women have reported being followed to their rooms at night, cornered, stalked, intimidated, and physically assaulted by bartenders, food servers, lifeguards, and security workers employed by island hotels. Following an investigation by the *Free Press* that found that sexual assaults in Jamaica are a "pervasive and unchecked" problem, TripAdvisor added a Safety Warning box to the review section of a property; the warning pops up if the resort has reviews mentioning sexual assault or misconduct within the last twelve months.

The newspaper article points out that "none of the flagged reviews mention sexual *harassment*," although on the site there have been multiple past reviews of Jamaican properties mentioning such conduct.[51] In response, TripAdvisor spokesperson Brian Hoyt stated: "We are looking at sexual harassment and how to address it in the future as we continue to enhance the travel safety information on our site; we had to start somewhere and we started with involuntary physical harm."[52]

TripAdvisor also points out that it does not investigate alleged crimes or post opinions on them, and it suggests that reviewed businesses and hotels need to take responsibility: "It's critical that businesses in the hospitality industry, including hotels and lodging, do their part—including making background checks and [adding a] safety training core to their hiring and labor practices; governments also need to continue to pass laws and commit resources to making tourists safe."[53]

VALUE GOAL: To communicate risks and promote traveler safety on travel review sites.

STRATEGY: Develop a strategy that would allow TripAdvisor to communicate reviews mentioning sexual harassment incidents in addition to sexual assault events to travelers using their site.

LAW: TripAdvisor is an Internet Service Provider (ISP) and, as such, it is subject to the protections of Section 230 of the Communications Decency Act (CDA). Examine the CDA and determine if your strategy would subject TripAdvisor to liability under this law. If yes, refine your strategy to provide TripAdvisor with continued protections under Section 230.☙

ETHICS: There are a number of stakeholders in this scenario that may be affected by your strategy, including TripAdvisor, travelers, reviewed resorts and their employees, communities, and governments. Keep these stakeholders and others in mind when examining your strategy for ethical issues, working through these four steps of ethical decision making: (1) describe the ethical dilemma, (2) identify the stakeholders involved, (3) analyze options (including how each group of stakeholders will be affected), and (4) make a decision based on your analysis. After examining ethical issues associated with the strategy, determine whether any modifications should be made.

☙ *Check for law research materials in the Appendix: Legal Resources for Business Decisions*

1   Bagley et al., "Who Let the Lawyers Out?: Reconstructing the Role of the Chief Legal Officer and the Corporate Client in a Globalizing World," 18 University of Pennsylvania Journal of Business Law 419 (2016).

2   Director's Roundtable, "Michael Solender," September 29, 2015.

3   "List of Areas of Law," http://en.wikipedia.org/wiki/List_of_areas_of_law.

4   Refo, "The Vanishing Trial," *Litigation*, Winter 2004.

5   "The Status of Law in Academic Business Study," http://cba2.unomaha.edu/faculty/mohara/web/ALSBsta8.htm.

6   "Value Creation by Lawyers," *The Yale Law Journal*, December 1984.

7   Harrison, "Champions of Change," *InsideCounsel*, November 1, 2014.

8   "2015 Travelers Business Risk Index," http://www.travelers.com/prepare-prevent/risk-index/business/2015/business-risk-index-report.pdf.

9   "Risk Management for an Era of Greater Uncertainty," http://www.accenture.com/us-en/~/media/Accenture/Conversion-Assets/DotCom/Documents/Global/PDF/Industries_6/Accenture-Global-Risk-Management-Study-2013.pdf.

¹⁰ "2015 Litigation Trends Annual Survey," http://www.nortonrosefulbright.com/files/20150514-2015-litigation-trends-survey_v24-128746.pdf.

¹¹ AlixPartners Litigation and Corporate Compliance Survey, http://www.alixpartners.com/en/LinkClick.aspx?fileticket=SO5aBoKEHDs%3d&tabid=635.

¹² "Legal Risk Benchmarking Survey," http://www.blplaw.com/download/BLP_Legal_Risk_Benchmarking_Report.pdf.

¹³ "Managing Complexity and Change in a New Landscape," http://www.ey.com/Publication/vwLUAssets/EY_-_7_big_changes_to_asset_management_operating_models/$FILE/EY-Managing-complexity-and-change in a new-landscape.pdf.

¹⁴ "Government and the Global CEO: Redefining Success in a Changing World," http://www.pwc.com/gx/en/industries/government-public-services/public-sector-research-centre/publications/government-19th-annual-ceo-survey.html.

¹⁵ "Rediscovering the Power of Law in Business Education," http://www.aacsb.edu/blog/2016/february/rediscovering-the-power-of-law-in-business-education.

¹⁶ "Building the Manager's Toolbox, *Journal of Legal Studies Education*, 2013.

¹⁷ *Skills for the 21st Century General Counsel* (2013).

¹⁸ *Id.*

¹⁹ Jessen, "Moving Beyond the 'Department of No,' " *Inside Counsel*, December 11, 2015.

²⁰ Legal Risk Benchmarking Survey," *supra.*

²¹ Khusainova, "Exploring Legal Strategy," unpublished paper.

²² "Law, Strategy and Competitive Advantage," *Connecticut Law Review*, November 2011.

²³ "Finding the Right Corporate Legal Strategy," Fall 2014.

²⁴ "Legal Risk Benchmarking Survey," *supra.*

²⁵ "Building Your Organization's Legal IQ," http://img.en25.com/Web/CEB/CEB_Legal_Building_Your_Organizations_Legal_IQ_Preview_Report.pdf?cid=70134000001A7ckAAC.

²⁶ The 190/MBA Program, The University of Chicago Booth School of Business, undated catalog.

²⁷ Bagley, et al., *supra.*

²⁸ Colby, Ehrlich, Sullivan and Dolle, *Rethinking Undergraduate Business Education* (2011).

²⁹ "A Seat at the Table," http://www.shell.com/global/aboutshell/media/speeches-and-articles/2014/a-seat-at-the-table-in-house-lawyers-are-business-partners.html.

³⁰ Bagley, et al., *supra.*

³¹ Russo and Schoemaker, *Decision Traps* (1990).

³² *Judgment in Managerial Decision Making* (2008).

³³ Siedel, *Negotiating for Success: Essential Strategies and Skills* (2014).

³⁴ "Managing Government Relations for the Future," http://www.mckinsey.com/insights/public_sector/managing_government_relations_for_the_future_mckinsey_global_survey_results.

³⁵ https://www.damninteresting.com/undark-and-the-radium-girls/; https://text-message.blogs.archives.gov/2018/01/04/the-radium-girls-at-the-national-archives/; http://radiumgirlsnhd.weebly.com/impact.html.

³⁶ https://www.nytimes.com/1987/10/04/nyregion/radium-from-wonder-drug-to-hazard.html.

³⁷ Lewis, *The Public Image of Henry Ford* (1976).

³⁸ "Why We Should Stop Teaching *Dodge v. Ford*," http://papers.ssrn.com/sol3/papers.cfm?abstract_id=1013744.

³⁹ https://www.fastcompany.com/90391743/top-ceo-group-business-roundtable-drops-shareholder-primacy.

⁴⁰ Elkington, John. Cannibals with Forks, Capstone Publishing Limited, 1997.

⁴¹ *Id.*

⁴² https://www.fastcompany.com/90391743/top-ceo-group-business-roundtable-drops-shareholder-primacy.

[43] Burton's Legal Thesaurus, 4E. S.v. "Business." Retrieved April 1, 2018 from https://legal-dictionary.thefreedictionary.com/business.

[44] https://www.azlyrics.com/lyrics/tracychapman/fastcar.html.

[45] https://segarlaw.com/blog/myths-and-facts-of-the-mcdonalds-hot-coffee-case/.

[46] https://injury.findlaw.com/product-liability/the-mcdonald-s-coffee-cup-case-separating-mcfacts-from-mcfiction.html.

[47] https://segarlaw.com/blog/myths-and-facts-of-the-mcdonalds-hot-coffee-case/.

[48] http://www.hotcoffeethemovie.com/default.asp?pg=mcdonalds_case.

[49] https://www.researchgate.net/publication/230106152_At_What_Temperatures_Do_Consumers_Like_to_Drink_Coffee_Mixing_Methods.

[50] Article Source: http://EzineArticles.com/50056.

[51] https://www.freep.com/story/news/local/michigan/detroit/2019/05/31/tripadvisor-sexual-misconduct-buried/1274528001/.

[52] https://www.freep.com/story/news/local/michigan/detroit/2019/05/31/tripadvisor-sexual-misconduct-buried/1274528001/.

[53] https://www.freep.com/story/news/local/michigan/detroit/2019/05/31/tripadvisor-sexual-misconduct-buried/1274528001/.

CHAPTER 3

Ethics: Icing on the Strategy-Law Pillar Cake

ADDING THE ETHICS PILLAR

In addition to closing the gap between the Strategy Pillar and the Law Pillar, alignment of these pillars with the Ethics Pillar is essential to improved business decision making and value creation. This is important because business leaders often fail to understand that what is *legal* is not necessarily the same as what is *ethical*, creating a schism in the decision making process. For example, imagine that one day you are walking past a local pond, and you see a young child in the pond water. As you move closer, you realize that there is no one else around. The child is in trouble and might drown if you do not intercede. Yet the general rule in the United States is that you do not have to stop and render aid, even if doing so is within your capacity—so, you could keep on walking and allow the child to be seriously injured or drown. Although this act of not rendering assistance would be *legal*, few would believe this decision to be *ethical*.

Many times, business decision-makers are faced with a similar conundrum, although the situation is rarely as clear-cut as the drowning child example. Once a business has formulated a strategy to achieve a goal and researched and understood the law, ethics becomes an indispensable part of the Three Pillar foundational approach.

Aligning the Ethics Pillar with the Strategy and Law Pillars is just simply good, responsible business practice. This section of the book addresses the following key ethics-related questions that every business leader—ranging from the owner of a start-up business to the leader of a multinational company—must address:

- How does the law influence ethical decision making within your company?

- What elements should your company include in its compliance program and code of conduct?

- How can you become an ethical leader in your business?

- Can your business meet societal needs while also creating value for shareholders?

Before moving to the first question, a big-picture perspective on business ethics programs is useful. According to Harvard Professor Lynn Paine and coauthor Christopher Bruner, companies use two types of programs when focusing on the Ethics Pillar: compliance programs and values programs. Compliance programs have a risk management orientation and emphasize meeting legal requirements to avoid liability. Values programs encourage ethical decision making even when it is not legally required.

The most effective programs blend both compliance and values elements. Paine and Bruner described the danger of relying on only one element: "Just as exclusive emphasis on compliance may result in a myopic focus on 'obeying the letter of the law,' vague statements of principles, without translation into concrete standards that are consistently enforced, may leave employees with little sense of what is expected. . . ."[1]

THE LAW'S INFLUENCE ON ETHICAL DECISION MAKING

The law influences ethical decision making in two ways. First, certain laws require companies to adopt programs designed to promote compliance with the law. Second, legal principles provide guidance to managers faced with ethical dilemmas.

Laws Requiring Compliance Programs

Several US laws require businesses to adopt compliance programs.[2] Some of these laws are included in legislation—for instance, the USA Patriot Act, which requires financial institutions to create programs to prevent money laundering. Other laws are embedded in regulations that government agencies develop. The Securities and Exchange Commission, for example, requires investment advisers and investment companies to adopt compliance programs designed to prevent violations of securities law.

Courts have also addressed the duty of company leaders to establish compliance programs. A key 1996 decision[3] involved healthcare company Caremark International. After the company pleaded guilty to mail fraud and paid about $250 million in damages, shareholders initiated a lawsuit claiming that individual members of the company's board of directors should pay for the losses. Although the Delaware Chancery Court approved a settlement of the lawsuit, it also noted that in some circumstances directors could be held liable for losses when they do not make a good faith attempt to ensure that the company has an adequate information and reporting system.

Even when companies are not technically required to adopt compliance programs, they have other incentives to do so. The US Organizational Sentencing Guidelines are especially important. The latest version of these guidelines provides that companies that have an "effective program to prevent and detect violations of law" are eligible for reduced fines following a criminal conviction.[4]

For example, assume that a company convicted of fraud for overcharging its customers paid restitution to its victims. Under the Sentencing Guidelines, the company would face a fine as low as $685,000 or as high as $54,800,000, depending on the quality of its compliance program and other Sentencing Guidelines that judges consider.[5] These guidelines are especially important because they provide a model that companies can use worldwide, even when not subject to US law. Later in this chapter, we will review a checklist of the guidelines.

Another incentive for companies to adopt compliance programs arises from rules that private organizations adopt. For example, to be listed on the New York Stock Exchange, companies must adopt a code of conduct that includes complying with the law.

In the case that follows, the repercussions of noncompliance are stark as a Brazilian subsidiary of Walmart, Inc. is found liable for improper payments for licenses and building permits related to the company's expansion efforts in Mexico, India, Brazil, and China. The resulting $137 million fine imposed on Walmart and $144 million profit disgorgement suggest that its strategy to pay bribes was very much a false economy.[6]

STRATEGY	
LAW	***Three Pillars Case: "Save Money. Live Better."***[7]
ETHICS	

It was determined through a US Department of Justice (DOJ) investigation that the retail giant Walmart failed to comply with the Foreign Corrupt Practices Act (FCPA). The FCPA prohibits companies and officers from influencing foreign officials by providing them with payments or rewards. In the following DOJ press release, the importance of compliance is clear, even when that adherence to the rules may interfere with timely expansion around the world.

Department of Justice
Office of Public Affairs

FOR IMMEDIATE RELEASE   Thursday, June 20, 2019

Walmart Inc. and Brazil-Based Subsidiary Agree to Pay $137 Million to Resolve Foreign Corrupt Practices Act Case

Walmart Inc. (Walmart), a U.S.-based multinational retailer and its wholly owned Brazilian subsidiary, WMT Brasilia S.a.r.l. (WMT Brasilia), have agreed to pay a combined criminal penalty of $137 million to resolve the government's investigation into violations of the Foreign Corrupt Practices Act (FCPA). WMT Brasilia pleaded guilty today in connection with the resolution.

. . . "Walmart profited from rapid international expansion, but in doing so chose not to take necessary steps to avoid corruption," said Assistant Attorney General Benczkowski. "In numerous instances, senior Walmart employees knew of failures of its anti-corruption-related internal controls involving foreign subsidiaries, and yet Walmart failed for years to implement sufficient controls comporting with U.S. criminal laws. As today's resolution shows, even the largest of U.S. companies operating abroad are bound by U.S. laws, and the Department of Justice will continue to aggressively investigate and prosecute foreign corruption."

. . . "The FBI will hold corporations responsible when they turn a blind eye to corruption," said FBI Assistant Director Johnson. "If there is evidence of violations of FCPA, we will investigate. No corporation, no matter how large, is above the law."

. . . In Mexico, a former attorney for Walmart's local subsidiary reported to Walmart in 2005 that he had overseen a scheme for several years prior in which Third Party Intermediaries (TPIs) made improper payments to government officials to obtain permits and licenses for the subsidiary and that several executives at the subsidiary knew of and approved of the scheme. Most of the TPI invoices included a code specifying why the subsidiary had made the improper payment, including: (1) avoiding a requirement; (2) influence, control or knowledge of privileged information known by the government official; and (3) payments to eliminate fines.

In India, because of Walmart's failure to implement sufficient internal accounting controls related to anti-corruption, from 2009 until 2011, Walmart's operations there were able to retain TPIs that made improper payments to government officials in order to obtain store operating permits and licenses. These improper payments were then falsely recorded in Walmart's joint venture's books and records with vague descriptions like "misc fees," "miscellaneous," "professional fees," "incidental" and "government fee."

In Brazil, as a result of Walmart's failure to implement sufficient internal accounting controls related to anti-corruption at its subsidiary, Walmart Brazil, despite repeated findings in internal audit reports that such controls were lacking, continued to retain and renew contracts with TPIs without conducting the required due diligence. Improper payments were in fact paid by some of these TPIs, including a construction company that made improper payments to government officials in connection with the construction of two Walmart Brazil stores in 2009 without the knowledge of Walmart Brazil. Walmart Brazil indirectly hired a TPI whose ability to obtain licenses and permits quickly earned her the nickname "sorceress" or "genie" within Walmart Brazil. Walmart Brazil employees, including a Walmart Brazil executive, knew they could not hire the intermediary directly because of several red flags. In 2009, the TPI made improper payments to government inspectors in connection with the construction of a Walmart Brazil store without the knowledge of Walmart Brazil. WMT Brasilia was a wholly-owned subsidiary of Walmart and was a majority-owner of Walmart Brazil, Walmart's wholly-owned subsidiary in Brazil, and the majority-owner of retail stores operating as Walmart Brazil.

In China, Walmart's local subsidiary's internal audit team flagged numerous weaknesses in internal accounting controls related to anti-corruption at the subsidiary between 2003 and 2011, sometimes repeatedly, but many of these weaknesses were not addressed. In fact, from 2007 until early 2010, Walmart and the subsidiary failed to address nearly all of the anti-corruption-related internal controls audit findings.

. . . Walmart did not voluntarily disclose the conduct in Mexico and only disclosed the conduct in Brazil, China and India after the government had already begun investigating the Mexico conduct. The $137 million penalty includes forfeiture of $3.6 million and a fine of $724,898 from WMT Brasilia.

In a related resolution with the U.S. Securities and Exchange Commission (SEC), Walmart agreed to disgorge $144 million in profits.

THREE PILLARS CASE QUESTIONS

(1)   The press release indicates that some of these violations were the result of TPIs taking action without Walmart's direct knowledge. Should this fact absolve the company of liability for these acts?

(2)   According to the investigators, Walmart's primary failure in the violations was a lack of internal controls. Read about the "Ten Most Important FCPA Internal Controls" at http://fcpamericas.com/english/anti-corruption-compliance/ten-important-fcpa-internal-controls-part-1-accounting-controls/# and http://fcp americas.com/english/anti-corruption-compliance/ten-important-fcpa-internal-controls-part-2-processes/. Which of the controls discussed would have helped prevent the Walmart violations?

(3)   Companies who violate the FCPA standards often point to the culture of the country in which they are operating as the reason for the payments. What is considered illegal by the FBI in the US might be business as usual in another country. Looking at the Brazil Walmart situation from this perspective, do you believe the practice is unethical?

(4)   Assuming that your company is expanding in a country where "greasing the wheels" with payments and gifts is the norm in order to make progress there, what is another strategy you could use to accomplish your goals without running afoul of the law and ethical practice?

Law-Based Ethical Standards

Often, you can resolve an ethical dilemma by basing your decisions on legal principles. Legal rules relating to fraud, fiduciary duty, and unconscionability provide especially useful guidelines.[8] These principles frequently come into play during business negotiations.

Fraud. Fraud is defined as a false representation of a material fact that is relied on by the other side. In other words, it is illegal to lie about facts that the other side relies on during business transactions.

The false representation must relate to a fact that goes beyond puffery, the subjective boasting that is common in advertising. For example, a group of consumers sued cyclist Lance Armstrong arguing that he committed fraud by claiming that certain energy products were his "secret weapon" leading to his success. They claimed that he lied, because his real secret weapon was doping. A Los Angeles judge dismissed the case in 2014 after concluding that Armstrong's statements were puffery.[9]

Sometimes, even statements that are technically true can be considered fraudulent if they need clarification. For example, a couple in Washington was interested in purchasing a hotel. During negotiations, the owner gave them accurate information about the monthly income they could make from the hotel.

After the couple completed the purchase, they learned that the hotel was being run as a house of prostitution, and the monthly income the seller had mentioned was based on this activity. When they sued the seller, the court allowed them to recover damages, noting that: "A representation literally true is actionable if used to create an impression substantially false. In the case at bar there was no misrepresentation as to the amount of the income. . . [The owner] deceived them to their damage by failing to reveal the source of the income."[10]

Fiduciary Duty. A fiduciary duty is the highest duty of trust and loyalty, which is the type of duty that agents (including employees) owe their principals. Suppose that a real estate developer hires you to obtain a $10 million loan commitment from a financial institution. The developer promises you a commission of $50,000. You successfully obtain the commitment, and the financial institution is so pleased with the deal that it pays you a finder's fee.

If the developer refuses to pay, are you entitled to the $50,000 commission? No, said a Georgia court.[11] The agent in that case violated the fiduciary duty owed to the developer by accepting the finder's fee. An agent cannot "compromise himself by attempting to serve two masters having a contrary interest. . . ." In this situation, the agent should have disclosed the dual agency to both principals.

Unconscionability. Unconscionability is an important concept in business negotiations when there is a power imbalance between the parties. In essence, the law requires you to act morally when you are the more powerful party.

Courts focus on two issues in deciding whether a contract is unconscionable. First, they look at the negotiation process (procedural unconscionability): was the weaker party forced to accept the contract terms because of unequal bargaining power? Second, they look at the substance of the deal (substantive unconscionability): are the terms of the deal so unreasonable that they violate principles of good conscience?

An example of unconscionability involved the restaurant Hooters, which forced employees to sign an "Agreement to arbitrate employment-related disputes." This agreement required them to arbitrate all employment disputes, including sexual harassment claims. A bartender at Hooters who signed the agreement filed suit in federal court claiming sexual harassment.

When Hooters argued that she had to use arbitration instead of going to court, the trial court concluded that the arbitration agreement was unconscionable and an appellate court agreed, noting that the rules in the arbitration agreement were "so one-sided that their only possible purpose is to undermine the neutrality of the proceeding."

Among the reasons for this decision: Arbitrators were selected from a list that Hooters created. Hooters could cancel the agreement to arbitrate, but employees could not. Furthermore, Hooters could change the rules of the arbitration at any time.[12]

KEY ELEMENTS IN YOUR COMPLIANCE PROGRAM

Even when you are not legally required to adopt a compliance program, it is sound business practice to do so. The Sentencing Guidelines mentioned earlier are the best starting point for developing your program. The Sentencing Commission Guidelines Manual states that "to have an effective compliance program" you must "promote an organizational culture that encourages ethical conduct and a commitment to compliance with the law." This means that, at a minimum, your company must:

- establish an effective compliance and ethics program,

- communicate the program to employees and provide them with training,

- monitor and evaluate the program, including mechanisms for employees to report criminal conduct,

- enforce the program through disciplinary actions,

- prevent criminal conduct from recurring.

In addition to taking their own disciplinary actions, companies who seek favorable treatment at sentencing in the United States must report to the Department of Justice facts about individuals within the company who have violated the law. The reason for this policy is that it is often difficult for law enforcement officials to prosecute individuals in large corporations that have many layers of decision making.

DEVELOPING YOUR CODE OF CONDUCT

The themes in the Sentencing Guidelines are process-oriented; they do not give details about the content of compliance and ethics programs. Companies can provide this content in the form of a code of conduct. Governmental authorities and other institutions worldwide—ranging from the European Commission to Hong Kong's Independent Commission Against Corruption to Brazil's Institute of Corporate Governance—have encouraged companies to develop codes of conduct.[13]

For companies that decide to heed this advice, what should be included in a code? The answer to this question is easy in situations where a code is required. For example, the New York Stock Exchange rule mentioned previously (under "Laws Requiring Compliance Programs") requires that codes of business conduct and ethics include provisions on confidentiality, fair dealing, and compliance with the law, among others.

Sometimes, court decisions are important to your determination of what should be included—or excluded—from a company code of conduct. For example, Chapter 5 will discuss sexual harassment risk management. The chapter emphasizes that companies should adopt an anti-harassment policy that includes examples of prohibited acts. But in covering wrongful discharge, Chapter 5 also mentions the importance of excluding from company policies any language that would imply that employees will be discharged only for cause. In other words, you should include a sexual harassment policy in your code of conduct but exclude any language that might override your employment-at-will policy.

Beyond these examples of required provisions, what should be included in your code of conduct? Professor Paine and her coauthors analyzed several sets of guidelines for multinational companies, the codes of some of the largest companies in the world, and legal requirements for codes. Based on this extensive research, they developed a global consensus based on eight key ethical principles. You can use this consensus list, which they call a "Codex," in developing a code of conduct for your business or in assessing your existing code. The following definitions are quoted from their article "Up to Code."[14]

1. **Fiduciary Principle:** Act as a fiduciary for the company and its investors. Carry out the company's business in a diligent and loyal manner, with the degree of candor expected of a trustee. [As discussed earlier, this principle is similar to a law-based ethical standard.]

2. **Property Principle:** Respect property and the rights of those who own it. Refrain from theft and misappropriation, avoid waste, and safeguard the property entrusted to you.

3. **Reliability Principle:** Honor commitments. Be faithful to your word and follow through on promises, agreements, and other voluntary undertakings, whether or not embodied in legally enforceable contracts.

4. **Transparency Principle:** Conduct business in a truthful and open manner. Refrain from deceptive acts and practices, keep accurate records, and make timely disclosures of material information while respecting obligations of confidentiality and privacy.

5. Dignity Principle: Respect the dignity of all people. Protect the health, safety, privacy, and human rights of others; refrain from coercion; and adopt practices that enhance human development in the workplace, the marketplace, and the community.

6. Fairness Principle: Engage in free and fair competition, deal with all parties fairly and equitably and practice nondiscrimination in employment and contracting.

7. Citizenship Principle: Act as responsible citizens of the community. Respect the law, protect public goods, cooperate with public authorities, avoid improper involvement in politics and government, and contribute to community betterment.

8. Responsiveness Principle: Engage with parties who may have legitimate claims and concerns relating to the company's activities, and be responsive to public needs while recognizing the government's role and jurisdiction in protecting the public interest.

In their detailed analysis, Paine and her colleagues emphasize that these principles relate to each of the four stakeholders discussed in Chapters 4 through 7—customers, employees, the government (which they called the "public"), and investors. The principles also relate to competitors and suppliers/partners.

A code of conduct is often described as the heart and soul of a company.[15] In the following case, Gap, Inc. is faced with the challenge of aligning its operational strategies with components of its Code of Business Conduct. In meeting this challenge, the words of Hewlett-Packard founders the Bill Hewlett and David Packard are instructive: "The biggest competitive advantage is to do the right thing at the worst time."[16]

STRATEGY	
LAW	***Three Pillars Case: A Gap in the Code***
ETHICS	

International clothier Gap, Inc. is proud of its Code of Business Conduct that urges all those associated with the company to participate in "Doing the Right Thing." The business, founded in 1969, strives—according to its Code—to adhere to the principle of "conducting business in a responsible, honest and ethical manner." In the situations described below, it becomes clear that what a company espouses and what it achieves might not always align in the idealized struggle to promote a responsible and ethical work environment.

Gap, Inc.'s Code of Business Conduct encourages employees to ask themselves the following questions:[17]

- Is this the right thing to do?

- Is this legal?

- Is this permitted under our Code of Business Conduct?

- Would I want to see this reported in the media?

Although the tenets of the Code align well with an ethical and law-abiding corporate image, there are reports that the company was not always the most socially responsible.

Review this excerpt, dated September 25, 2007, from a young woman in El Salvador, which was published on the North American Congress on Latin America (NACLA) website. NACLA is an "independent, nonprofit organization founded in 1966 that works toward a world in which the nations and peoples of Latin America and the Caribbean are free from oppression and injustice."

> *My name is Judith Yanira Viera. I am from El Salvador and I am 18 years old. For over a year, I worked in the Taiwanese-owned Mandarin International maquiladora factory in the San Marcos Free Trade Zone, where we made shirts for the Gap, Eddie Bauer and J.C. Penney. From Monday to Thursday, our work shift went from seven in the morning until nine at night. On Fridays, we would work straight through the night, starting at 7 a.m. and working until 4 a.m. We would sleep overnight at the factory on the floor. The following day, we would work from 7 a.m. until 5 p.m. Despite these very long hours, the most I ever earned was 750 colones [about $43] per month. The supervisors often screamed at the women. They would hit us with the shirts and tell us to work faster. Even though we worked a 14-hour day, we were only permitted to go to the bathroom twice. It gets very hot in the plant, and the ventilation is poor. In the factory, there is no purified water, and the drinking water they give us is contaminated. There are many minors—girls aged 14, 15 and 16—who work in Mandarin. They would like to continue their studies, but the company does not permit it. They make the children work the same long shifts as the adult workers.*[18]

NACLA investigators added further details to Judith's story:

> At the Mandarin plant, women like Judith are paid 18 cents for every Gap shirt they make. The Gap sells these shirts for $20 each in the United States. In other words, the women's wages amount to under 1% of the sale price of the shirts in the United States. Like a number of other U.S.-apparel firms, the Gap has established much-touted Corporate Codes of Conduct that require contract shops with whom it does business to abide by their countries' labor laws. Despite ample

evidence of labor-rights violations by Mandarin, the Gap has consistently maintained that in its investigations, including several trips to visit the plant in El Salvador, it has found Mandarin to be a "model" operation that treated its workers with "decency and respect." Under intense pressure from the growing evidence of abuses at Mandarin, the Gap announced its decision to pull out of El Salvador in November (2007). The Gap continues to deny its role in the exploitation. Labor organizers, however, say the company's decision to pull out is tantamount to recognizing its incapacity to monitor its contractors and enforce its own codes of conduct. Organizers argue that the company should use its leverage as a major buyer to demand improved working conditions for maquiladora workers. By pulling out, they say, the Gap further punishes poor workers in developing countries.[19]

THREE PILLARS CASE QUESTIONS

(1)   Read Gap, Inc.'s Code of Business Conduct at the US Securities and Exchange Commission (SEC) website: https://www.sec.gov/Archives/edgar/data/39911/000119312504053618/dex14.htm. What aspects of Gap's Code are violated by the above narratives?

(2)   Charles Kernaghan, Executive Director of the National Labor Committee, first publicized Gap's use of sweatshop labor in El Salvador more than a decade before the 2007 reports featured above. Kernaghan has expressed wishes that the company (Gap) "would protect its workers as vigorously as it protects its trademark. The garment is protected but not the human being who made it. There are no laws to protect these human beings in the global economy."[20] What steps could Gap take to bring its company values in line with the grim realities of some aspects of its global business?

(3)   Gap has blamed unauthorized subcontractors hired by its vendors for some of the poor working conditions and child labor. Is this a valid excuse for Gap to avoid complicity in these issues?

(4)   Do you agree with labor organizers that Gap's decision to simply leave El Salvador is a mistake and that it should stay and try and make conditions better? If it did stay, what strategies could it implement to manage the situation effectively and create value for the company?

BECOMING AN ETHICAL LEADER

Developing a compliance program and a code of conduct is necessary to create an ethical company, but it is not sufficient to do so. An additional element is needed because of what Paine and her colleagues call the "Conduct Gap." This phrase stems from their surveys of employees at companies worldwide, which revealed that there is a gap between what companies should do and what they actually do.[21]

For example, according to a KPMG survey (with more than thirty-five hundred respondents from a wide variety of industries), 73 percent of employees had observed misconduct in the workplace. Most of this misconduct (reported by 56 percent of respondents) was serious—"possibly resulting in a significant loss of public trust." The most commonly-cited cause of misconduct is "pressure to do 'whatever it takes' to meet business goals," coupled with a belief that company codes of conduct are not taken seriously.[22]

One problem with codes of conduct is that companies use a top-down approach when creating them. This approach ignores the reality that "executives cannot just descend from some ethical mountaintop with a couple of stone tablets and expect immediate compliance."[23] In contrast, standards of conduct that are linked to the Strategy Pillar and the Law Pillar become automatically embedded in everyday decision making.

Here are two suggestions for closing the "Conduct Gap":

(1)   Use the Three Pillar model to embed the principles from the Codex into everyday ethical decision making.

(2)   Provide employees with a practical decision making process and related ethical guidelines.

Three Pillar Model to Embed Ethical Principles into Everyday Decisions

Closing the gaps between pillars requires that you understand the interests of key company stakeholders—customers, employees, government, and investors.

A company that understands and acts on stakeholder interests can use the Three Pillars to produce guidelines that parallel the eight principles in the Codex. Unlike the Codex principles, which sound as though they were handed down from the mountain top where senior executives reside, Three Pillar guidelines originate on the front line of business decision making. In other words, using the Three

Pillar model enables you to operationalize the more abstract principles in the Codex.

In Chapters 4 through 9, you will observe examples of how Three Pillar guidelines parallel the Codex principles. Here are examples.

Chapter	Codex Principles
Chapter 4: Develop safe products that meet customer needs.	**Codex #5:** Protect the health and safety of others and enhance human development in the marketplace.
Chapter 5: Use honesty and management by fact to attract and retain the best talent.	**Codex #4:** Conduct business in a truthful and honest manner. **Codex #5:** Enhance human development in the workplace.
Chapter 5: Eliminate all forms of discrimination to enable employees to achieve success.	**Codex #5:** Respect the dignity of all people. Enhance human development in the workplace. **Codex #6:** Practice nondiscrimination in employment and contracting.
Chapter 6: Participate in the law-making process. Embrace the law through strong compliance programs. Manage political risks in countries that do not follow the rule of law. Operate on the Regulatory Frontier to identify emerging social issues.	**Codex #5:** Enhance human development in the community. **Codex #7:** Act as responsible citizens of the community. Respect the law, cooperate with public authorities, avoid improper involvement in politics and government, and contribute to the community. **Codex #8:** Be responsive to public needs while recognizing the government's role and jurisdiction in protecting the public interest.
Chapter 7: Protect your property rights. Consider ways to work cooperatively with other companies by sharing intellectual property.	**Codex #2:** Respect property and the rights of those who own it. Safeguard the property entrusted to you.
Chapter 8: Focus on creating contracts that build relationships and	**Codex #3:** Honor commitments. Be faithful to your word and follow through on promises, agreements, and

create value through commercial affinity instead of legalities.	other voluntary undertakings,[24] [24] whether or not embodied in legally-enforceable contracts.
Chapter 9: Consider using alternatives to litigation for resolving disputes, such as mediation and arbitration.	**Codex #8:** Engage with parties who have legitimate claims.

Use a Practical Decision Making Process and Related Ethical Guidelines

A second approach to closing the Conduct Gap is to supplement the code of conduct with a practical decision making process and related ethical guidelines that employees can use in day-to-day decisions. A simple four-step process is useful for ethical decision making:

1. Define the ethical dilemma and alternatives.

2. Get facts, including the impact on stakeholders.

3. Analyze your alternatives, using ethical guidelines.

4. Make your decision.

There are many practical ethical guidelines that you and company employees can use at Step 3.[25] Here are four examples.

First, develop a credo or pledge that clearly states company beliefs. For example, the credo of Johnson & Johnson (J&J) tracks the organization of this book (Chapters 4–7) by first emphasizing the company's responsibilities to consumers of its products and then, in descending order, its responsibilities to employees, the community, and stockholders. Here are the opening lines of the J&J credo: "We believe our first responsibility is to the doctors, nurses and patients, to mothers and fathers and all others who use our products and services." Former company CEO Robert Wood Johnson wrote the credo in 1943, and it has guided the company ever since.

Second, when confronted with an ethical concern, think of someone you admire and ask yourself what that person would do to resolve the dilemma. This could be, for example, someone you read about—perhaps an historical figure— or someone you observe at work.

An attorney for Qualcomm once explained why he admired Qualcomm CEO Irwin Jacobs. During negotiations the attorney was involved in, the other side accidentally sent him a fax that appeared to provide their confidential information about the negotiations. As he tells the story, "I ran into Irwin's office with the fax. But before I could even start to read it, he asked, 'Was it meant to go to us?' When I told him it wasn't, he said, 'Send it back.' I left with my tail between my legs. He's a very ethical person. Most people would have read that document."[26]

Third, think about how you would feel telling your family about your business decisions. Or how you would feel reading about your actions on the front page of the local newspaper? Sometimes, these "family" and "newspaper" tests are combined. As legendary investor Warren Buffett put it: "After they first obey all rules, I then want employees to ask themselves whether they are willing to have any contemplated act appear the next day on the front page of their local paper, to be read by their spouses, children, and friends."

Fourth, consider using the Golden Rule, which is part of every major religion in the world. Although the precise wording differs, the rule basically suggests that you should treat others as you want to be treated.

Your challenge as an ethical leader does not stop here. After encouraging employees in your business to use the simple process and guidelines for making day-to-day decisions, you must also "walk the talk." For example, in 1982, beginning with the death of a twelve-year-old girl, seven people in the Chicago area died suddenly over a three-day period. Someone had obtained bottles of Tylenol, added cyanide, and returned the bottles to the shelves of various stores. The crime was never solved and is still under investigation.

Before the murders, the manufacturer of Tylenol, J&J, held a 35 percent market share. After the murders, the market share plunged to 7 percent. The ethical dilemma (Step One of the decision making process) J&J faced was clear: the company had to decide what action to take for a problem it did not cause. At Step Two, the company worked closely with the Chicago Police and the FBI in reviewing facts and developing possible courses of action, including a product recall.

In analyzing the alternatives (Step Three), J&J leaders realized that a recall would have a huge financial impact, as it would involve pulling thirty-one million bottles of Tylenol (with a value of $100 million, which is over $250 million in today's dollars) from shelves nationwide. But they also had the benefit of the clear credo described earlier. In the words of company CEO James Burke, "The credo made it very clear at that point exactly what we were all about. It gave me the ammunition I needed to persuade shareholders and others to spend the $100 million on the recall. The credo helped sell it."[27]

With this credo to guide the company's leaders, their decision (Step Four) to recall the product became clear. The company then quickly developed tamper-proof packaging, reintroduced the product, and eventually regained its market share leadership.

In addition to resolving specific ethical dilemmas in a beneficial manner, when company leaders like Burke establish a culture of integrity by "walking the talk," they have an opportunity to create value for their companies. A recent study of employees concluded that "when employees perceived high levels of integrity at work, their companies were more productive, more attractive to potential new hires, and more profitable."[28]

Beyond Business Decision Making: Corporate Social Responsibility

This chapter has emphasized the elements that encourage company leaders and employees to make ethical decisions in their daily work: use law-based and ethical standards, develop a compliance program and a code of conduct, and use a simple decision making process that includes practical ethical guidelines. But what about large-scale strategic decisions that change the direction of the company? Can and should business leaders decide to use company resources to serve society in addition to creating value for shareholders?

These questions bring us back to Chapter 2, which concluded that the law does not require company leaders to maximize shareholder value. Indeed, most state laws authorize them to consider the interests of all stakeholders, including the community at large. Furthermore, some laws now even require companies to engage in some form of corporate social responsibility (CSR), ranging from regulations covering conflict minerals to the European Union requiring companies to report on sustainability. According to two legal experts, "we are now witnessing a transition from voluntary CSR measures to hard law by means of . . . law and regulations in the United States and around the globe."[29]

Regardless of whether CSR strategies are voluntary or required by law, many business leaders undoubtedly would like to develop strategies that benefit both shareholders and society. This involves reframing strategies in order to consider the interests of both the company and society. When this happens, companies can achieve the desired overlap among the Three Pillars and create a zone of sustainable competitive advantage.

A strategy that has the goal of benefitting society while also creating shareholder value obviously brings into play the Strategy Pillar and the Ethics

Pillar. But what is the role of the Law Pillar? This question was addressed implicitly by Harvard strategy professor Michael Porter and his coauthor Mark Kramer in their article "Strategy and Society." The ideas in their article are closely aligned with this chapter in that they propose "a new way to look at the relationship between business and society that does not treat corporate success and social welfare as a zero-sum game."[30]

According to the authors, this "new look" arises from the two forms of interdependence between companies and society: inside-out links and outside-in links. Inside-out links focus on the ways in which companies affect society through their normal business operations, whereas outside-in links deal with how social conditions impact companies. An understanding of these links enables companies to "set an affirmative CSR agenda that produces maximum social benefit as well as gains for the business."[31]

The authors draw on Porter's earlier work to show how companies can prioritize the social issues they want to address. Inside-out links include a number of these issues that relate to the law, such as discrimination, government regulations, lobbying, privacy, safe working conditions, truthful advertising, and worker safety. Outside-in links provide the context for firm strategy and include these law-related examples:

- Fair and open local competition (e.g., fair regulations)
- Intellectual property protection
- Transparency (e.g., corruption)
- Rule of law (e.g., protection of property)
- Meritocratic incentive systems (e.g., anti-discrimination)

So, achieving the twin goals of business success and social responsibility, like the other business goals to be discussed throughout this book, requires considering all three pillars of decision making—Strategy, Law, and Ethics. Exploring stakeholder interests through the lens of the Three Pillar model enables companies to benefit others while also benefitting themselves. In this way, companies have an opportunity to embody at a company level the advice on happiness that economist John Stuart Mill gave to individuals: "Those only are happy . . . who have their minds fixed on some object other than their own happiness; on the happiness of others, on the improvement of mankind. . . . Aiming thus at something else, they find happiness by the way."[32]

As discussed in this chapter, the success of a business requires thoughtful decision making that incorporates strategy, law, and ethics. In the following case,

Kuehn v. Pub Zone, business owner Maria Kerkoulas attempted to establish a legal and ethical strategy to protect her company and its customers by setting what she believed to be reasonable rules in her public bar. Unfortunately, when the business failed to adhere to established safety measures, tragic consequences resulted and compromised the "happiness" of both her patrons and her popular nightspot. This case demonstrates that after a strategy is implemented, even one aligned with law and ethics, the key to continued benefit from the decision requires adherence, monitoring, and sometimes subsequent adjustment.

STRATEGY LAW ETHICS	*Three Pillars Case: Pagans in the Danger Zone*

Citation: *Kuehn v. Pub Zone*, 364 N.J. Super. 301 (N.J. Super. 2003)

Business owners often strive to find a balance between serving the needs of customers and their own self-interests. Making decisions that incorporate law and ethics helps a business to create value for customers and the company, but only if those decisions include consistency and follow-through. In this case, pub owner Maria Kerkoulas learned the hard way that her strategy is only as good as its implementation. What follows are excerpts from the decision of Justice Payne of the New Jersey Superior Court Appellate Division.

PAYNE, J.A.D.

Plaintiff Karl Kuehn was severely injured when attacked in the men's room of a tavern in the Township of Union known as the Pub Zone by three members of the Pagan motorcycle gang. Following trial, a $300,000 verdict in plaintiff's favor was entered against the Pub Zone. However, the trial judge granted judgment notwithstanding the verdict (JNOV) to it, finding the facts established that no foreseeable danger was posed by the Pagans and that the tavern owed no duty to plaintiff that was breached. Plaintiff has appealed from the JNOV. The Pub Zone has filed a cross-appeal, arguing in the event that the jury's verdict is reinstated that the court committed error in its decisions during trial to bar any claim of comparative negligence on plaintiff's part and to permit testimony by plaintiff's expert. If the JNOV is not sustained, it also seeks a new trial claiming the jury's award of damages to have been so unreasonably high as to shock the judicial conscience. We reverse the trial court's determination to grant a JNOV and deny the relief sought in the Pub Zone's cross appeal.

. . . Plaintiff Karl Kuehn was severely injured when attacked in the men's room of a tavern in the Township of Union known as the Pub Zone by three members of the Pagan motorcycle gang. . . . At the time, Maria Kerkoulas was the Pub Zone's co-owner . . . Prior to Kerkoulas's ownership of the bar, it had been taken over as a biker hangout, and frequent incidents had occurred that included destruction of property. During this period, Kerkoulas had served as a bartender. Upon purchasing the establishment, Kerkoulas sought the assistance of the Union police in ridding the bar of its biker clientele.

Kerkoulas testified that the Union police advised her to put up a sign stating that persons wearing "colors" (a term meaning gang insignia) were not allowed in the premises. She did so and instructed her doormen to deny entry to persons fitting that description. When asked why she adopted these measures, Kerkoulas testified that if bikers wearing insignia were not present, no disturbances would occur, and people would not get beaten up. Kerkoulas stated that strict enforcement of her policy and calls to the police when insignia-wearing bikers gained entry had eliminated "a lot" of the trouble at the bar, and that the clientele had changed.

On the night at issue, three bikers . . . pushed past Petey, the doorman, and had entered the Pub Zone wearing their colors. . . . Plaintiff testified that he recognized Pagans as part of a "drifter, criminal element," he was "concerned" by their entry, and he stated to Petey that he didn't think their presence was a "great idea." However, after a discussion with plaintiff and Petey, Kerkoulas permitted the three to remain for one drink.

All agreed that the Pagans consumed one drink without incident and proceeded toward the stairs leading toward the downstairs bar and men's room and toward the exit. Kerkoulas assumed the three were leaving, but did not witness them doing so. In fact, they did not. Instead, they either entered the men's room with plaintiff or followed him there, and shortly thereafter, they viciously attacked him. . . . Plaintiff sustained injuries in the attack including loss of consciousness, traumatic subarachnoid brain hemorrhage, a C-5, -6 disc herniation with pressure on the spinal cord and radiculopathy, a right orbital fracture, maxillary fractures, and a basilar skull fracture manifesting as the presence of blood behind the tympanic membrane of the ear.

At the time of the attack, approximately 125 to 130 patrons were present in the bar, with approximately 80 patrons participating in classic disco night upstairs and the remainder at the downstairs bar, where a band was playing. The bar had one doorman, Petey, stationed at the front entrance, which was located at the opposite end of the front facade from the exit by which Kerkoulas assumed the Pagans were leaving. There was one bartender in the downstairs bar and two bartenders, including Kerkoulas, upstairs. No other security was present, no training in security techniques had been provided to bar personnel, and no background in security measures was required for employment.

. . . In this case, Kerkoulas had actual knowledge of a risk of injury from bikers as the result of her experiences as a barkeeper prior to and immediately following her purchase of the Pub Zone. She admitted that she had received additional information regarding the Pagans from a nearby tavern owner and from the Union police. As a result, she understood that they were troublemakers who were known to assault people for no known reason. In Kerkoulas's mind, the foreseeable risk of Pagan violence was sufficient to cause her to place a sign at the entrance to her premises warning that Pagans wearing colors would be barred from entry and to summon the police if unauthorized entry were gained. . . . "Business owners and landlords have a duty to protect patrons and tenants from foreseeable criminal acts of third parties occurring on their premises."

. . . The imposition of a duty is further justified by the fact that the Pub Zone derived an economic benefit from affording protection to its patrons in circumstances such as these. Indeed, testimony suggests that the Pub Zone ceased business shortly after plaintiff's attack as a direct result of its patrons' new-found perception that the tavern was dangerous. Moreover, we do not find the cost of reasonable security measures to be prohibitive in this context. . . . To fulfill its duty in this context, the Pub Zone was merely required to employ "reasonable" safety precautions. It already had in place a prohibition against entry of Pagans and other bikers who were wearing their colors, and that prohibition, together with the practice of calling the police when a breach occurred, had been effective in greatly diminishing the occurrence of biker incidents on the premises. The evidence establishes that the prohibition was not enforced on the night at issue, that three Pagans were permitted entry while wearing their colors, and the police were not called.

The order of judgment notwithstanding the verdict is reversed and the verdict in plaintiff's favor is reinstated. The relief sought by defendant the Pub Zone in its cross appeal is denied.

THREE PILLARS CASE QUESTIONS

(1)   According to the court, what was Pub Zone's duty to customers? How did the business try and fulfill this duty?

(2)   From the language of the decision, what indications are there from Justice Payne that the precautions the pub took to protect customers were inadequate?

(3)   Pub Zone owner Kerkoulas testified in court "that plaintiff had been the one to urge that the Pagans be admitted, and that she had relied on plaintiff's assessment in permitting them to remain. She [also] testified that she would have called the police

immediately if plaintiff had not vouched for the three bikers." Do you believe that this evidence, if true, absolves Kerkoulas of liability? Why?

(4) Do you believe Kerkaoulas' precautions, such as posting a sign in the bar, were sufficient to prevent biker violence? If you were the owner of Pub Zone, what strategy or additional safety measures would you implement?

THE THREE PILLARS MANTRA

To summarize what we have covered so far, business decisions are made within the Three Pillar model framework. The major challenge in using the model is the gap between the Strategy Pillar and the Law Pillar. Closing this gap enables businesses to create a sweet spot at the intersection of the Three Pillars—the zone of sustainable competitive advantage.

Regardless of whether you are starting your own business or making decisions within a large organization, the key to closing the gap is for you to become a legally savvy decision maker. This will enable you to understand the Law Pillar and manage the legal risks associated with your strategic plan. Becoming legally savvy will also allow you to ascend the balcony to reframe your decisions relating to creating shareholder value (Strategy Pillar), managing risk (Law Pillar), and considering ethical perspectives (Ethics Pillar). As part of the reframing process, you should consider the interests of all stakeholders and try to develop opportunities for mutual value creation.

In shorthand, your mantra should be Understand, Protect, and Create. You should *understand* the Law Pillar, *protect* your company through legal risk management and ethical considerations, and *create* value with an interest-based mindset that results in a larger pie for the company and its stakeholders.

KEY TAKEAWAYS

Law and ethics are not synonymous. Businesses must take extra steps beyond their understanding of legal principles to ensure their decisions are also ethical. A business may foster alignment of legal and ethical considerations through:

1. **Compliance Programs.** This involves promoting an organizational culture that encourages ethical conduct and a commitment to compliance with the law. Your company should develop and promote seven requirements as set out by the Sentencing Commission Guidelines Manual.

2.   Codes of Conduct. Use the Three Pillars to develop a Code of Conduct that aligns with the eight principles in the Codex.

3.   An Ethical Decision Process. This four-step process should be applied to every business decision: (1) describe the ethical problem, (2) identify ramifications for stakeholders, (3) analyze alternatives, and (4) make a decision.

STRATEGY	
LAW	***Three Pillars Decision: All Hands on Deck***
ETHICS	

As discussed early in this chapter, actions or lack of actions may be legal but not necessarily ethical. Companies frequently struggle when trying to make ethical decisions that protect and promote the interests of all stakeholders.

In the early morning hours of Friday, May 13, 2016, thirty-three-year-old Samantha Broberg disappeared from the Carnival Cruise ship *Liberty* while en route to Mexico. Friends of Samantha, a mother of four, reported her missing to the crew at about noon that day. While an onboard search ensued, ship camera surveillance footage showed Samantha sitting on, and then falling backward from, the tenth-floor deck railing at 2:00 a.m. After twenty hours and forty-three hundred square miles of searching, the Coast Guard suspended all recovery efforts, and Samantha joined the statistics of the twenty-five persons on average who fall from cruise ships each year and are lost at sea.

In recent years, concerns have been raised as to whether the cruise line industry is taking appropriate safety steps to prevent such incidents. In Samantha's case, for example, even though her fall overboard was filmed, no one was monitoring the video feed.

Additionally, cruise lines have been criticized for not installing Man Overboard (MOB) Technology, which could potentially detect a fall overboard and alert crew members of such events immediately. According to the Federal Register, the Coast Guard has indicated that the cost of installing MOB technology ranges from $62,500 to $700,000 per ship depending upon the vessel's size and capacity, and it requires additional costs in ongoing maintenance.[33] However, the technology has not been perfected and can trigger false alarms and can also be affected by the corrosive elements of the ocean (salt, water, etc.). Cruise lines have also been targeted for encouraging risky behavior by their promotion of "booze cruise" itineraries, which provide passengers with as many as fifteen alcoholic drinks in a twenty-four-hour period.

VALUE GOAL: To reduce/prevent overboard falls from cruise ships while preserving passenger enjoyment.

STRATEGY: Develop a strategy that would increase the prevention and detection of MOB incidents on cruise ships while preserving enjoyment for passengers.

LAW: Research the "Cruise Vessel Security and Safety Act of 2010" (CVSSA). Does this research affect or alter the strategy you developed? Now examine bill H.R. 3142, titled the "Cruise Passenger Protection Act," by going to its location on the Congress.gov website at https://www.congress.gov/bill/114th-congress/house-bill/3142. Does this proposed legislation alter your strategy? When faced with a situation where there is a potential imminent change in the law, should you align your strategy with the current law or the proposed law (which might never be passed)? Also, considering the proposed legislation, what suggestions or changes would you make with regard to the bill H.R. 3142, and why?৵০

ETHICS: There are significant ethical concerns in this scenario, especially in striking a balance between the existing technology, potential technology, the law, customs of the industry, and the value of human life. Apply ethics to your strategy by working through these four steps of ethical decision making: (1) describe the ethical dilemma, (2) identify the stakeholders involved, (3) analyze options (including how each group of stakeholders will be affected), and (4) make a decision based on your analysis. After examining ethical issues associated with the strategy, determine whether any modifications should be made.

৵০ *Check for law research materials in the Appendix: Legal Resources for Business Decisions*

STRATEGY	
LAW	***Three Pillars Decision: Redefining "Haute" Cuisine***
ETHICS	

As the law changes with regard to the use of recreational drugs, businesses that add these products are being presented with a wide spectrum of ethical considerations—not unlike those faced for many years by purveyors of alcohol and cigarettes.

Laws are changing with respect to the recreational use of marijuana, a plant that contains a psychoactive (mind-altering) chemical ingredient known as tetrahydrocannabinol (THC). A number of restaurants and chefs have begun incorporating derivatives from marijuana, such as hemp and cannabidiol, into food and drink menus at their establishments. A restaurant in Colorado, one of the first states to legalize the recreational use of the famous intoxicating "weed," plans to add cannabis derivatives to both food items and drinks, including coffee.

VALUE GOAL: Incorporate marijuana plant extracts into a Colorado restaurant menu to take advantage of this haute (French for "high cooking") cuisine trend.

STRATEGY: Develop a strategy for a Colorado restaurant to incorporate marijuana into their food and drink menu.

LAW: Research the Colorado law related to the use of marijuana in food and drink sold to the public. How does the Colorado law differ from the law in other locations where recreational marijuana use is allowed, such as California or Maine? How does it differ from Federal law? How does this research affect or alter the strategy you developed?&

ETHICS: Apply ethics to your strategy by working through these four steps of ethical decision making: (1) describe the ethical dilemma, (2) identify the stakeholders involved, (3) analyze options (including how each group of stakeholders will be affected), and (4) make a decision based on your analysis. After examining ethical issues associated with the strategy, determine whether any modifications are necessary.

& *Check for law research materials in the Appendix: Legal Resources for Business Decisions*

STRATEGY	
LAW	***Three Pillars Decision: Droning for Drugs***
ETHICS	

This decision focuses on the ethical and legal considerations raised by rapidly-changing technology.

A primary focus of the business world is to improve the quality of people's lives. As a result, efforts from businesses to minimize time and effort for their clients and customers are cropping up everywhere these days, including grocery pick-up services, delivered home meal prep kits, live chat customer service, and automated twenty-four-hour account access.

When researchers asked two thousand individuals to name the top inventions that have made life easier, the responses mentioned some ingenious age-old marvels, including "washing machines," "refrigerators," and "microwaves."[34] Also among the answers were more modern developments such as "smartphones," "laptops," and even "online banking." Missing from the list, yet being contemplated more and more for commercial convenience, is the delivery of purchases through modern remote-controlled, pilotless aircraft—the *drone*. Several years ago, a drone company formed in California to deliver prescription and over-the-counter drugstore items, with the goal of making waiting in line or a midnight dash to the "open-all-night" pharmacy historical memory.

VALUE GOAL: To replace the current pharmacy model with a drone delivery approach.

STRATEGY: Develop a strategy that would allow drones to deliver prescription drugs.

LAW: Research the laws related to commercial use of drones. Does this research affect or alter the strategy you developed? If necessary, refine your strategy to align it with the law.&

ETHICS: As happens with many other developments, the application of drone technology has resulted in some misuse. Drones are being used to deliver illegal drugs and other contraband to prison yards, and there are reports that Chinese-made drones are sending intelligence gathered through use in other countries back to Chinese manufacturers. Conversely, drones have recently been used to carry life-saving routine and emergency vaccines to countries like Ghana, where distribution would otherwise be difficult. Keep these points in mind when examining your strategy for ethical issues, working through these four steps of ethical decision making: (1) describe the ethical dilemma, (2) identify the stakeholders involved, (3) analyze options (including how each group of stakeholders will be affected), and (4) make a decision based on your analysis. After examining ethical issues associated with the strategy, determine whether any modifications should be made.

& *Check for law research materials in the Appendix: Legal Resources for Business Decisions*

STRATEGY	
LAW	***Three Pillars Decision: Lighter than Air***
ETHICS	

This next decision scenario focuses on maintaining a balance between law and ethics when strategizing to integrate a popular trend within your business operations.

Following its invention in the late eighteenth century, the toy balloon has been an important part of children's birthday parties and other festive celebrations. The typical balloon is brightly colored, constructed of plastic or foil, and filled with a lighter-than-air gas that allows it to float when released. Helium-filled balloons have been known to rise as high as twenty miles above Earth's surface and theoretically may traverse a distance of one thousand miles or greater.

The sentimental release of large numbers of balloons is an increasing trend to recognize events such as funerals, anniversaries, and wedding services. However, environmental concerns and a worsening shortage of helium are complicating this practice and creating a logistical headache for party planners. A florist in the state of Virginia has been asked to provide a large-scale balloon release (five hundred balloons with flowers and silk ribbon streamers attached) as part of an outdoor wedding service. These requests are becoming more and more common in the industry.

VALUE GOAL: To accommodate the rising trend of providing large-scale balloon releases.

STRATEGY: Develop a strategy for a Virginia-based florist to provide large-scale balloon releases as a part of its service menu for clients.

LAW: Research the Virginia law related to large-scale balloon releases, as well as the use of alternative (other than helium) balloon gases. Also review the environmental concerns related to the outdoor release of balloons. How does this research affect or alter the strategy you developed? Refine your strategy to align with the law and public concerns.&

ETHICS: There have been environmental concerns for a number of years with respect to the release of balloons outdoors. With this concern in mind, apply ethics to your strategy by working through these four steps of ethical decision making: (1) describe the ethical dilemma, (2) identify the stakeholders involved, (3) analyze options (including how each group of stakeholders will be affected), and (4) make a decision based on your analysis. After examining ethical issues associated with the strategy, determine whether any modifications should be made.

& Check for law research materials in the Appendix: Legal Resources for Business Decisions

---

STRATEGY
LAW   ***Three Pillars Decision: Flying the Friendly Skies***
ETHICS

The following decision scenario describes a typical dilemma faced by airlines, and raises questions about whether they can strike a better balance between law and ethics in the industry.

The airline industry has been increasingly profitable in recent years due to consolidation, low fuel prices, and rising passenger demand. Despite this change in fortunes, airlines were hit particularly hard by the 2008 US recession, and air travel companies are still facing problems that create increasingly complex dilemmas. Congestion at airports is at its worst level ever, resulting in long waits, crowded terminals, and intensified delays due to weather and security. Dependency on technology brings advantages but also increased vulnerability.

Passenger scrutiny of airline policies is also on the rise—made evident by the posting of complaints and videos on social media. For example, several years ago, United Airlines was the focus of criticism for its overbooking policy, which is the practice of selling more tickets than available capacity. Statistics show that an average of fifty thousand air passengers are involuntarily denied boarding each year due to overbooking.[35] When film of a United passenger being forcibly removed from a flight at Chicago's O'Hare International Airport surfaced in April 2017, the overbooking issue moved directly into the public consciousness. (See the video at: https://www.bing.com/videos/search?q=video+of+dr.+david+ dao+taken+off+plane&&view=detail&mid=93F98E1BA30929658A6793F98 E1BA30929658A67&&FORM=VRDGAR.)

VALUE GOAL: To provide a passenger-friendly solution to overbooking air flights.

STRATEGY: Develop a strategy that would allow airline companies to avoid overbooking or at least have a satisfactory contingency plan available when passengers are displaced.

LAW: Research the Department of Transportation regulations related to flight reservations and overbooking at https://www.transportation.gov/airconsumer/ fly-rights. Does this research affect or alter the strategy you developed? If necessary, refine your strategy to align with the law.&

ETHICS: The United flight where Dr. David Dao was forcibly removed was overbooked because airline employees gave his pre-booked seat to a flight attendant who was scheduled to cover another trip at the flight's destination. Dr. Dao refused to give up his seat because he needed to see patients at his clinic the next day. Consider these facts as you review your strategy for ethical issues, working through these four steps of ethical decision making: (1) describe the ethical dilemma, (2) identify the stakeholders involved, (3) analyze options (including how each group of stakeholders will be affected), and (4) make a decision based on your analysis. After examining ethical issues associated with the strategy, determine whether any modifications should be made.

& *Check for law research materials in the Appendix: Legal Resources for Business Decisions*

---

1   "Legal Compliance Programs," Harvard Business School 9-306-014 (2005).

2   The examples in this section are drawn from "Corporate Compliance Survey," *The Business Lawyer*, August 2005.

3   *In re Caremark International, Inc. Derivative Litigation.*

4   "Legal Compliance Programs," *supra.*

5   Paine, "Managing for Organizational Integrity," *Harvard Business Review*, March–April 1994.

6   https://www.justice.gov/opa/pr/walmart-inc-and-brazil-based-subsidiary-agree-pay-137-million-resolve-foreign-corrupt.

7   Walmart slogan.

8   This section is adapted from Siedel, *Negotiating for Success: Essential Strategies and Skills* (2014).

9   Schrotenboer, "Lance Armstrong Wins Endorsement Lawsuit," *USA Today*, February 26, 2014.

10   *Ikeda v. Curtis* (1953).

11   *Spratlin v. Hamm* (1967).

12   *Hooters v. Phillips* (1998).

13   Paine, Deshpande, Margolis and Bettcher, "Up to Code," *Harvard Business Review*, December 2005.

14   *Id.*

15   https://www.thebalancecareers.com/code-of-conduct-1918088.

16   https://philmckinney.com/10-quotes-from-bill-hewlett-and-david-packard-that-every-executive-should-read/.

17   https://www.gapinc.com/content/gapinc/html/investors/corporate_compliance/cobc_policies/your_role.html.

18   https://nacla.org/article/gap-and-sweatshop-labor-el-salvador.

19   *Id.*

20   https://www.cbsnews.com/news/the-gap-falls-into-child-labor-controversy/.

21   Paine, Deshpande and Margolis, "A Global Leader's Guide to Managing Business Conduct," *Harvard Business Review*, September 2011.

22   KPMG, "Integrity Survey," http://www.kpmg.com/CN/en/IssuesAndInsights/Articles Publications/Documents/Integrity-Survey-2013-O-201307.pdf.

23   Gibeaut, "Getting Your House in Order," ABAJ, June 1999.

24   https://www.hsnsudbury.ca/portalen/Portals/0/InternalPostings/Code%20of%20Conduct.pdf).

25   Adapted from Siedel, *supra.*

26   Foster, "Qualcomm Counsel Hits the Jackpot," *National Law Journal*, January 31, 2000.

27   "Tylenol and the Legacy of J&J's James Burke," http://knowledge.wharton.upenn.edu/article/tylenol-and-the-legacy-of-jjs-james-burke/. Another source used in summarizing the Tylenol case is "Chicago Tylenol Murders," http://en.wikipedia.org/wiki/Chicago_Tylenol_murders.

28   "Corporate Culture Gets Real," *BizEd*, September–October 2015.

29   Walter and Shackelford, "Our Mini-Theme: Corporate Social Responsibility Is Now Legal," *Business Law Today*, http://www.americanbar.org/publications/blt/2015/01/intro.html.

30   *Harvard Business Review*, December 2006.

31   *Id.*

32   *Autobiography of John Stuart Mill* (1873).

33   https://www.gpo.gov/fdsys/pkg/FR-2015-01-16/pdf/2015-00464.pdf.

34   https://q92hv.iheart.com/content/2019-04-10-the-10-modern-conveniences-that-have-improved-our-lives-the-most/.

35   https://www.npr.org/sections/thetwo-way/2017/04/10/523275494/passenger-torcibly-removed-from-united-flight-prompting-outcry.

Transform Product Liability into Product Innovation

This chapter examines a key business risk, product liability, as it relates to your customers. As Chapter 2 noted, a McKinsey survey of stakeholders showed that customers have the most significant effect on a company's economic value. Other studies have identified torts, in general, and product liability, specifically, as key customer-related risks to a company's success.

The opening section of this chapter provides an overview of product liability and its impact on customers, companies, and society. The second section provides a legal briefing on tort law and product liability, which is designed to help you become legally savvy about these important topics. The third section covers risk management (the key focus of the Law Pillar)—that is, how you can minimize product liability. The final section merges the Law Pillar and Strategy Pillar, by showing how even a contentious area of law like product liability can be used to create value for businesses by focusing on customer interests. The last section also discusses how attention to the Ethics Pillar preserves and magnifies the alignment among all three decision making considerations.

IMPACT OF PRODUCT LIABILITY

Product liability is an especially controversial topic because of its impact on companies, customers, and society in general.

Impact of Product Liability on Companies

Product liability as we know it today is the result of changes in the law over the last third of the twentieth century. These changes left in their wake the bankruptcy of a large number of companies, including industrial giants such as Johns Manville Corporation, A. H. Robins Co., and Dow Corning Corp. Product liability is often front-page news as companies manufacturing cars, drugs, tobacco, and a variety of other products face lawsuits where claims can exceed billions of dollars.

Less well publicized is the impact of product liability on smaller companies that are forced out of business because they cannot compete effectively while paying high product liability insurance premiums. Few people know about Havir Manufacturing, a small punch press manufacturer that was based in St. Paul, Minnesota several years ago. Havir was doing fine until, in one year, its product liability insurance premium jumped 1,900 percent, which equaled 10 percent of the company's sales. The company could not afford to stay in business, so it auctioned off its equipment and laid off its workers.[1]

Impact of Product Liability on Consumers

From a consumer perspective, product liability forces companies to act responsibly in manufacturing and selling products. The size of jury awards often reflects the consumer perspective. For example, Patricia Anderson purchased a used Chevrolet Malibu. While she was driving home from a Christmas Eve church service with her four children, a speeding drunk driver rear-ended her vehicle. Anderson escaped serious injury, but the four children, who were sitting in the back seat, were horribly disfigured when the gas tank erupted in flames.

Anderson sued General Motors (GM), and a jury held the company liable for $107 million in compensatory damages and another $4.8 billion in punitive damages. A judge later ruled that the punitive damage award was excessive and reduced the amount to "only" $1.09 billion. (GM appealed the decision and, as often happens, it is likely that the two parties reached a private settlement.)

The jury based the award in part on a finding that GM wanted to reduce costs by placing the car's gas tank under the trunk, where it was vulnerable to rupture. An internal GM memorandum concluded that placing the gas tank in a different location would cost $8.59 more per car. In another internal memorandum, a young GM engineer conducted a "value analysis," which assumed a maximum of five hundred deaths per year in GM cars and a "value" (that is, the cost to GM) of $200,000 per death. Multiplying five hundred times $200,000 and dividing the result by the number of GM cars on the road (forty-one million) the engineer came up with a cost per automobile of $2.40, which was less than the $8.59 cost of relocating the fuel tank.[2]

The *General Motors* case illustrates the controversial nature of product liability. Why should the company be responsible for injuries triggered by an accident that a speeding drunk driver caused? Did the engineer's memo actually influence company decisions? Did placing the gas tank under the trunk create greater danger than placement in other locations? What was the Malibu's safety record compared to other cars?

Though these are legitimate questions, it is also important to keep in mind that business leaders wear two product liability hats. In your role as a business leader, you are concerned about the impact of product liability on your company. But as a consumer, you want safe products for yourself and your loved ones.

A case in Texas illustrates these two hats. A forty-two-year-old attorney who specialized in defending companies in product liability cases went hunting with his sixteen-year-old son and two judges. After the hunt, the son entered their car holding a high-powered Remington rifle. One of the judges suggested that he unload the gun. The son released the safety, which was necessary to unload the rifle. The gun fired, wounding his father and leaving him paralyzed from the waist down. The father proceeded to sue Remington, claiming that it should not be necessary to release the safety to unload a rifle. The company paid him $6.8 million to settle the case.[3]

Impact of Product Liability on Society

Beyond the impact of product liability on individual companies and customers is the concern that product liability might inhibit innovation and new-product development. Based on responses from the CEOs of 264 companies, a Conference Board study (at the time when product liability litigation first became a major problem for companies) concluded that 47 percent of the companies had discontinued product lines and 39 percent had decided not to introduce new products because of product liability. More than 40 percent of the CEOs indicated that product liability had a major impact on the companies' ability to compete.[4]

The examples discussed above illustrate not only the impact of product liability issues on the various stakeholders, but also the complexity of these cases. When a company fails due to product liability claims, is it a result of company inaction? Skyrocketing insurance premiums? Lack of innovation? Consumer misuse? The case below is one of many that were launched against gas container manufacturer Blitz USA before the company filed for bankruptcy protection in 2012. If you had a red gas container in your garage, chances are it would bear the Blitz label, as the company had 75 percent of the market before its downfall. The combination of factors that spelled demise for Blitz is still a topic debated by analysts even years after the company closed its doors.

STRATEGY	
LAW	***Three Pillars Case: The Blazing of Blitz USA***
ETHICS	

Citation: *Calder v. Blitz USA*, 2011 WL 542224 (USDC D. Utah 2011)

The shuttering of gas can manufacturer Blitz USA in Miami, Oklahoma was blamed on idiot consumers, frivolous litigation by greedy lawyers, lack of a five-cent engineering fix, too-high insurance premiums, and a host of other causes. What follows are excerpts from a decision in this especially tragic product liability case (one of many against Blitz), demonstrating the impact these complex cases have on companies, consumers, and society.

TENA CAMPBELL, DISTRICT JUDGE.

On December 28, 2005, David Calder used a gas container manufactured by Blitz U.S.A. to start a fire in a wood-burning stove in his trailer home. The fire that resulted killed Mr. Calder's two-year-old daughter and severely burned Mr. Calder. Mr. Calder sued Blitz alleging (1) defective design (2) defective warning (3) breach of implied warranty (4) negligent misrepresentation and (5) negligence under Utah law. The gravamen of all of Mr. Calder's claims, except his defective-warning claim, was that the gas container Mr. Calder used lacked a flame arrestor, and that because the container did not have a flame arrestor, vapors from outside the container ignited and caused a flashback explosion.

Trial began on November 1, 2010. During the trial, Blitz moved for judgment as a matter of law twice, and the court denied both motions. The jury found that Mr. Calder was 30 percent at fault for the accident and that Blitz was 70 percent at fault. The jury awarded Mr. Calder damages of $6,167,943.00, reduced by 30 percent for Mr. Calder's fault. The damages included $650,000 for Mr. Calder's lost earning capacity.

Blitz now renews its motion for judgment as a matter of law under Federal Rule of Civil Procedure 50, claiming that (1) Mr. Calder failed to present evidence that Blitz's gas container is "unreasonably dangerous" under Utah law; and that (2) Mr. Calder failed to present evidence that Blitz misrepresented an important fact upon which Mr. Calder relied when he used the gas container on December 28, 2005.

. . . Specifically, Blitz alleges that the court's rulings resulted in: "(1) the improper exclusion of material and relevant causation evidence that refuted Plaintiff's causation case and established alternative causation; (2) the admission of evidence violating the state of the art doctrine and the refusal to give a state of the art jury instruction, notwithstanding the Court's proper pretrial recognition of the state of the art standard and Blitz U.S.A.'s reliance upon it; (3) the failure to give a jury instruction on compliance with governmental and industry standards and the resultant rebuttable presumption that should have flowed to Blitz U.S.A.; and (4) the inconsistent enforcement of evidentiary rulings and improper admission of evidence regarding explosion containment systems, inadequate warning content, and other similar incidents."

. . ."Unreasonably dangerous" is defined under Utah law as follows: "[U]nreasonably dangerous" means that the product was dangerous to an extent beyond which would be contemplated by the ordinary and prudent buyer, consumer, or user of that product in that community considering the product's characteristics, propensities, risks, dangers, and uses together with any actual knowledge, training, or experience possessed by that particular buyer, user, or consumer.

. . . Glen Stevick, Plaintiff's engineering expert, testified that a flame arrestor would have prevented the explosion that injured Mr. Calder and killed his daughter. Dr. Stevick also testified that other manufacturers have been putting flame arrestors in consumer gas cans since the 1970's. Cy Elmburg, the owner and CEO of Blitz at the time the gas container that is the subject of the litigation was made, told the jury that he knew since the 1960's that people had been burned by "gasoline or gasoline vapors found with the use of gasoline containers."

. . . Considering this evidence in the light most favorable to the jury verdict, the court concludes that there is ample basis in the record to support the jury's finding that the Blitz gas container was unreasonably dangerous under Utah law.

. . . There is [also] sufficient evidence in the record for the jury to have found that Blitz misrepresented that its gas containers were safe, and that Mr. Calder relied on that misrepresentation when he used the gas container.

. . . Because the court finds no error in its evidentiary rulings or in its instructions to the jury, the court denies Blitz's motion for a new trial.

THREE PILLARS CASE QUESTIONS

(1)   Which allegation by Mr. Calder is best supported by Dr. Stevick's testimony that "other manufacturers have been putting flame arrestors in consumer gas cans since the 1970s"? Explain.

(2)   One of Blitz's contentions was that "the failure to give a jury instruction on compliance with governmental and industry standards" and "refusal to give a state of the art jury instruction" compromised the manufacturer's case. This reference relates to the Environmental Protection Agency's (EPA) 2009 requirements for gas

containers, including: (1) a single, self-venting opening for filling and pouring with no separate vents or openings; (2) a permeation-resistant container that permits no more than 0.3 grams per gallon per day of hydrocarbon emissions; (3) automatic closure, such as a nozzle that automatically springs to the closed position when the user is not pouring from the container; and (4) childproof features as outlined by the Children's Gasoline Burn Prevention Act.[5] What role could the above regulations have played in the Calder event?

(3)   The court believed that Blitz CEO Cy Elmburg's testimony was evidence supporting the gas container as being "unreasonably dangerous." Do you agree? Why?

(4)   Similar to what happened in the Havir manufacturing case mentioned earlier, Blitz USA's demise was partially due to increased insurance premiums. Do you believe it is ethical for insurance companies to increase premiums for companies that face product liability claims? Are there any alternative options for insurers in this type of situation?

(5)   There were several hundred claims for injuries and deaths against Blitz USA, primarily related to the lack of a "flame arrestor." Dozens of claims also stated that a defective warning was partially to blame for consumer misuse of the container. Blitz's warning on its product was embossed into the plastic siding and stated "KEEP AWAY FROM FLAMES, PILOT LIGHTS, STOVES, HEATERS, ELECTRIC MOTORS, AND OTHER SOURCES OF IGNITION." Could Blitz USA have reduced its liability risk by rewording the warning? Why?

LEGAL BRIEFING ON TORT LAW AND PRODUCT LIABILITY

Understanding product liability requires some background on the fundamental nature of tort law. This section provides a legal briefing on tort law and explains how it relates to product liability.

Tort Law Fundamentals

A tort is a wrongful act that injures someone's property, body, or reputation. There are three basic types of torts: intentional torts, negligence, and strict liability.

Intentional Torts. As the name implies, intentional torts result when someone intends to cause injury. In addition to being subject to damages in a civil lawsuit, someone who commits an intentional tort might face criminal charges because most intentional wrongs are both torts and crimes.

Negligence. In everyday language, negligence is carelessness that results in injury. A plaintiff who sues you for negligence must prove four key elements: (1) you owed a duty of care to the plaintiff, (2) you breached your duty of care, (3) the plaintiff suffered injury, and (4) the breach of the duty of care caused the injury.

The automobile accident is probably the most common source of tort liability worldwide. Drivers owe a duty of care to other drivers and to pedestrians. When they drive carelessly and injure someone, they breach the duty of care, and there is a causal link between this breach and the injury.

Strict Liability. In some situations, there is tort liability even though the person sued did not intentionally injure someone and was not negligent. This form of liability arises when someone is engaged in an especially dangerous activity, such as housing wild animals. As discussed in the next section, in recent years, strict liability theory has been used to hold businesses liable for making and selling defective products.

Legal Elements of Product Liability

A plaintiff in a typical product liability case will assert two of the three basic tort theories—negligence and strict liability—along with breach of warranty, which is based on contract law. From a business perspective, there are three types of product defects that can lead to liability under these tort and contract theories: design defects, manufacturing defects, and marketing defects.

Design Defects. Your company is responsible for injuries resulting from defective product design. Your duties in designing a product are governed by reasonableness: is the design reasonable given your customers' foreseeable uses of the product?

Courts recognize that requiring your company to develop a perfectly safe product is often unrealistic. For example, automobile manufacturers have the ability to design cars that would virtually eliminate personal injuries in automobile accidents. But what would these cars look like? Probably a lot like army tanks. These tank-like cars would be inefficient (with mileage measured in gallons to the mile rather than miles to the gallon), unattractive, prohibitively expensive, and slow. In short, no one would want to buy them.

As a result, most courts have adopted a balancing test that considers, on the one hand, the risks associated with a product, and, on the other, the benefits (or utility) of the product. The Supreme Court of Georgia summarized the balancing test in a case involving a nine-year-old child who died after eating rat poison. The poison did not contain a bitter element that would deter human consumption or cause people to vomit if they mistakenly swallowed the poison. The court reversed a lower court decision in favor of the manufacturer of the rat poison and ordered a new trial.

The court first noted that the case involved a design defect—rather than a manufacturing or marketing defect. The court then observed that the risk-utility analysis represents the "overwhelming consensus" on the law of defective design: "This risk-utility analysis incorporates the concept of 'reasonableness,' i.e., whether the manufacturer acted reasonably in choosing a particular product design, given the probability and seriousness of the risk posed by the design, the usefulness of the product in that condition, and the burden on the manufacturer to take the necessary steps to eliminate the risk."[6]

After reviewing numerous sources, the court developed a list of general factors that are considered in a risk-utility analysis. The factors, presented in question format, provide a checklist you can use when designing products:

- How useful is the product?

- Does the design create serious dangers?

- Is injury likely?

- Is the danger avoidable?

- Does the customer have an ability to avoid the danger?

- What is the state of the art (at the time of manufacture)?

- Can the danger be eliminated without impairing the utility of the product or making it prohibitively expensive?

- Can the losses sustained by injured customers be spread through higher prices or insurance?

- Are alternative designs feasible, taking into account cost and adverse effects of the alternative?

- What are the benefits of the product—for example, appearance, attractiveness, usefulness for multiple purposes, and convenience?

Manufacturing Defects. Manufacturers, like other defendants, are liable for carelessness that results in injury to others (that is, negligence). Over the last half of the twentieth century, American courts crafted an additional theory of liability—called strict liability—that makes it much easier for an injured consumer to win a case against a manufacturer. Under this theory, businesses that sell defective products that injure consumers are liable even if they exercise "all possible care" in preparing and selling the product. In other words, the customer no longer has to prove that the manufacturer was negligent, and the manufacturer can no longer successfully defend a lawsuit by asserting that it exercised all care humanly possible in producing the product.

Countries around the world have followed the United States in adopting the strict liability theory. Why would these countries expand traditional tort law by fashioning this rule of strict liability? One view is that the law is based on the ability of companies to pay damage awards because they have "deep pockets." Judges and legal scholars, however, claim that the law is designed to shift losses from one person (the injured consumer) to society in general. This loss-shifting occurs because of manufacturers' supposed ability to raise prices after incurring product liability costs. As one scholar observed: "[Strict liability] is not a 'deep pocket' theory but rather a 'risk-bearing economic' theory. The assumption is that the manufacturer can shift the costs of accidents to purchasers for use by charging higher prices for the costs of products."[7]

The cost-shifting aspect of product liability is illustrated by a case involving a high school student who was paralyzed when his spinal cord was severed while playing football. His lawsuit against the helmet manufacturer, Riddell, resulted in a $5.3 million judgment. Riddell's insurance company proceeded to raise the company's annual product liability insurance premiums from $40,000 to $1.5 million. Riddell responded by raising the price of helmets over the next few years by 33 percent, virtually all of which was attributed to product liability costs.

Football teams faced with higher helmet prices undoubtedly raised the price of tickets and advertising so that ultimately the cost fell on consumers. In other words, costs of the accident are spread among a large number of consumers rather than falling entirely on the player and his family.[8] Riddell continues to face litigation involving football injuries. In 2015, a federal judge approved the settlement of head trauma litigation brought by professional football players against the National Football League but decided that the settlement did not apply to their claims against Riddell.[9]

One problem with strict liability theory is that many companies, unable to raise prices enough to cover product liability costs, are forced out of business. For example, the number of companies manufacturing football helmets has dropped dramatically in recent years. Companies that survive are then better able to pass on product liability costs to customers through price increases.

In the case that follows, Coca-Cola Bottling Company was found liable for an exploding glass bottle that severely injured a restaurant waitress. This liability was based on a theory of negligence known by the Latin phrase *res ipsa loquitur* (the thing speaks for itself), yet the case (through Justice Traynor's concurring opinion) was one of the first to introduce the idea of strict liability for manufacturers.

STRATEGY	
LAW	***Three Pillars Case: Under Pressure***
ETHICS	

Citation: *Escola v. Coca-Cola Bottling Company of Fresno*, 24 Cal.2d 453 (S.C. Cal. 1944)

The "pressure" on manufacturers for product defect responsibility evolved from a series of cases such as the one below. The California Supreme Court decided that restaurant waitress Gladys Escola should prevail in her allegation of negligence against Coca-Cola.

GIBSON, CHIEF JUSTICE.

Plaintiff, a waitress in a restaurant, was injured when a bottle of Coca Cola broke in her hand. She alleged that defendant company, which had bottled and delivered the alleged defective bottle to her employer, was negligent in selling 'bottles containing said beverage which on account of excessive pressure of gas or by reason of some defect in the bottle was dangerous . . . and likely to explode.' This appeal is from a judgment upon a jury verdict in favor of plaintiff.

Defendant's driver delivered several cases of Coca Cola to the restaurant, placing them on the floor, one on top of the other, under and behind the counter, where they remained at least thirty-six hours. Immediately before the accident, plaintiff picked up the top case and set it upon a near-by ice cream cabinet in front of and about three feet from the refrigerator. She then proceeded to take the bottles from the case with her right hand, one at a time, and put them into the refrigerator. Plaintiff testified that after she had placed three bottles in the refrigerator and had moved the fourth bottle about 18 inches from the case 'it exploded in my hand.' The bottle broke into two jagged pieces and inflicted a deep five-inch cut, severing blood vessels, nerves and muscles of the thumb and palm of the hand. Plaintiff further testified that when the bottle exploded, 'It made a sound similar to an electric light bulb that would have dropped. It made a loud pop.' Plaintiff's employer testified, 'I was about twenty feet from where it actually happened and I heard the explosion.' A fellow employee, on the opposite side of the counter, testified that plaintiff 'had the bottle, I should judge, waist high, and I know that it didn't bang either the case or the door or another bottle . . . when it popped. It sounded just like a fruit jar would blow up. . . . ' The witness further testified that the contents of the bottle 'flew all over herself and myself and the walls and one thing and another.'

. . . One of defendant's drivers, called as a witness by plaintiff, testified that he had seen other bottles of Coca Cola in the past explode and had found broken bottles in the warehouse when he took the cases out, but that he did not know what made them blow up.

Plaintiff then rested her case, having announced to the court that being unable to show any specific acts of negligence she relied completely on the doctrine of *res ipsa loquitur*. . . . *Res ipsa loquitur* does not apply unless (1) defendant had exclusive control of the thing causing the injury and (2) the accident is of such a nature that it ordinarily would not occur in the absence of negligence by the defendant.

Many authorities state that the happening of the accident does not speak for itself where it took place some time after defendant had relinquished control of the instrumentality causing the injury. Under the more logical view, however, the doctrine may be applied upon the theory that defendant had control at the time of the alleged negligent act, although not at the time of the accident, provided plaintiff first proves that the condition of the instrumentality had not been changed after it left the defendant's possession. . . . Upon an examination of the record, the evidence appears sufficient to support a reasonable inference that the bottle here involved was not damaged by any extraneous force after delivery to the restaurant by defendant. It follows, therefore, that the bottle was in some manner defective at the time defendant relinquished control, because sound and properly prepared bottles of carbonated liquids do not ordinarily explode when carefully handled. . . . Although it is not clear in this case whether the explosion was caused by an excessive charge or a defect in the glass there is a sufficient showing that neither cause would ordinarily have been present if due care had been used. Further, defendant had exclusive control over both the charging and inspection of the bottles. Accordingly, all the requirements necessary to entitle plaintiff to rely on the doctrine of *res ipsa loquitur* to supply an inference of negligence are present.

. . . The judgment is affirmed.

TRAYNOR, JUSTICE.

I concur in the judgment, but I believe the manufacturer's negligence should no longer be singled out as the basis of a plaintiff's right to recover in cases like the present one. In my opinion it should now be recognized that a manufacturer incurs an absolute liability when an article that he has placed on the market, knowing that it is to be used without inspection, proves to have a defect that causes injury to human beings.

THREE PILLARS CASE QUESTIONS

(1)   Is the bottle defect described in this case a design defect or a manufacturing defect? Explain how you can distinguish between these two types.

(2)   Coca-Cola insisted in this case that evidence was insufficient to support the claim made. What evidence supports Gladys' story?

(3)   There is a heightened burden on the manufacturer with strict liability because the company may be found liable even if it took every precaution in the product's manufacture. In this case, a chemical engineer testified that Coca-Cola used standard methods for testing bottle pressure, and he described the tests as "pretty near infallible." What else then could a manufacturer do to ensure product safety?

(4)   Justice Traynor states that "a manufacturer incurs an absolute liability when an article that he has placed on the market, knowing that it is to be used without inspection, proves to have a defect that causes injury to human beings." Do you believe this statement places too much responsibility on the manufacturer? Is this fair to companies? Why?

——————

Marketing Defects. Two types of marketing defects can lead to product liability. Liability can result either from express or implied warranties that your company provides to your customers or from your company's failure to warn customers of hidden dangers associated with the product.

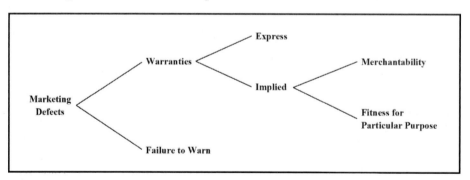

Warranties. Your warranty liability is often based on statements—called express warranties—that you make to consumers. When you state a fact, make a promise, or describe your product, you are giving express warranties. The information that you provide does not have to be distributed with the product and does not have to use the word "warranty" in order to create liability.

For example, an advertisement can create an express warranty. At one time, cigarette companies emphasized the safety of smoking with ads like the following from a US Supreme Court decision.[10] The Supreme Court ruled that a smoker could sue tobacco companies because, through these ads, cigarette companies gave express warranties that cigarettes are safe:

- Play Safe—Smoke Chesterfield

- Nose, Throat and Accessory Organs Not Adversely Affected by Smoking Chesterfields

- [Chesterfields are] entirely safe for the mouth

- [L&M filters are] Just What the Doctor Ordered

Even when your company does not give express warranties, the law automatically gives purchasers two warranties, called implied warranties. One of these implied warranties is the warranty of merchantability. With this warranty, businesses must provide products that are of average quality and fit for ordinary purposes. The other implied warranty is the warranty of fitness for a particular purpose, which applies to all sellers—even if they aren't in business. You give this warranty in situations where you know that the buyer (1) needs the product for a particular purpose and (2) is relying on your skill and judgment in providing a product that will meet the buyer's needs.

Warnings and Failure to Warn. Your company has a legal duty to warn customers about the dangers associated with the foreseeable uses of your product. This liability can arise even when products are not otherwise defective. For example, in 2013, a jury decided that Riddell was liable for $3.1 million for failing to provide an adequate warning about possible head trauma to a football player who was injured in a high school game. As a result of cases like this, helmet manufacturers have strengthened their warnings. Here is an example: "No helmet system can protect you from serious brain and/or neck injuries including paralysis or death. To avoid these risks, do not engage in the sport of football."[11]

Your company's warnings should also take into account the risk of potential psychological harm. In one case, a doctor replaced the heart valve of a patient named Bravman with a mechanical valve. The mechanical valve made a loud noise that, in some patients, could be heard in a quiet room from as far as twenty feet away. When Bravman sued the manufacturer, the court decided that there was (1) no design defect, because the product's usefulness outweighed the noise problems and (2) no manufacturing defect.

The court determined, however, that the manufacturer could be held liable for failing to warn the patient of the noise problem. Evidence surfaced that the manufacturer knew that its mechanical valves were noisy. Other patients had complained, and one patient attempted suicide because of the noise. Bravman alleged that he had lost sleep, become despondent, and been forced to take early retirement because of the noise. The court concluded that: "Unlike the purely psychological terror suffered by the protagonist in Edgar Allan Poe's The Tell-Tale Heart, Bravman's complaint, that his artificial heart valve creates excessive noise that prevents him from sleeping, among other things, is objectively verifiable."[12]

THE LAW PILLAR: PRODUCT LIABILITY RISK MANAGEMENT

Managing product liability risk to achieve competitive advantage involves three fundamental approaches: (1) a strategic approach, (2) an organizational approach, and (3) an operational approach.

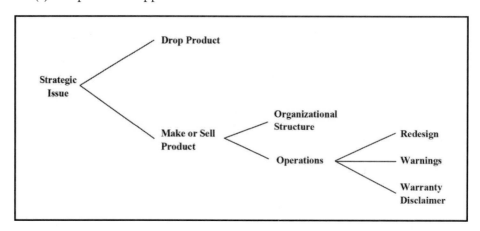

Strategic Approach

The strategic approach focuses on your fundamental business strategy and addresses this question: should you continue to make products that subject the company to potential liability? In answering this question, you might decide to drop products on the basis of your litigation experience and the size of damage awards. But this decision might be an overreaction that would result in the loss of significant business opportunities.

For a deeper strategic analysis, consider the rationale for strict liability (a theory providing that companies are liable for selling a defective product even when they are not negligent). This theory is based on the assumption that companies are simply intermediaries that can raise prices to pass on product liability costs to customers. With this rationale in mind, your strategic analysis should focus on whether your company can indeed pass on its product liability costs (as the theory predicts) or whether it must bear the costs because of an inability to increase prices. In other words, the analysis should focus on who pays, rather than on whether there is liability.

To illustrate this analysis, let's assume that you work for a company in the tobacco industry, which has incurred high product liability costs over the years. Settlements and jury verdicts have pushed the product liability in this industry to hundreds of billions of dollars. Faced with this immense liability, a knee-jerk reaction might lead you to decide that your company should drop cigarettes as a product.

But a deeper analysis should focus on whether your company can pass this liability on to customers. For example, after tobacco companies agreed to a $206 billion settlement with forty-six states in 1998, the companies raised their prices by seventy-six cents a pack. This allowed them to fund the settlement despite a 7 percent drop in cigarette consumption. As a *Wall Street Journal* article noted: "Where does the [state settlement] money come from? Generally speaking, not the bottom line. . . . Viewed from the consumer perspective, the settlements effectively transfer vast wealth from smokers to states and lawyers on both sides."[13] This analysis, by the way, is not to suggest that companies should manufacture and sell cigarettes. Other factors in addition to an economic analysis should determine that decision!

Organizational Approach

After you make the strategic decision to continue a product line, you should review your organization's structure. This review will bring into play one of the foundations of capitalism—the concept of limited liability. Under this concept, when you buy stock in a corporation, the most you can lose is your investment. If the company fails and declares bankruptcy, creditors cannot seize your—or other stockholders'—personal assets. In other words, the company is a "corporate veil" that protects you from liability.

This concept also applies when one company (a "parent") owns another company (a "subsidiary"). If the subsidiary fails, the parent is not liable for the subsidiary's debts. This creates an opportunity for a company to isolate product liability risks in a subsidiary. Your lawyers will create the subsidiary as an independent corporation. Your company, the parent, will typically own 100 percent of the subsidiary's stock. If, in the worst-case scenario, major product liability damage awards are levied against the subsidiary, the parent company might lose its investment in the subsidiary but will not be liable beyond this investment.

Exceptions to the principle of limited liability are especially important to managers involved with company operations. For example, if the parent corporation does not treat a subsidiary as an independent corporation, courts will "pierce the corporate veil" and hold the parent liable for the subsidiary's creditors.

Several years ago, world-class race car driver Mark Donohue was killed when a tire manufactured by Goodyear blew out during a race. When his estate sued Goodyear in the United States, the company argued that because the tire was manufactured by its United Kingdom subsidiary, the lawsuit should be filed in England. But the trial judge allowed the case to proceed against the parent company on the grounds that Goodyear dominated the subsidiary rather than treating it as an independent corporation.

A comment on the case in *Forbes* observed that: "One of the reasons companies set up subsidiaries, in fact, is to use the corporate form to limit legal liability. For the same reason that you can't sue GM shareholders if a Chevrolet's brakes fail, you can't sue Goodyear if a tire made by its subsidiary has a blowout. . . . [But] companies get into trouble over the question of whether they have dominated subsidiaries to the extent that they are indistinguishable from the parent."[14]

Courts are also inclined to pierce the corporate veil when a subsidiary is inadequately capitalized, when the parent describes a subsidiary as a department or division (rather than as a corporation), when a subsidiary does not follow normal legal requirements such as holding regular board meetings, or when a parent uses the subsidiary's property as its own.

The general message for managers is clear. Your attorneys will be able to incorporate a subsidiary that can be used to sell products that carry significant product liability risks. But to be protected by the corporate veil that your attorneys have created, you should allow the subsidiary to operate as an independent entity.

Operations Approach

In addition to considering your organizational structure, you should review your operations. Your operations approach to minimizing product liability costs should relate to the three types of product defects discussed previously in this chapter: design, manufacturing, and marketing. The importance of eliminating manufacturing defects is obvious and has already received considerable attention as a result of quality programs that many companies worldwide have adopted. This section will focus instead on a process companies can use to eliminate design and marketing defects, which are especially common forms of product liability. The design/marketing process has six key steps.

1. **Form a product safety team.** In assembling teams, you might be inclined to invite participants with engineering backgrounds who understand product design. The risk is that engineers, while bright and logical, might be too focused on the product's intended purpose and uncomfortable thinking about how "real" people (that is, non-engineers) actually use products. For reasons discussed in the next step, your product safety team should include representatives from functions throughout the company. You should also include potential customers on the team and invite them to describe how they might use your product.

2. **Identify foreseeable uses.** Recall that you must design a product and develop warnings based on the foreseeable ways in which customers might use your product—not just the ways you intend them to use the product. Thus, the product safety team should consider *all* possible ways customers might use the product. For example, author Siedel has led simulations where product safety teams composed of experienced managers brainstorm possible uses of a hairdryer. Within a matter of seconds, team members think of uses such as:

- Dry clothing
- Start barbeques
- Shrink plastic
- Dry glue and paint
- Defrost refrigerators
- Thaw frozen pipes
- Dry pets
- Remove stickers
- Dry fingernail polish
- Dust
- Defrost locks

You might notice when examining foreseeable uses that some of those uses are really *misuses* of the product. For example, we all know that chairs are manufactured for the purpose of sitting, yet many people stand on a chair to change a lightbulb or to reach something on a high shelf. The use of a chair for standing, and not sitting, is a misuse of the intended purpose for chairs, so you would think that if people who stand on a chair fall or the chair breaks they would be wholly responsible for their own injuries. Yet the law in most states says that a manufacturer cannot escape liability for a product that has been misused by a plaintiff if that misuse is reasonably foreseeable. Chair manufacturers know that people use their product for standing as well as sitting, and the manufacturers therefore must make sure that their chairs will be safe when misused or provide adequate warnings or instructions with respect to that potential misuse. Although manufacturers are not expected to anticipate and take precautions against every potential misuse or abuse of their product by consumers, courts will still hold them responsible for those which, like intended uses, are reasonably "foreseeable."

3.   Identify risks. The product safety team should next identify risks associated with all the foreseeable uses. For example, in reviewing the hairdryer's foreseeable uses, you might decide there are risks associated with using the hairdryer to dry glue and paint but that using the hairdryer to defrost locks creates little risk of injury.

4.   Redesign the product. The product safety team should then determine whether the product can be redesigned to eliminate the identified risks. In considering design issues, the team should focus generally on a risk-utility analysis and the questions noted previously in this chapter in the section on design defects.

5.   Develop warnings. The team should develop warnings (and safety instructions) for the risks that cannot be eliminated through redesign. In conducting simulations with product safety teams, author Siedel has found that team members tend to skip discussing redesign (Step 4) and move directly to developing warnings once risks have been identified. This is a mistake, because a court might not allow warnings as a defense if a safer design is available.

For example, a worker suffered a brain injury when a 16-inch Goodrich tire exploded as he attempted to mount it on a 16.5-inch rim. A prominent warning label attached to the tire contained the following warnings in red and yellow highlights. The worker ignored these warnings:

DANGER

NEVER MOUNT A 16" SIZE DIAMETER TIRE ON A 16.5" RIM. Mounting a 16" tire on a 16.5" rim can cause severe injury or death. While it is possible to pass a 16" diameter tire over the lip or flange of a 16.5" size diameter rim, it cannot position itself against the rim flange. If an attempt is made to seat the bead by inflating the tire, the tire bead will break with explosive force.

Failure to comply with these safety precautions can cause the bead to break and the assembly to burst with sufficient force to cause serious injury or death.

In the worker's lawsuit against Goodyear, the Supreme Court of Texas affirmed a jury award of $5.5 million in damages.[15] The court noted that "a product may be unreasonably dangerous because of a defect in manufacturing, design, or marketing." In this case, because there was evidence that the tire was designed defectively, the warning label did not excuse the design defect. As the court observed (quoting a legal authority): "*Warnings are not, however, a substitute for the provision of a reasonably safe design.*" (The court added the italics for emphasis.)

6.   **Review warranties.** Finally, product safety teams should determine what, if any, warranties should accompany the product. Your company can avoid liability for express warranties simply by not giving them. In marketing your products, you can also attempt to disclaim express warranties, but the disclaimer will not work if it conflicts with an express warranty.

For example, a warranty from a clothing manufacturer stated that the company would provide a replacement if the product did not provide "one year of normal wear." Below this statement, in small type, was a disclaimer stating that the warranty would not apply if the garment was "worn out." If tested in court, the one-year warranty should prevail over the disclaimer.

You can also disclaim warranties that the law provides automatically—the implied warranties discussed earlier in this chapter. To disclaim the implied warranty of merchantability, the disclaimer must specifically mention the word "merchantability" and, if in writing, must be conspicuous. The implied warranty of fitness for a particular purpose can be disclaimed through a conspicuous disclaimer in writing. For examples of disclaimers, simply visit your favorite website. Chances are that you will find disclaimers similar to those found at Amazon.com (in print twice as large as other print at the website):

> . . . AMAZON.COM DISCLAIMS ALL WARRANTIES, EXPRESS OR IMPLIED, INCLUDING, BUT NOT LIMITED TO, IMPLIED WARRANTIES OF MERCHANTABILITY AND FITNESS FOR A PARTICULAR PURPOSE.

Attention to the issues described above is a critical focus for a company demonstrating a commitment to consumer safety. In the next case, a Michigan district court examines a plaintiff's claims against Proctor & Gamble for her injuries incurred while using a Tide laundry detergent POD. Much can be learned from the court's rationale in this recent action.

STRATEGY	
LAW	*Three Pillars Case: Turning of the Tide*
ETHICS	

Citation: *Swartz v. Procter & Gamble Manufacturing Company*, 2018 WL 2239558 (E.D. Mich. 2018)

The following trial court decision illustrates the importance of company warnings. Although it decided for the company on the plaintiff's failure-to-warn claim, the court allowed the case to proceed on other grounds.

MATTHEW F. LEITMAN, UNITED STATES DISTRICT JUDGE.

In this action, Plaintiff Ariana Swartz alleges that a Tide laundry detergent POD designed and manufactured by Defendants The Proctor & Gamble Manufacturing Company and Proctor and Gamble Distributing, LLC (collectively, "P&G") "exploded" and "sprayed" its contents onto her clothes and body, causing a chemical burn on her left breast. . . . Instead of using liquid or powder laundry detergent to wash her clothes, Swartz used a Tide POD. A POD contains concentrated detergent in a dissolvable packet. . . . After Swartz "pulled [the] Tide POD out of the package," it "just popped," partially exploding in her hand. About one-half of the concentrated detergent in the POD "squirted on [Swartz], [her] neck, [and on her] hands." The detergent also sprayed on her shirt. . . . Swartz realized that the concentrated detergent from the POD had seeped through her shirt onto her bra, and she concluded that the detergent on her bra came into contact with, and a caused a chemical burn on, her breast. Swartz seeks damages related to that burn in this action.

The Court turns first to Swartz's claim that P&G negligently and/or defectively designed the PODs. In this claim, Swartz asserts that the design of the PODs "cause[d] the film on the [PODs] to weaken over time" when exposed to water and moisture, "resulting in a compromised shelf life of the product." Swartz says that this design created an unacceptable risk that the PODs would "ruptur[e] through [their] ordinary course of use."

"Michigan has adopted what its courts have come to call the 'risk-utility' test for determining whether a plaintiff has made out a case for a product liability claim based upon a claimed design defect." Peck v. Bridgeport Machines, Inc., 237 F.3d 614, 617 (6th Cir. 2001). In order to prevail on a design defect claim under Michigan law, a plaintiff must establish that:

(1) the severity of the injury was foreseeable by the manufacturer;

(2) the likelihood of occurrence of [the plaintiff's] injury was foreseeable by the manufacturer at the time of distribution of the product;

(3) there was a reasonable alternative design available;

(4) the available alternative design was practicable;

(5) the available and practicable reasonable alternative design would have reduced the foreseeable risk of harm posed by defendant's product; and

(6) the omission of the available and practicable reasonable alternative design rendered defendant's product not reasonably safe.

... Swartz's negligent design claim fails because she has not presented any evidence that there was a reasonable and safer alternative design of the PODs or that such a reasonable alternative design was practicable. Swartz points only to opinions offered by D. J. Hartwig, a purported expert in product safety, but he did not opine about alternative possible designs. Indeed, he did not offer opinions about design issues at all. Instead, he opined that P&G "did not adequately test the safety" of the PODs, that "P&G knew of the hazardous nature of the POD ingredients," that "the film covering the POD could rupture," and that "P&G's cautionary wording on the POD packaging was inadequate." Thus, Hartwig's opinions cannot support Swartz's design defect claim, and the claim fails for lack of the required expert testimony.

... Swartz's claim that P&G failed to warn her that the PODs could rupture when they are removed from their packaging fails because Swartz did not read any of the warnings on the POD packaging before she took the POD out of its package. She testified as follows at her deposition:

Q: Did you read any of the words down here where it says caution or attention or anything like that? Did you read any of those words before you used the Tide PODs?

A: Possibly. [. . . .] I definitely remember looking at the back of the Tide PODs container after the incident. I do remember that, but remembering exactly what words I read, no.

Q: I'm talking about before the incident.

A: I didn't read it before. I had no reason to.

[. . . .]

Q: Did you or did you not read the words on the package before you used the product? [. . . .] Did you read any of the words on the back of this package before you used the product?

A: Wash instructions. Not the caution. [. . . .] Not the cautions.

[. . . .]

Q: Had there been a caution about a pod bursting in this caution section of the label, you would not have read it because you didn't feel the need to read the caution section before you used the product, right? [. . . .]

A: I would not have—no, I would not have seen it because I did not read it.

. . . [T]he POD packaging did instruct Swartz that if her "skin or clothing" was exposed to the chemicals from the POD, that she should "remove [the] contaminated clothing and rinse the skin with water.". . . Because Swartz did not read the relevant warnings, she cannot establish the required proximate cause element of her failure-to-warn claim. Indeed, her testimony establishes that even if P&G had provided an expansive, detailed warning about the risks of the PODs exploding, Swartz, in her own words, "would not have seen it." P&G is therefore entitled to summary judgment with respect to this portion of Swartz's failure-to-warn claim.

THREE PILLARS CASE QUESTIONS

(1) Which of the "risk-utility" test elements did the plaintiff's case for negligent design fail to support here, and why?

(2) For the Michigan Court to find in favor of negligent design, it stated that "expert testimony is required to demonstrate the existence of a reasonable alternative design that would satisfy the elements of a plaintiff's claim." How can a company take steps to ensure that it has the safest design for its product?

(3) Was Swartz successful in her failure-to-warn claim? Why or why not?

(4) One claim that the Court allowed to go forward was the plaintiff's breach of implied warranty. The elements of this claim are to show: "(1) the product in question was defective when the defendant sold or otherwise placed it in the stream of commerce, and (2) that the defect caused her injury." To satisfy the defectiveness element, a plaintiff must show that a product was not "reasonably fit for its intended, anticipated, or reasonably foreseeable use." Which of the two types of implied

warranty is this? What evidence did Schwartz present that shows that the Tide POD was not "reasonably fit"?

(5)   Following (or during) liability cases, companies can learn about defects in their products and make adjustments to improve their safety and efficiency. What do you think Procter and Gamble may consider as improvements, if any, to the Tide POD based on this case?

This section has examined three business approaches—strategic, organizational, and operational—that you can use to seize competitive advantage by minimizing product liability risks. You are now ready to climb to the balcony in an attempt to reframe product liability to meet the interests of both your company and its customers.

ALIGN STRATEGY AND LAW: USE PRODUCT LIABILITY TO CREATE VALUE

When running simulations involving the six-step new-product process, author Siedel has discovered that managers can become agitated when discussing product liability, especially when the law enables customers to recover damages for injuries that result from using products for purposes other than those the manufacturer intended. Often, the simulations bring to mind stories managers have heard or experiences they have had with their own customers' misuse of products. Some of these stories are urban myths (or at least the authors cannot locate them in published case reports)—such as the one about the person whose cat exploded when he attempted to dry it in a microwave.

But other stories, often drawn from the executives' experiences and from case examples, are true—including the Goodyear case described previously in which the plaintiff ignored tire warnings. Managers are often especially critical of judges who push the boundaries of foreseeability and of customers who misuse products. These negative reactions can cloud opportunities to create value based on customer interests.

To illustrate, let's return to the hairdryer example. You might consider the list of foreseeable uses as examples of customer stupidity, because it shows that customers use hairdryers for purposes other than drying hair. But what if you changed your mindset to focus on your customers' interests? What are they trying to tell you when they use hairdryers for a variety of purposes? The common theme in the list is that customers need warm, moving air. They do not have access to products on the market that meet this need and must use hairdryers for this purpose.

Companies that move beyond a purely legal focus in their design review (that is, beyond focusing on developing designs that minimize liability) and use information from the process to develop new products have an opportunity to meet customer interests while creating shareholder value. As legendary General Motors executive Alfred Sloan stated in a letter to shareholders:

> To discuss Consumer Research as a functional activity would give an erroneous impression. In its broad implications it is more in the nature of an Operating Philosophy, which to be fully effective, must extend through all phases of the business [and] serve the customer in ways [in] which the customer wants to be served.[16]

"All phases of the business" should include considering the Law Pillar of decision making. In other words, law should be used not only to control costs but also to generate new-product ideas.

Identifying customer needs extends beyond initial development of new products. Once your product is on the market, it becomes important for you to review your customers' complaints about your product, their warranty claims, and their lawsuits against your company. Recognizing your customers' use of products, their positive and negative experiences, and their needs also shows an understanding of Codex Principle #5 from Chapter 3, which focuses on protecting the health and safety of others and enhancing human development in the marketplace. Adding the Ethics Pillar by analyzing the potential uses of your product, both intended and unintended, helps to ensure that the welfare of the consumer is at the forefront of company motivations.

The best approach to product liability claims is to have an aggressive and responsive program within the company—even before the product enters the marketplace. Then proactive and ongoing evaluation of product complaints and issues is an essential component of the ethical commitment to consumer well-being. This form of data mining and analysis is especially useful as you continue to redesign your products to maintain competitive advantage.

Opportunities for you to create or retain value extend to product delivery. For example, at one time, Domino's Pizza guaranteed pizza delivery within thirty minutes or customers would receive a discount. After several traffic accidents involving Domino's drivers, the company faced public criticism and lawsuits.

If you were a Domino's executive, how might you handle this problem? One response might be to require continuous training of your drivers. But it is likely that training would be costly and might not significantly reduce the number of accidents. Better screening of potential drivers would probably lead to the same result. Another approach would be to drop your thirty-minute guarantee. But you might lose a significant marketing advantage and the opportunity to provide the best service to your customers.

Domino's opted for the last approach, dropping the thirty-minute guarantee. In doing so, however, rather than complaining about the negative impact the law had on its ability to serve customers, the company asked the question Alfred Sloan suggested: "What do our customers really want?" The company discovered that although customers want their pizza delivered as soon as possible, an important reason for that speedy delivery is that they want their pizza served hot. The solution? A new service-enhancing product—a bag that contains heating coils that keeps the pizza hot until delivery.

KEY TAKEAWAYS

Product liability is one of the most important risks facing businesses worldwide. This risk relates especially to a key business stakeholder—your customers. Despite its negative impact on companies, product liability enables opportunities to create value. To develop these opportunities, you should:

1.   **Become legally savvy about product liability.** You should understand the three basic legal theories that form product liability and how they apply to the three product defects that lead to liability: design defects, manufacturing defects, and marketing defects.

2.   **Manage product liability risks.** Once you decide to make or sell a product, you should decide whether to isolate liability within a subsidiary. You should also make operational decisions relating to warranty disclaimers and use the six-step design and marketing process.

3.   **Create value by using product liability to identify customer needs and interests.** For example, your foreseeable use (and misuse) analysis provides valuable data on your customers' needs for new products.

STRATEGY	
LAW	***Three Pillars Decision: Pulling Some Strings***
ETHICS	

This decision making analysis emphasizes why it is important for companies to understand the law and not make assumptions regarding the manufacturing and marketing of products. Use of the operational design steps discussed in this chapter is critical to a favorable outcome in the scenario described below.

Debuting in the 2017 spring/summer fashion year, adult clothing with drawstrings made a big retro comeback on fashion runways. According to the British online newspaper *The Independent*, famous design houses embraced the use of drawstrings in everything from jackets to hemlines and sleeves. The newspaper reported that "At Versace, dresses were given a sultry, almost athletic vibe with jewel-toned techo fabrics threaded with drawstrings" and at "Maxmara, they nipped in waists on sporty cropped jackets."[17]

Children's clothing manufacturers are increasingly influenced by adult fashions and look to incorporate these trends as a way to maximize profits in a $400 billion a year global industry. The luxury and designer market for young people is especially active, fueled primarily by older parents in US markets who tend to have children later in life. These well-established adults, generally further along in their careers, are likely to have higher disposable incomes—resulting in lavish spending on their offspring.

This phenomenon has also been seen in China as a result of the one-child policy, when "increased spending power within households and parents' desire to give their children benefits the previous generation lacked, gave rise to *Little Emperor Syndrome*, a term coined to describe the tendency of Chinese households to spend heavily on only children."[18]

VALUE GOAL: To allow children's clothing manufacturers to take advantage of adult fashion trends.

STRATEGY: Develop a strategy that would incorporate the popular drawstrings trend into children's clothing designs.

LAW: Research the laws related to the use of drawstrings in children's clothing. Do these provisions affect or alter the strategy you developed? If necessary, refine your strategy to align with the law.❧

ETHICS: Apply ethics to your strategy by working through these four steps of ethical decision making: (1) describe the ethical dilemma, (2) identify the stakeholders involved, (3) analyze options (including how each group of stakeholders will be affected), and (4) make a decision based on your analysis. After examining ethical issues associated with the strategy, determine whether any modifications should be made.

❧*Check for law research materials in the Appendix: Legal Resources for Business Decisions*

STRATEGY	
LAW	***Three Pillars Decision: Lunch at the Laundromat***
ETHICS	

Procter & Gamble's Tide POD has been both vilified and celebrated. In this chapter, we discussed one case of related product liability for the POD, and in this decision making analysis, we see the ongoing complex spectrum of issues for this single laundry product.

Following its introduction in 2012, Proctor & Gamble's Tide laundry detergent POD has made all kinds of news headlines—and not many of them good. The palm-sized, liquid-filled tablet and packaging were launched after eight years of research, 450 sketches, six thousand consumer tests, and hundreds of millions of development dollars. However, despite all the marketing and R&D study, by the end of 2013, the American Association of Poison Control Centers was awash with poisoning complaints as over ten thousand children tried to eat the brightly-colored, candy look-alike.

As Proctor & Gamble redesigned the POD and packaging to include locks and warnings, the product see-sawed between being wildly successful ($2 billion in sales by 2015) and devastatingly fraught with intense product liability issues. To make matters worse, just when the poisonings began trending downwards in 2017, eating the PODSs became a social media meme among teenagers, evolving into the Tide Pod Challenge. Videos of individuals putting the pod in their mouths went viral, and reports of poisonings spiked.

VALUE GOAL: To retain and further advance Proctor & Gamble's Tide POD product.

STRATEGY: Develop a strategy to retain the Tide POD product and discourage misuse. Apply the process to minimize product liability, outlined in Chapter 4's "Operations Approach" section, as a part of your strategy. Focus on identifying foreseeable uses (and misuses), risks of those uses, and potential redesigns and warnings.

LAW: Research the cases and causes of action against Proctor & Gamble (such as *Swartz v. Procter & Gamble Manufacturing*, discussed earlier in this chapter) that relate to the Tide POD. How does this research affect or alter the strategy you developed? Refine your strategy to align with the law and consumer safety.&

ETHICS: The public, courts, and consumer safety experts have expressed concern about the Tide POD product, even with the continual changes to packaging. With these concerns in mind, apply ethics to your strategy by working through these four steps of ethical decision making: (1) describe the ethical dilemma, (2) identify the stakeholders involved, (3) analyze options (including how each group of stakeholders will be affected), and (4) make a decision based on your analysis. After examining ethical issues associated with the strategy, determine whether any modifications should be made.

☜*Check for law research materials in the Appendix: Legal Resources for Business Decisions*

STRATEGY LAW ETHICS	*Three Pillars Decision: Golfing with Gizmo*

Hauter v. Zogarts (1975) illustrates the type of guarantees that companies should avoid.

In 1966, Louise Hauter purchased a device known as the "Golfing Gizmo" for her thirteen-year-old son Fred to use when practicing his golf swing. The Gizmo consisted of two metal pegs, two cords (one elastic and one cotton), and a regulation golf ball. After the pegs were driven into the ground, the elastic cord was stretched and looped over them. The cotton cord with the golf ball attached at the end was added to the middle of the elastic cord, forming a "T" shape. When a golfer hit the ball, it was supposed to fly out and then return close to the point of impact. "A label on the Gizmo shipping carton and the cover of the instruction booklet urged players to 'drive the ball with full power' and further stated: 'Completely Safe Ball Will Not Hit Player.' "[19]

While using the Golfing Gizmo according to the instructions, Fred was hit in the head by the ball when it looped over the club on a drive, knocking him unconscious. He sustained permanent brain damage. A safety engineer at the trial against the manufacturer stated that the device was a "major hazard." The court determined that the manufacturer expressly warranted the safety of its product and was liable for Fred Hauter's injuries that resulted from a breach of that express warranty.

VALUE GOAL: To improve the safety of the "Golfing Gizmo."

STRATEGY: Develop a strategy to increase safer use of the Golfing Gizmo and avoid liability. Use the images of the Gizmo instruction manual (found at https://lawprofessors.typepad.com/tortsprof/files/Gizmo0001.PDF) and apply the process to minimize product liability, outlined in Chapter 4's "Operations Approach" section, as a part of your strategy. Focus on identifying risks of consumer uses and potential warnings and instructions.

LAW: Read *Hauter v. Zogarts,* 534 P. 2d 377 (1975) at https://scocal.stanford.edu/opinion/hauter-v-zogarts-27822. Does your reading of the case affect or alter the strategy you developed? If necessary, refine your strategy to align with the law and consumer safety.℘

ETHICS: Even with adjustments to the instructions and packaging, the Golfing Gizmo may still not be safe for consumer use. With these concerns in mind, apply ethics to the question of keeping the product on the market (including your strategy to avoid breach of warranty) by working through these four steps of ethical decision making: (1) describe the ethical dilemma, (2) identify the stakeholders involved, (3) analyze options (including how each group of stakeholders will be affected), and (4) make a decision based on your analysis. After examining ethical issues associated with the strategy, determine whether any modifications should be made.

℘*Check for law research materials in the Appendix: Legal Resources for Business Decisions*

---

1   Wysocki, "Manufacturers Are Hit with More Lawsuits," *Wall Street Journal*, June 3, 1976.

2   Zeman and Fix, "When Secrecy Explodes," *Detroit Free Press*, July 7, 2000.

3   Geisel, "Gun Firm Pays $6.8 Million to Attorney," *Business Insurance*, November 13, 1978.

4   McGuire, *The Impact of Product Liability* (1988).

5   https://www.thespruce.com/regulations-for-portable-fuel-containers-2153054.

6   *Banks v. ICI* (1994).

7   *Prosser and Keeton on the Law of Torts* (1984).

8   Edgerton, "How One Firm Learned Its Lesson in Liability Cases," *Detroit Free Press*, March 19, 1978.

9   Perlman, "Riddell Severed From NFL Claims in Concussion MDL," *Law 360*, December 1, 2015.

10   *Cipollone v. Liggett Group, Inc.* (1990).

11   Belson, "Warning Labels on Helmets Combat Injury and Liability," *The New York Times*, August 4, 2013.

12   *Bravman v. Baxter Healthcare Corporation* (1993).

13   Geyelin, "Yes, $145 Billion Deals Tobacco a Huge Blow, But Not a Killing One," July 17, 2000.

14   Greene, "Peeking Beneath the Corporate Veil," August 13, 1984.

15   *Uniroyal v. Martinez* (1998).

16   Barksdale (ed.), *Marketing in Progress* (1964).

17   https://www.independent.co.uk/life-style/fashion/how-to-wear-drawstring-trend-fashion-style-spring-summer-2017-a7741821.html.

18   https://www.businessoffashion.com/articles/intelligence/the-childrenswear-market-comes-of-age.

19   https://scocal.stanford.edu/opinion/hauter-v-zogarts-27822.

CHAPTER 5

Use Employment Law to Attract and Retain the Best Business Talent

The worldwide McKinsey report mentioned in Chapter 2 concluded that employees are key stakeholders who, along with customers, government, and investors, have the greatest effect on a company's economic value. In the past, an organization's assets were measured in terms of land, buildings, and equipment. In today's information-based economy, the intellectual capital employees create is a key asset. As such, your ability to find and retain the best employees is a critical element in creating value. Your success in this endeavor depends in large part on your understanding of employment law, which touches every aspect of a company's relationship with its employees.

As noted in Chapter 2, employment law covers many areas, including collective bargaining, discrimination, employee benefits, health and safety, pay, and work hours. To illustrate the Three Pillar model, this chapter addresses two of the most important and controversial areas: wrongful discharge and discrimination. A Chubb Private Company Risk Survey concluded that a high percentage of the surveyed companies were concerned about the topics covered in this chapter: "a lawsuit for wrongful termination, sexual harassment, discrimination or retaliation."[1] Many of the companies also felt that an employment lawsuit would cause significant damage. The first half of this chapter covers wrongful discharge, and the second half focuses on discrimination.

LEGAL BRIEFING ON WRONGFUL DISCHARGE LAW

As a starting point, you should be familiar with the basic legal concepts relating to wrongful discharge. The fundamental principle that governs wrongful discharge in the United States is the employment-at-will rule. Under this rule, you can hire and fire employees at will in all states but Montana (which requires good cause for dismissals after a probationary period). This rule does not apply to employees governed by union collective bargaining agreements, but the overwhelming majority of US employees in private industry do not belong to unions.

Most other countries do not follow the employment-at-will rule. Instead, the typical approach is that employers must provide advance notice when employees are discharged and might have to compensate employees who are fired without cause. The length of the notice varies from country to country. In Japan, for instance, thirty days' notice is required, while in India the notice period is one to three months, depending on the employer's size.[2]

In recent years, various US states have moved closer to the law in other countries as courts have developed three exceptions to the employment-at-will rule. First, in most states, the rule does not apply when companies make statements to employees or in company documents that create contractual rights that override the rule. For example, during a company's negotiations with a prospective employee (who was later hired as Director of Marketing), a company officer mentioned that "if you are doing the job, you can be assured that you will not be discharged." When the employee was later discharged, he sued the company claiming that the oral statement prevented the company from firing him without cause and that there was no cause for the dismissal. He recovered $300,000.[3]

Second, in some states, a company must act ethically, in "good faith," when dismissing employees. This exception to employment-at-will is illustrated by the case below.

STRATEGY	
LAW	***Three Pillars Case: Cashing in on a Fortune***
ETHICS	

Citation: *Fortune v. National Cash Register Co.*, 373 Mass. 96 (1977)

In this case, the National Cash Register Company (NCR), an organization that began operating in 1884, fired a salesperson who had worked for the company for twenty-five years. The court decided that the company was liable to its former successful employee.

ABRAMS, J.

Orville E. Fortune (Fortune), a former salesman of The National Cash Register Company (NCR), brought a suit to recover certain commissions allegedly due as a result of a sale of cash registers to First National Stores Inc. (First National) in 1968.

. . . Fortune was employed by NCR under a written "salesman's contract" which was terminable at will, without cause, by either party on written notice. The contract provided that Fortune would receive a weekly salary in a fixed amount plus a bonus for sales made within the "territory" (i.e., customer accounts or stores) assigned to him for "coverage or supervision," whether the sale was made by him or someone else.

. . . On November 29, 1968, First National [a client of Mr. Fortune] signed an order for 2,008 Class 5 machines to be delivered over a four-year period at a purchase price of approximately $5,000,000. Although Fortune did not participate in the negotiation of the terms of the order, his name appeared on the order form in the space entitled "salesman credited." The amount of the bonus credit as shown on the order was $92,079.99.

On January 6, 1969, the first working day of the New Year, Fortune found an envelope on his desk at work. It contained a termination notice addressed to his home dated December 2, 1968. Shortly after receiving the notice, Fortune spoke to the Boston branch manager with whom he was friendly. The manager told him, "You are through," but, after considering some of the details necessary for the smooth operation of the First National order, told him to "stay on," and to "[k]eep on doing what you are doing right now."

Commencing in May or June, Fortune began to receive some bonus commissions on the First National order. . . . Approximately eighteen months after receiving the termination notice, Fortune, who had worked for NCR for almost twenty-five years, was asked to retire. When he refused, he was fired in June of 1970. Fortune did not receive any bonus payments on machines which were delivered to First National after this date.

. . . The contract at issue is a classic terminable at will employment contract. It is clear that the contract itself reserved to the parties an explicit power to terminate the contract without cause on written notice. It is also clear that under the express terms of the contract Fortune has received all the bonus commissions to which he is entitled. Thus, NCR claims that it did not breach the contract, and that it has no further liability to Fortune. According to a literal reading of the contract, NCR is correct.

However, Fortune argues that, in spite of the literal wording of the contract, he is entitled to a jury determination on NCR's motives in terminating his services under the contract and in finally discharging him. We agree. We hold that NCR's written contract contains an implied covenant of good faith and fair dealing, and a termination not made in good faith constitutes a breach of the contract.

We do not question the general principles that an employer is entitled to be motivated by and to serve its own legitimate business interests; that an employer must have wide latitude in deciding whom it will employ in the face of the uncertainties of the business world; and that an employer needs flexibility in the face of changing circumstances. We recognize the employer's need for a large amount of control over its work force. However, we believe that where, as here, commissions are to be paid for work performed by the employee, the employer's decision to terminate its at will employee should be made in good faith. NCR's right to make decisions in its own interest is not, in our view, unduly hampered by a requirement of adherence to this standard.

Recent decisions in other jurisdictions lend support to the proposition that good faith is implied in contracts terminable at will. In a recent employment at will case, *Monge v. Beebe Rubber Co.*, 114 N.H. 130, 133 (1974), the plaintiff alleged that her oral contract of employment had been terminated because she refused to date her foreman. The New Hampshire Supreme Court held that "[i]n all employment contracts, whether at will or for a definite term, the employer's interest in running his business as he sees fit must be balanced against the interest of the employee in maintaining his employment, and the public's interest in maintaining a proper balance between the two. . . . We hold that a termination by the employer of a contract of employment at will which is motivated by bad faith or malice . . . constitutes a breach of the employment contract. . . . Such a rule affords the employee a certain stability of employment and does not interfere with the employer's normal exercise of his right to discharge, which is necessary to permit him to operate his business efficiently and profitably."

It is clear . . . a finding is warranted that a breach of the contract occurred. Where the principal seeks to deprive the agent of all compensation by terminating the contractual relationship when the agent is on the brink of successfully completing the sale, the principal has acted in bad faith and the ensuing transaction between the principal and the buyer is to be regarded as having been accomplished by the agent. . . . In our view, the Appeals Court erroneously focused only on literal compliance with payment provisions of the contract and failed to consider the issue of bad faith termination. . . .

Judgment of the Superior Court affirmed.

THREE PILLARS CASE QUESTIONS

(1) Mr. Fortune's actual firing from NCR, if in good faith, would not be actionable. Why?

(2) Do you believe that NCR operated in "bad faith" with regard to Mr. Fortune? What evidence from the case supports your answer?

(3) In an essay submitted to the Mackinac Center for Public Policy, legal analyst and attorney Jürgen Skoppek writes about the *Fortune* decision:

> [This] case constitutes the threshold to a complete judicial takeover of the employment relationship. There is no limitation of any kind on judicial intervention, no reference to statute, no articulation of boundaries which might guide employer behavior. Instead, the court simply says, if we don't like a reason for termination, we'll hold you as the employer liable. Every employment contract becomes subject to ever-changing judge or jury standards of "fairness" and "good faith." A "covenant of good faith and fair dealing" is imagined in order to justify the desirable result. . . . The practical effect is to destroy employment-at-will and replace it with a "just cause" standard, since the absence of "just cause" can in almost every case be interpreted as bad faith.

> Do you agree with attorney Skoppek? Why?

(4) What could happen if there were no exceptions to the employment-at-will rule?

Closely associated with adherence to the covenant of "good faith and fair-dealing" is the third exception to employment-at-will, which states that a dismissal may not violate public policy. For example, a hospital hired a nurse as an at-will employee. She went on a camping trip with her supervisor and employees of other hospitals. During the trip, members of the group staged a parody of the song "Moon River," which allegedly featured them "mooning" the audience. The nurse refused to participate in this parody and in other activities that made her feel uncomfortable. Before the trip, the nurse had received favorable performance evaluations. Shortly after the trip, she was terminated.

When the lower courts dismissed a lawsuit filed by the nurse, she appealed to the Supreme Court of Arizona. The Court held that "an employer may fire for good cause or for no cause. He may not fire for bad cause—that which violates public policy." Does refusal to participate in mooning violate public policy? The Supreme Court justices admitted that, "We have little expertise in the techniques of mooning." But, citing the state's indecent exposure law, the court concluded that "termination of employment for refusal to participate in public exposure of one's buttocks is a termination contrary to the policy of this state. . . ."[4]

In addition to these three exceptions—contractual rights, good faith, and public policy—fired employees often allege that they have been defamed in connection with the discharge. Defamation occurs when someone makes untrue statements that harm another person's reputation.

In one case, an employer fired an insurance salesperson named Larry. When he was unable to find employment with other firms, he hired an investigator. Posing as a prospective employer, the investigator contacted the office manager of the firm where Larry had worked. The office manager told the investigator that Larry was "irrational, ruthless, and disliked by office personnel. . . a classical sociopath. . . a zero, a Jekyll and Hyde person who was lacking. . . scruples." Because the statements were untrue, this conversation cost the employer $1.9 million in damages when Larry filed suit for defamation.[5]

Performance reviews are a fertile source of potential defamatory statements. The following statements, allegedly from actual performance evaluations, illustrate the danger.[6]

- "He's so dense, light bends around him."

- "Since my last report, the employee reached rock bottom and began to dig."

- "He would argue with a signpost."

- "If you stand close enough to him you can hear the ocean."

- "Takes an hour and a half to watch 60 Minutes."

- "If he were any more stupid he'd have to be watered twice a week."

- "His men would follow him anywhere, but only out of morbid curiosity."

The combination of the exceptions to the employment-at-will rule with the defamation claims has produced a judicial lottery in which some employees win large damage awards and many win nothing. California is notorious for large awards in wrongful discharge cases. Several years ago, when one of the authors was a visiting professor at Stanford University, an article in the local paper told the story of a Silicon Valley employee, David, who was fired by an electronics firm. According to the article, David, a top salesperson for the company, was replaced by someone who had financial ties to the manager who fired David. Company representatives investigated the matter but then claimed that they lost their file. When David sued the company for wrongful discharge, he also claimed that the company distributed defamatory information about him. Based on this combination of factors, the jury awarded David $61 million in damages. The article indicated that the company planned an appeal.[7]

Large awards are not limited to California. A jury in Kentucky awarded two former Ashland Oil employees $70 million (more than half of the company's annual earnings) after the company wrongfully discharged them when they protested illegal foreign payments. The case was eventually settled for "only" $25 million.[8] And a Texas jury awarded a former energy company employee $124 million for wrongful discharge after the employee refused to prepare documents that contained misleading information. The Texas case also eventually settled for $25 million.[9]

THE LAW PILLAR: WRONGFUL DISCHARGE AND DEFAMATION RISK MANAGEMENT

Given the high financial risks associated with wrongful discharge litigation, most companies have taken numerous measures to minimize liability. Consider in particular three approaches for preventing potential liability: (1) review your hiring practices, (2) train managers and review your documents, and (3) minimize defamation liability.

Review Your Hiring Practices

First, review your hiring practices. Careful screening of prospective employees to eliminate those who might be candidates for dismissal down the road is an obvious approach. Unfortunately, obtaining employment histories from former employers can be difficult. They are often reluctant to discuss job performance because of defamation risks.

Another hiring strategy is to hire temporary employees. Companies outside the United States have long used this strategy in countries where the costs of dismissal are high because the law provides automatic compensation when employees are discharged without cause. For example, a few years ago, author Siedel helped open a University of Michigan center in Paris. Before he interviewed potential staff members, a French lawyer emphasized the importance of hiring staff on short-term contracts. At the end of such contracts, she explained, the University could decide whether to renew or terminate the contracts without the costs that would be associated with dismissing a regular employee. In France, more than 80 percent of new employment contracts signed each year are for temporary employment.[10]

Training and Document Review

A second strategy for minimizing liability is directed toward statements that might create an exception to the employment-at-will rule. You should train and constantly remind managers that statements to staff such as "as long as you do well, you'll have a job" create an expectation that the company will only fire employees when there is good cause.

You should also review company documents and delete language that might overturn the employment-at-will rule. A few years ago, author Siedel gave a presentation at a large utility company in Texas. In preparing the talk, he reviewed the company's recruiting brochure in the MBA Career Development Office at the Ross School of Business. A statement in the brochure read (paraphrased): "After joining the company, you will first participate in an orientation program. You then will be assigned to a permanent position that is consistent with your career goals." The problem here is with "permanent"—a word that should be *permanently* avoided in all company documents. During the presentation, Siedel quoted the brochure. Immediately afterward, two human resource managers mentioned their concern about this language and asked for a copy of the brochure.

The following year, the company invited Siedel back for another presentation. Once again, he visited the Ross Career Development Office to review the recruiting brochure, and he noticed that the company had a new brochure and that the language quoted above had been "slightly" altered. Paraphrasing again, it now read: "At the end of the orientation program, an interesting career *may* be waiting for you" (our emphasis). Clearly, the company understood the problem with the language in the original brochure!

Minimize Defamation Liability

The third strategy is to try to reduce your company's liability for defamatory statements by instructing your staff that they should not comment on the job performance of former employees. In fact, they should make no comments at all but should, instead, direct all inquiries about a former employee to human resources. A human resources professional will then provide very limited information regarding the time of employment and title but will not discuss performance matters.

But even when communications about a former employee are handled by human resources, a "no comment" approach can have drawbacks. One problem is the difficulty prospective employers face when trying to investigate someone's employment history. Another problem arises when you dismiss someone for reasons unrelated to performance (for example, when you downsize your business) and want to say something positive about the former employee to a prospective employer. Furthermore, as discussed in the next section, a "no comment" approach will not eliminate all types of liability. Nevertheless, all respondents in a survey of Fortune 500 firms indicated that they do not provide references.[1112]

ALIGN STRATEGY AND LAW: USE WRONGFUL DISCHARGE LAW TO CREATE VALUE

The fear of a headline damage award like those rendered by juries in California, Texas, Kentucky, and elsewhere has caused managers to focus on the risk management approaches just described. However, these approaches have limitations that are illustrated by the "no comment" strategy.

Problems with the "No Comment" Strategy

The "no comment" approach to requests for information from prospective employers might reduce your company's liability based on conversations with outsiders, but it overlooks other types of conversation. For example, what would you say if one of your staff asks why an employee is no longer with the company? A "no comment" response is likely to cause morale problems and unrest among remaining employees.

On the other hand, if you do choose to comment, a statement that is untrue opens the door to a defamation lawsuit. For example, an employee who had worked for a company for forty-one years was fired after the company accused him of stealing a thirty-five dollar company phone. The employee, who claimed that the phone belonged to him, sued the company for defamation after it posted notices on company bulletin boards accusing him of theft. A jury awarded the employee $15.6 million in damages, and the case was later settled.[13]

What if you say nothing to either outsiders or insiders? Might there be defamation liability for actions alone? Yes, said an Illinois federal court in a case involving a trader on the Chicago Board of Trade who had worked for a brokerage firm for twelve years. The broker claimed that one afternoon, three of the firm's officials unexpectedly came to his office and, in plain view of other employees, interrogated him about his expense reports. They then escorted him from the office without allowing him to speak to his staff or take his belongings. He alleged that other brokerage firms would not discharge a high-level employee in this manner unless there had been a violation of criminal law or a breach of ethics. When the firm asked the court to dismiss the case, the judge denied the request.[14]

Still another flaw with the "no comment" approach is the risk of liability for what you say to the discharged employee, even if no one else is present. For example, let's assume that you fire one of your employees, Frank, and you advise him privately that the reason for the discharge is that he is a classic sociopath, which is not true. Frank then applies for a job with another company. A manager from that company calls you and asks why Frank was fired. You refuse to comment, in accordance with company policy. The manager then asks Frank to explain why he left the company. Frank's choice is to explain honestly that you told him he is a classic sociopath or to lie about the reasons you gave, which is not an acceptable alternative.

After hearing Frank explain the truth, the manager understandably decides not to hire Frank. Frank then sues you for defamation. "Wait a minute," you say. "I did not defame Frank. He defamed himself by passing on the information." This is still defamation, according to courts in several states, because Frank had no choice. He was compelled to defame himself.

In one "compelled self-defamation" case, four insurance company employees were terminated for what the company called "gross insubordination." The company policy was to provide prospective employers with only dates of employment and the final job titles of former employees. When these employees told prospective employers the reasons they were given for the discharge, they had difficulty finding jobs. The Supreme Court of Minnesota upheld a damage award of $300,000 to the employees.[15]

In summary, the conventional "no comment" approach overlooks potential liability based on (1) conversations with internal staff, (2) actions that might be defamatory, and (3) comments made privately to an employee.

Manage by Fact

Conventional risk management strategies tend to address a symptom (potentially large damage awards) of a deeper problem that is revealed when you climb to the balcony to gain perspective: the real cost of wrongful discharge litigation. The Rand Corporation conducted an in-depth empirical study that assessed the impact of employment-at-will rule erosion following development of the exceptions discussed in the Legal Briefing that opens this chapter. The study concluded that the indirect costs of these exceptions are one hundred times greater than the direct legal costs that receive the most attention from managers—that is, jury awards, settlements, and attorney fees. The indirect costs include keeping poor performers, making large severance payments, and forcing managers to use complex and time-consuming processes before discharging anyone. The view from the balcony demonstrates that company expenditures to avoid litigation far exceed actual litigation costs.[16]

By reframing the legal concern (high litigation costs) as a business concern (the impact of keeping poor performers or giving them large severance packages), you can then reexamine your risk management solutions with an eye toward value creation. One solution that should immediately come to mind is a key feature of a quality program: manage by fact. In other words, tell the truth. The greatest overall advantage of this approach is that a *truthful* company is nearly universally regarded as an *ethical* company.

Honesty also aligns with the Ethics Pillar in its adherence to the Codex principles of transparency, dignity, and fairness discussed in Chapter 3. As researcher, author, and CEO John Gerzema wrote: "Transparency, honesty, kindness, good stewardship. . . work in businesses at all times." This solution is especially attractive because it meets the interests of both your company and its employee stakeholders. It is a true win-win scenario.

When truth is the focus of interactions with employees, the benefits are reciprocal and multi-fold. For example, aspects of truth-telling are especially vital in the context of wrongful termination. First, telling the truth about an employee's poor performance is critically important in the performance review process, because your ability to show cause for discharge reduces a poor performer's chances for a successful lawsuit under the exceptions to the employment-at-will rule. According to a human resources director at a large utility company, "We are an at-will company, but we always try to show cause."

Honesty is sometimes easier said than done. It is often difficult for managers to be completely candid when they sit down with employees to review performance. For example, one company rated employees on a scale of one to ten, with ten as the best rating. No supervisor at this company gave employees a rating of lower than eight, and the average score was nine.[17] In an environment where managers are not candid and honest, even poor performers might walk into court with performance reviews indicating that their work has been "great." The solution is to use candid, fact-based statements when you conduct performance reviews. Employees appreciate the honesty of these reviews as well; specific, truthful feedback tailored to the individual and tied to company goals tends to have a positive motivational effect.[18]

In light of the difficulty and hazards associated with communicating negative feedback, many companies have recently decided on another approach—they have abandoned performance reviews altogether. Cigna Corporation, for example, eliminated its performance review system in 2015. In its place, the company encourages managers to meet frequently with employees, with an emphasis on coaching them. According to the company's chief learning officer, "Employees are saying, 'This is the first real honest conversation I've had with my manager about me, about what I should do, instead of these goals that aren't really related to me.' "[19]

Another aspect of truth-telling that is important in the context of wrongful termination is that truth is a defense in a defamation action. As we have seen, the "no comment" approach that dominates business today is only partially effective because it focuses on external communications, whereas liability may extend to comments made within the company. The "no comment" approach also makes it difficult for companies to uncover information about prospective employees. In contrast, a truth-telling approach will protect a company across the board—whether the communication is with prospective employers, other employees within the firm, or the discharged employee.

Beyond its impact in wrongful termination cases, truth-telling is important in establishing trust. In a world of flat, lean organizations and new forms of business alliances, trust is essential to achieve competitive advantage. As noted in an article in *The Economist*:

> The arguments in favour of trust seem overwhelming. Trust reduces the costs and delays associated with traditional monitoring systems and formal legal contracts. It enables companies to engage the hearts and minds of their employees, not just their passive compliance.[20]

In short, replacing "no comment" policies with management by fact and truth-telling in your internal and external communication represents a major step toward creating an environment of trust.

LEGAL BRIEFING ON DISCRIMINATION

We now turn to the second important and controversial employment law topic covered in this chapter—discrimination. Managers need a clear understanding of anti-discrimination law. Depending on country or local law, the following categories might be protected from employer discrimination: age, appearance, disability, marital status, national origin, pregnancy, race, receipt of welfare, religion, sex, and sexual orientation. To illustrate company approaches toward addressing discrimination concerns, this section focuses generally on sex discrimination and specifically sexual harassment.

The #MeToo movement brought considerable attention to the widespread prevalence of sexual harassment in the workplace. The moniker for "MeToo" was derived from use of the phrase by social activist and community organizer Tarana Burke. Burke said "she was inspired to use the phrase after being unable to respond to a thirteen-year-old girl who confided to her that she had been sexually assaulted. Burke said she later wished she had simply told the girl, "Me too."[21] The phrase went viral in 2017 following allegations of predatory sexual abuse by Hollywood magnate Harvey Weinstein. The awareness created in the wake of these events has spurred reform among companies in the handling of sexual harassment complaints in the workplace.

Sex discrimination and sexual harassment cases are fraught with psychological, emotional, and physical trauma for all the parties involved. Lawsuits can also be financially devastating, as they can result in huge damage awards. For example, in 2010 a jury awarded $250 million to several female staff members in a sex discrimination case. In 2011 an employee who alleged sexual harassment was awarded $95 million. In 2012 a physician's assistant won $168 million in a sexual harassment lawsuit.[22] And in 2016 the company that owns Fox News settled a sexual harassment lawsuit filed by broadcaster Gretchen Carlson for $20 million. Although plaintiffs in cases such as these often receive less than the jury award as a result of caps on damages, appeals or negotiated settlements, the financial impact on business can still be severe. Even allegations of sexual harassment can destroy a business, which happened to a public relations firm in late 2015.[23]

United States sexual harassment law is grounded in the Civil Rights Act of 1964, which makes sex discrimination illegal. While sex discrimination includes sexual harassment, the definition of sexual harassment was unclear until a landmark Supreme Court decision in 1986, *Meritor v. Vinson*. According to the Court, a key fact in determining whether conduct is lawful is whether it is welcome. Conduct that is welcomed does not constitute harassment; unwelcomed conduct is harassment. In the words of the US Equal Employment Opportunity Commission (EEOC), "Harassment is unwelcome conduct that is based on race, color, religion, sex (including pregnancy), national origin, age (40 or older), disability or genetic information."[24]

The Supreme Court explained that there are two types of unwelcome conduct. One type is *quid pro quo* (or "this for that") sexual harassment. The "this" is an economic benefit that a manager might offer someone in exchange for "that," which is a sexual relationship. The classic example is the "casting couch" scenario, where a movie director says to a young starlet, "Sleep with me, and I'll make you a star."

The second type of sexual harassment results when the work environment is hostile because of sexual misconduct. In defining "hostile environment" sexual harassment, the Supreme Court quoted guidelines developed by the EEOC. These guidelines provide that "sexual misconduct constitutes prohibited 'sexual harassment,' whether or not it is directly linked to the grant or denial of an economic *quid pro quo*, where 'such conduct has the purpose or effect of unreasonably interfering with an individual's work performance or creating an intimidating, hostile, or offensive working environment.' "

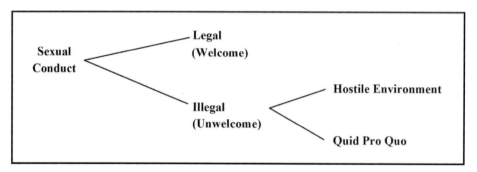

Laws in other countries now reflect the US Supreme Court's definition of sexual harassment. For example, French law defines sexual harassment as putting someone in an intimidating, hostile, or offensive situation. Penalties for violating the law are harsh and include a possible three-year prison sentence.[25] Companies have also responded to the ruling by developing internal codes of conduct. As an article in *The Economist* noted: "A Supreme Court ruling in 1986 made firms liable if they allow a 'hostile environment' in which harassment is tolerated. This led to the near-universal adoption of codes of conduct. . . ."[26]

STRATEGY
LAW   ***Three Pillars Case: Equal Opportunity Harassment***
ETHICS

Citation: *Oncale v. Sundowner Offshore Services, Inc.*, No. 96-568 (1990)

In this case, the US District Court for the Eastern District of Louisiana originally decided against the Plaintiff Joseph Oncale, saying "Mr. Oncale, a male, has no cause of action under Title VII for harassment by male co-workers." Oncale appealed, and the US Court of Appeals for the Fifth Circuit affirmed the decision. Later, the US Supreme Court reversed lower court decisions when it decided that same-sex sexual harassment is actionable under Title VII.

JUSTICE SCALIA delivered the opinion of the court.

This case presents the question whether workplace harassment can violate Title VII's prohibition against "discriminat[ion] . . . because of . . . sex," when the harasser and the harassed employee are of the same sex.

The District Court having granted summary judgment for respondent, we must assume the facts to be as alleged by petitioner Joseph Oncale. . . . In late October 1991, Oncale was working for respondent Sundowner Offshore Services on a Chevron U. S. A., Inc., oil platform in the Gulf of Mexico. He was employed as a roustabout on an eight-man crew which included respondents John Lyons, Danny Pippen, and Brandon Johnson. Lyons, the crane operator, and Pippen, the driller, had supervisory authority. On several occasions, Oncale was forcibly subjected to sex related, humiliating actions against him by Lyons, Pippen and Johnson in the presence of the rest of the crew. Pippen and Lyons also physically assaulted Oncale in a sexual manner, and Lyons threatened him with rape.

Oncale's complaints to supervisory personnel produced no remedial action; in fact, the company's Safety Compliance Clerk, Valent Hohen, told Oncale that Lyons and Pippen "picked [on] him all the time too," and called him a name suggesting homosexuality. Oncale eventually quit-asking that his pink slip reflect that he "voluntarily left due to sexual harassment and verbal abuse." When asked at his deposition why he left Sundowner, Oncale stated "I felt that if I didn't leave my job, that I would be raped or forced to have sex."

. . . We see no justification in the statutory language or our precedents for a categorical rule excluding same-sex harassment claims from the coverage of Title VII. As some courts have observed, male-on-male sexual harassment in the workplace was assuredly not the principal evil Congress was concerned with when it enacted Title VII. But statutory prohibitions often go beyond the principal evil to cover reasonably comparable evils, and it is ultimately the provisions of our laws rather than the principal concerns of our legislators by which we are governed. Title VII prohibits "discriminat[ion] . . . because of . . . sex" in the "terms" or "conditions" of employment. Our holding that this includes sexual harassment must extend to sexual harassment of any kind that meets the statutory requirements.

. . . Courts and juries have found the inference of discrimination easy to draw in most male-female sexual harassment situations, because the challenged conduct typically involves explicit or implicit proposals of sexual activity; it is reasonable to assume those proposals would not have been made to someone of the same sex. The same chain of inference would be available to a plaintiff alleging same sex harassment, if there were credible evidence that the harasser was homosexual. But harassing conduct need not be motivated by sexual desire to support an inference of discrimination on the basis of sex. A trier of fact might reasonably find such discrimination, for example, if a female victim is harassed in such sex-specific and derogatory terms by another woman as to make it clear that the harasser is motivated by general hostility to the presence of women in the workplace. A same-sex harassment plaintiff may also, of course, offer direct comparative evidence about how the alleged harasser treated members of both sexes in a mixed-sex workplace. Whatever evidentiary route the plaintiff chooses to follow, he or she must always prove that the conduct at issue was not merely tinged with offensive sexual connotations, but actually constituted "discrimina[tion] . . . because of . . . sex."

. . . We have emphasized, moreover, that the objective severity of harassment should be judged from the perspective of a reasonable person in the plaintiff's position, considering "all the circumstances." In same-sex (as in all) harassment cases, that inquiry requires careful consideration of the social context in which particular behavior occurs and is experienced by its target. A professional football player's working environment is not severely or pervasively abusive, for example, if the coach smacks him on the buttocks as he heads onto the field-even if the same behavior would reasonably be experienced as abusive by the coach's secretary (male or female) back at the office. The real social impact of workplace behavior often depends on a constellation of surrounding circumstances, expectations, and relationships which are not fully captured by a simple recitation of the words used or the physical acts performed. Common sense, and an appropriate sensitivity to social context, will enable courts and juries to distinguish between simple teasing or roughhousing among members of the same sex, and conduct which a reasonable person in the plaintiff's position would find severely hostile or abusive.

Because we conclude that sex discrimination consisting of same-sex sexual harassment is actionable under Title VII, the judgment of the Court of Appeals for the Fifth Circuit is reversed, and the case is remanded for further proceedings consistent with this opinion.

It is so ordered.

THREE PILLARS CASE QUESTIONS

(1) Find the section of Title VII that the Court refers to in this case at https://www.eeoc.gov/laws/statutes/titlevii.cfm. Why does the Court believe that this clause covers both genders?

(2)   What do you believe the Court meant by the statement, "As some courts have observed, male-on-male sexual harassment in the workplace was assuredly not the principal evil Congress was concerned with when it enacted Title VII"?

(3)   What did the Court suggest had to be the basis for a violation of Title VII? What would not constitute a violation?

(4)   The Court suggested there would be a major difference between "[a] professional football player's working environment if the coach smacks him on the buttocks as he heads onto the field" compared to the same action "experienced by the coach's secretary (male or female) back at the office." Do you agree with this assessment? Explain.

(5)   What strategy could Sundowner employ in this environment to avoid sexual harassment in the future?

THE LAW PILLAR: SEXUAL HARASSMENT RISK MANAGEMENT

In decisions after *Meritor*, the Supreme Court provided companies with guidelines that can minimize liability for sexual harassment. A leading case was brought by an ocean lifeguard who worked for the City of Boca Raton, Florida. She claimed that her two supervisors created a "sexually hostile atmosphere" by subjecting her and other female lifeguards to "uninvited and offensive touching." She also alleged that they made lewd remarks and spoke of women in offensive terms. The trial court found that one of the supervisors:

> repeatedly touched the bodies of female employees without invitation, would put his arm around Faragher, with his hand on her buttocks, and once made contact with another female lifeguard in a motion of sexual stimulation. He made crudely demeaning references to women generally, and once commented disparagingly on Faragher's shape. During a job interview with a woman he hired as a lifeguard, Terry said that the female lifeguards had sex with their male counterparts and asked whether she would do the same.[27]

Based on these findings, the trial court held that Boca Raton was liable for sexual harassment. The Supreme Court upheld this decision. The Court noted that employers are liable when they take tangible action—for example, causing economic injury to an employee such as denying a promotion or raise. But even when the employer does not take action, as in this case, an employer is liable unless it can prove two elements: "(a) that the employer exercised reasonable care to prevent and correct promptly any sexually harassing behavior, and (b) that the plaintiff employee unreasonably failed to take advantage of any preventive or corrective opportunities provided by the employer."[28]

The practical message from this language is that employers should take three measures to prevent liability. First, adopt an anti-harassment policy. Ideally, the policy will provide examples of the acts that are prohibited by the company. Here is an example of prohibited acts listed in one company's policy: "Repeated, offensive sexual flirtations, advances, propositions; continued or repeated verbal abuse of a sexual nature; graphic verbal commentaries about an individual's body; sexually degrading words used to describe an individual; display of sexually suggestive objects or pictures."[29]

Second, employers should establish a complaint procedure that will result in prompt correction of any suspect behavior. This procedure should provide alternative avenues for complaint—for example, to a supervisor, to human resources, or to a peer group. Both the anti-harassment policy and the complaint procedure should be communicated effectively to employees.

Third, employers should provide sexual harassment training. The law in California, for example, requires companies with fifty or more employees to provide supervisors with sexual harassment training.

Through training, employees should understand that actions and statements are perceived differently by men and women. For example, how would you feel about being sexually propositioned in the workplace? A study cited by a Florida court found that around two-thirds of men would be flattered while fifteen percent would feel insulted. These proportions are reversed for women. As a result, the court decided that the test to determine whether a hostile environment exists depends on how a reasonable woman would view the workplace.[30] With this perspective in mind, the Golden Rule (do unto others as you would have them do unto you) is not a useful guideline. A better guide is the Platinum Rule: do unto others as they would want done to themselves.

A company that takes these three measures should have a greater chance of success in defending a sexual harassment case. For example, in one case decided after the Supreme Court stated its guidelines, an employee was assigned to a new shift. One of her coworkers made comments (among others) "in front of other co-workers that if Fenton had any more children she would be wider than the Grand Canyon and that she would have to use shims off of one of the machines in the shop to make any man want her again; that he was going to call 1-900 numbers and 'play with himself', and that men 'only want one thing from you.' "

The employee reported the coworker's comments to a supervisor, who the same day met with the plant superintendent. A report was immediately made to a human resources manager, who met with the complaining employee the next day. The manager investigated the matter, and within four days, the coworker who made the comments was reassigned to another area. The coworker was also advised that if the comments continued, he would be subject to disciplinary action. The court concluded that the employer was not liable because it took prompt corrective action.[31]

Even with these responsive measures in place, however, employee plaintiffs may still claim "retaliation" that can result in employer liability. It is illegal for employers to retaliate against employees who file discrimination complaints or who complain to an employer about discrimination. Retaliation encompasses actions beyond firing the employee and could come in the form of decisions relating to pay, work assignments, or training opportunities.

Retaliation claims can even be made by an associate of the person who filed a complaint. For example, a company fired an engineer three weeks after his fiancé filed a sex discrimination complaint. He then sued the company, alleging retaliation. The US Supreme Court decided that his lawsuit could proceed to trial, noting that, "We think it obvious that a reasonable worker might be dissuaded from engaging in protected activity if she knew that her fiancé would be fired."[32]

The EEOC offers several risk management guidelines companies can use to try to prevent retaliation claims, including the following:[33]

- Avoid publicly discussing the allegation.

- Be mindful not to isolate the employee.

- Avoid reactive behavior such as denying the employee information/equipment/benefits provided to others performing similar duties.

- Do not threaten the employee, witnesses or anyone else involved in processing a complaint.

ALIGN STRATEGY AND LAW: USE SEXUAL HARASSMENT LAW TO CREATE VALUE

Just the mention of sexual harassment often brings thoughts of litigation and large damage awards to a manager's mind. Some managers even consider sexual harassment training to be a necessary evil that pulls employees away from productive work and is forced on companies by the legal system. As the president of a high-tech company commented following a US Supreme Court sexual harassment decision, "I have to lay something out very bluntly. I have had very little use for lawyers. They cause more problems than they solve."[34]

But is sexual harassment a legal problem or a business problem? If there were no laws governing sexual misconduct, would it still make sense for businesses to follow the approaches that are currently mandated by law? When you climb to the balcony to move away from the legal fray and gain a broader perspective, a different picture might emerge. This perspective was best summarized by an executive vice president for a major power company who noted that sexual harassment "is a business issue. It doesn't have to do [only] with law or morality but about having a productive workforce."[35]

Simply stated, your employees cannot be productive if they must worry about the abuse of power that sexual harassment represents. Studies on the incidence of sexual harassment reach varying conclusions depending on the country and the type of work at issue. For example, one study concluded that 90 percent of female restaurant workers in the United States have experienced sexual harassment.[36] More generally, an estimated 40 percent to 60 percent of women in United States-based companies have experienced harassment.[37] Outside the workplace, sexual harassment is more rampant. A study concluded that harassment caused 75 percent of women around the world to change their transportation.[38]

Women comprise half of the workforce worldwide. If 50 percent of women experience or witness sexual harassment on the job, 25 percent of your employees must worry about something other than doing a good job. And this figure does not include sexual harassment of men. According to the United States Equal Employment Opportunity Commission, over 16 percent of sexual harassment charges are filed by men.[39]

Companies that eliminate sexual harassment have the opportunity to seize competitive advantage by allowing their employees to focus on company interests while at the same time enhancing their career prospects by performing to their full potential. As one expert on sexual harassment noted, "there's quite a consistent body of literature that shows that [with sexual harassment] work performance declines, and as a result quality of performance, and attendance [also decline]. All of that ultimately has to hurt the company."[40]

From your perspective on the balcony, you can see that the real issue for your company extends beyond complying with the laws against sexual harassment to removing barriers that prevent your employees from being as productive as possible. As a result, your sexual harassment policy should not be limited to "We will not tolerate sexual harassment." Instead, the spirit of the policy should be "We will create a productive work environment that will enable our employees to achieve company and career success."

With this perspective, your horizon broadens to eliminating barriers beyond sexual harassment. As an employment law expert once put it, companies tend to "broadcast their sexual-harassment policies, but they have nothing in them about any other kind of harassment."[41] Yet it is clear that the Supreme Court guidelines apply to other types of harassment covered by the Civil Rights Act of 1964, such as race and religion.

For example, an African-American employee brought suit against Budget Rent-a-Car alleging racial discrimination. A federal court denied Budget's motion to dismiss the case, noting that the employee's claims, if proven, could result in a finding of racial harassment. The employee alleged that his supervisor treated him more harshly than other employees and used racial epithets. This is testimony from another employee:

> I was in [the supervisor's] office one morning and he was looking out the window and pointed to the black service agents and remarked how lazy they were and how slow they worked and said that was typical of blacks. . . . [He] said that he wanted to get Anthony to quit because it would be difficult to fire him because he was black.[42]

The court noted that under the post-*Meritor* Supreme Court guidelines, Budget did not prove that it distributed its harassment policy to employees or that it offered racial harassment training to its managers. Budget also did not prove that it promptly corrected complaints of racial harassment.

With a company policy that takes a broader perspective focusing on productivity, it is easier for all employees to understand that harassment is not limited to the acts of managers and other employees; the company even has a duty to prevent customers from engaging in discriminatory conduct. For example, a waitress sued the Pizza Hut franchise where she worked, claiming hostile environment sexual harassment. Two "crude and rowdy" male customers had eaten at the restaurant several times and had made sexually offensive remarks to the waitress, such as "I would like to get into your pants."

One evening, when no one on the wait staff wanted to serve these customers, the shift manager ordered the waitress to serve them. One of the customers said "that she smelled good and asked what kind of cologne she was wearing." When she told the customer that it was "none of his business," he grabbed her by the hair. When she told the manager what happened, and that she did not want to wait on them, he responded: "You wait on them. You were hired to be a waitress. You waitress." When she delivered a pitcher of beer to the customers, one of them "pulled her by the hair, grabbed her breast, and put his mouth on her breast."

The waitress then told the manager that she was quitting and called her husband, who picked her up. At trial, an expert witness testified that the waitress, who had been sexually assaulted by a friend of her father when a teenager, "exhibited classic symptoms of post-traumatic stress disorder and major depression." In upholding a jury verdict for the waitress, an appellate court concluded that an employer should be held liable regardless of whether a hostile environment is created by "a co-employee or a nonemployee, since the employer ultimately controls the conditions of the work environment."[43]

According to a federal court of appeals ruling, companies have a duty to follow their usual anti-discrimination policies even when there is an anonymous harasser. In that case, an African-American flight attendant alleged that United Airlines failed to take adequate measures after she reported a racist death threat.[44]

In cases involving sexual, racial, or religious harassment by employers or their customers, there is a clear violation of the law. But harassment in any form, whether legal or not, is harmful to employees (and their companies) because it prevents them from focusing on their work. This is the way Dow Chemical puts it when describing its policy toward lesbian, gay, bisexual, and transgender (LGBT) workers:

> While many states in the US and abroad have yet to pass laws protecting LGBT people from being fired based on their sexual orientation or gender identity, Dow's global Respect and Responsibility policy provides the Company's employees with this protection and helps create an environment in which all employees can focus on their jobs rather than fear of being discriminated [against] for who they are.[45]

Beyond eliminating discrimination, companies that move women and minorities to leadership positions have the opportunity to create value in the form of a "diversity dividend." According to a 2015 McKinsey study of public companies in Europe and the Americas, there is a "statistically significant relationship between companies with women and minorities in their upper ranks and better financial performance."[46]

As discussed in this chapter, best-practice risk management for sexual harassment involves establishing an anti-discrimination policy, implementing a complaint channel with prompt corrective action, and providing training for both employees and management. What follows below is a case where the company took these actions but failed to implement its policies.

STRATEGY	
LAW	***Three Pillars Case: "Delightfully Tacky, Yet Unrefined"*** [47]
ETHICS	

Citation: *Ciesielski v. Hooters of America, Inc.*, 2004 WL 1699020 (N.D. Ill. 2004)

Employers should not only establish policies to help prevent harassment in the workplace but also ensure that these risk management actions are failsafe through careful monitoring. In this case, which involved a waitress at the restaurant chain Hooters, maintaining a professional work environment became difficult when guidelines and corrective actions were disregarded.

St. Eve, J.

Defendants Hooters Management Corporation and Hooters on Higgins, Inc. (collectively "Hooters") move the Court . . . to grant judgment as a matter of law regarding Plaintiff's punitive damages award. For the following reasons, the Court denies Defendants' motion.

On February 18, 2003, Plaintiff Joanna Ciesielski filed a four-count complaint against Defendants alleging a hostile work environment claim, failure to supervise, intrusion upon the seclusion of another, and intentional infliction of emotional distress. . . . The case then proceeded to trial on the hostile work environment claim. . . . On November 23, 2004, after a seven day jury trial, the jury found in favor of Plaintiff and awarded her $25,000 in compensatory damages and $250,000 in punitive damages. . . . Defendants do not challenge the amount of the punitive damages that the jury awarded, but argue that punitive damages cannot be awarded in the first instance. The Court now turns to whether judgment as a matter of law is appropriate. . . .

Title VII allows for punitive damages awards when a plaintiff demonstrates that her employer engaged in discrimination "with malice or with reckless indifference to the federally protected rights of an aggrieved individual.". . . The Supreme Court has articulated a three-part framework for determining whether punitive damages are appropriate. . . . First, a plaintiff must demonstrate that the defendant acted with knowledge that its actions may have violated federal law. . . . A plaintiff can establish this requirement by demonstrating that the relevant employees knew or were familiar with anti-discrimination laws and the employer's anti-discrimination policies. . . . Second, the plaintiff must establish a basis for imputing liability to the employer. . . . A plaintiff establishes this element by demonstrating that the employees who discriminated against her were managerial agents acting within the scope of their employment. . . . Whether an employee acts in a managerial capacity is a fact-intensive inquiry based on the authority the employer gives the employee, the employee's discretion, and the manner in which the employee carries out his duties. . . .

Even if these two requirements are met, an employer may avoid liability for punitive damages if it can establish that it engaged in a good faith effort to implement an anti-discrimination policy. . . . The existence of an anti-discrimination policy alone, however, is insufficient to fulfill this requirement. . . . The employer must also engage in good faith efforts to comply with Title VII after it becomes aware of any discrimination complaints. . . . This requirement exists so that employers do not insulate themselves from punitive damages by simply implementing anti-discrimination policies without actually enforcing them.

. . . Ciesielski must demonstrate that Hooters acted with the requisite mental state, that is, with knowledge that its actions may have violated federal law. . . . Ciesielski can establish this element by demonstrating that the relevant employees knew or were familiar with anti-discrimination laws and Hooters' anti-discrimination policies.

At trial, there was testimony that every new Hooters' employee received an employee manual containing Hooters' policy prohibiting sexual harassment in the workplace. . . . Hooters also made its employees aware that they were subject to disciplinary actions for violations of the non-harassment policy. . . . There was also undisputed trial testimony that Hooters' management employees participated in annual training programs that addressed sexual harassment in the workplace. . . . Managers Douglas Gleichner, Jimmy Rabbit, Arlen Chung, Lisa Cooper, and Clint Unrue all testified that they were required to attend annual sexual harassment seminars in which Hooters trained them about unfair labor practices, including claims of discrimination and harassment.

. . . [T]he Court turns to whether there was sufficient trial evidence for a reasonable jury to conclude that Hooters engaged in a good faith effort to implement an anti-discrimination policy. . . . As discussed above, Defendants point to undisputed testimony that Hooters had a non-harassment policy. Evidence in the record reveals that at the outset of her employment, Hooters gave Ciesielski a new hire package containing the Hooters' non-harassment policy and the new hire manual, both of which set forth Hooters' policies regarding sexual harassment. . . . The "Statement on Harassment" contained in the employee handbook provided details of the types of conduct that constituted harassment, as well as the complaint procedure. . . . In addition, Hooters' managers participated in annual training programs addressing sexual harassment in the workplace. . . . Hooters' President and CEO, Neil Kiefer, testified that Hooters required all managers. . . to attend sexual harassment seminars every year. . . . According to Kiefer, Hooters had a procedure to address harassment complaints, including an employee's right to contact him directly. . . . Based on this undisputed testimony, a reasonable jury could have found that Hooters had a formal anti-discrimination policy.

Although the implementation of a formal anti-discrimination policy is relevant in evaluating whether Hooters made a good faith effort to comply with Title VII, the Court must also determine whether there was sufficient evidence for a jury to believe that Hooters did not engage in a good faith effort to comply with Title VII after it became aware of Ciesielski's sexual harassment complaints. . . . At trial, the jury heard testimony that after complaints were made about the recurring holes in the changing room walls, Hooters' management did not respond in a timely fashion.

. . . General Manager Cooper testified that there was no investigation into the original hole in the changing room walls. . . . Cooper testified that instead of interviewing the staff and others who had access to the building, she thought patching the hole was the most efficient way to rectify the situation. . . . Her further testimony reveals, however, that no investigation took place after the second or third set of holes appeared. . . . In fact, she testified that she did not report the holes in the changing room walls to anyone else in management because she did not feel like there was anything to report. . . .

There is additional evidence in the trial record that the kitchen staff and assistant managers made sexual comments and touched other Hooters' employees. . . . For example, "Hooters Girls" complained about the kitchen staff's sexual comments and behavior to Assistant Manager Unrue in May 2001. . . . Melissa Frankfort testified that Assistant Manager Jimmy Rabbitt touched other employees, such as tickling them or patting them on the butt. . . . In fact, after Rabbitt had touched Frankfort on the butt, she asked him to stop touching her. . . . Frankfort also testified that because it took Hooters months to fix the holes in the changing room walls, she felt uncomfortable working at Hooters and eventually left her job there. . . .

Based on this evidence in the trial record, the jury could have believed that after Ciesielski and other "Hooters Girls" complained about the sexual comments, touching, and holes in the changing room walls, management such as Cooper, Gleichner, Unrue, and Rabbitt did not cure the problem. As such, viewing the facts and drawing all reasonable inferences in favor of Ciesielski . . . the jury could have concluded that Hooters failed to engage in a good faith effort to comply with

Title VII after it became aware of Ciesielski's complaints of the recurring holes in the changing room walls, and the sexual comments and touching by other Hooters' staff.

In sum, there was sufficient evidence presented at trial for the jury to conclude that punitive damages . . . were appropriate under the circumstances.

THREE PILLARS CASE QUESTIONS

(1)   Punitive damages are intended to "punish" defendants and act as a deterrent to such conduct in the future. What is the standard for determining if punitive damages are appropriate in a discrimination case, and how can plaintiffs demonstrate their case meets this standard?

(2)   Can an employer avoid liability for punitive damages in a discrimination case even if company managers have violated the law? If so, how?

(3)   Did Hooters make a good faith effort to implement anti-discrimination policies? Use evidence from the court's ruling to support your answer.

(4)   Did Hooters make a good faith effort to comply with anti-discrimination policies after it became aware of Ciesielski's sexual harassment complaints? Use evidence from the court's ruling to support your answer.

(5)   A number of Hooter employees pointed to harassment as a primary reason why they left the company. If you were a member of Hooters' management, what strategy could you use to comply with anti-discrimination laws, promote ethics, and create value for the company?

KEY TAKEAWAYS

Employees are especially important stakeholders in your company. Your efforts to attract and retain the best talent depend on a solid understanding of employment law. This chapter shows how your company can create value even when addressing two of the most controversial areas of employment law—wrongful discharge and discrimination. Creating value requires that you should:

> 1.   **Become legally savvy about employment law.** Understand the fundamental differences between the United States-based approach to firing employees (the employment-at-will rule and its exceptions) and the approach used elsewhere. And understand that sexual harassment liability extends beyond *quid pro quo* to hostile environment claims.

2.   **Manage employment law risks.** Managing wrongful discharge risk requires a review of hiring practices and company documents. To manage sexual harassment risk, develop anti-harassment policies, along with procedures to enforce those policies, and provide company training.

3.   **Create value by using employment law to meet employee interests while also benefitting your company.** Managing by fact, as it relates to wrongful discharge, has the potential to improve the quality of your talent while also building employee trust in your company. Addressing harassment as a business problem and not just a legal problem creates an environment in which employees can focus on their work—which benefits them and your company.

STRATEGY	
LAW	***Three Pillars Decision: Frozen in 9-to-5 Time***
ETHICS	

Although we focus primarily on sex discrimination and sexual harassment in this chapter, other forms of discrimination are also prevalent in the workplace. Policies intended to benefit employees, like the oocyte cryopreservation perk discussed below, must be carefully designed to both avoid discriminatory effects and provide equal advantages to all.

Beginning in 2014, Apple, Facebook, and Google (among others) began offering female employees an unprecedented benefit—subsidized oocyte cryopreservation, also known as "egg freezing." The rationale for this costly perk, which may exceed $10,000 per employee in expense, was to provide fast track women within the company the opportunity to delay childbirth as they work to advance their careers. The benefit has been both lauded as accommodating employee planning timelines and criticized for suggesting that work is more important than family. Some analysts have additionally identified potential discrimination and inequity issues relating to the benefit.

VALUE GOAL: To offer an equitable employment policy that provides for subsidized oocyte cryopreservation.

STRATEGY: Develop a strategy that would provide the benefit of oocyte cryopreservation to company employees in a fair and equitable manner.

LAW: Review the 2016 journal article on legal and discriminatory issues related to oocyte cryopreservation located at this link: https://repository.uchastings.edu/cgi/viewcontent.cgi?article=1379&context=hwlj.

Does this information affect or alter the strategy you developed? If necessary, refine your strategy to align with the law.☙

ETHICS: Your strategy in the above scenario could raise significant ethical considerations for both employer and employee. Apply ethics to your strategy by working through these four steps of ethical decision making: (1) describe the ethical dilemma, (2) identify the stakeholders involved, (3) analyze options (including how each group of stakeholders will be affected), and (4) make a decision based on your analysis. After examining ethical issues associated with the strategy, determine whether any modifications should be made.

☙*Check for law research materials in the Appendix: Legal Resources for Business Decisions*

STRATEGY LAW ETHICS	***Three Pillars Decision: Good Samaritan—"You're Fired!"***

At-will employment and the judicially-created public policy exception are at issue in this next decision making analysis.

In the last decade, social media and news reports are replete with tales of employees who are fired from their positions for "doing the right thing":

- A Walmart employee in Michigan is fired after helping prevent a woman in the store parking lot from being physically assaulted;[48]

- A Home Depot employee in Oregon is fired after helping a woman whose child was being kidnapped;[49]

- A Nationwide Truck Brokers (NTB) Trucking employee in Texas is fired after helping a disabled customer fix his truck (during the employee's lunch hour break);[50]

- Four Home Depot employees in Florida are fired after following a suspected shoplifter to obtain the man's vehicle license plate number;[51]

- A Meijer employee in Michigan is fired after helping a customer extinguish a car fire; the employee said he was told by a supervisor that, "my heart was in the right place [but] my brain wasn't."[52]

The customers who have been helped by the terminated employee are often incredulous that someone who is aiding another in an emergency situation could lose their job because of those actions. Many of the employers interviewed have stated that the fired employees were not following company policy, which is strictly adhered to for the safety of both customers and employees.

VALUE GOAL: To allow for emergency assistance while promoting customer and employee safety.

STRATEGY: Design a strategy that would allow employees to assist customers in emergencies.

LAW: Research the Good Samaritan law in your state. Do the provisions of the Good Samaritan law have any impact on your strategy? Some analysts have argued that terminating an employee for a Good Samaritan act is a violation of the public policy exception to at-will employment. Do you agree or disagree?&

ETHICS: It has been contemplated that moral action should play a greater role in employment decisions. In your strategy/ethics analysis, keep this key factor in mind as you work through these four steps of ethical decision making: (1) describe the ethical dilemma, (2) identify the stakeholders involved, (3) analyze options (including how each group of stakeholders will be affected), and (4) make a decision based on your analysis. After examining ethical issues associated with the strategy, determine whether any modifications should be made.

&*Check for law research materials in the Appendix: Legal Resources for Business Decisions*

STRATEGY	
LAW	***Three Pillars Decision: Controlling the Demon*[53]**
ETHICS	

Artificial Intelligence (AI)—machine learning—can be a powerful tool to solve problems and improve human life quality. The recent use of AI in hiring, however, has created a number of issues related to discrimination that companies contemplating this technology would be wise to consider.

In the last few years, we've brought Artificial Intelligence (AI) into our offices, manufacturing facilities, smartphones, and homes through devices like Amazon's Alexa. Having an AI hiring manager—a machine that can learn to make important employment decisions—seems like a natural progression for our highly technological planet. By using artificial intelligence in employee hiring programs, there can be distinct advantages: increasing efficiency, reducing the drudgery of sifting through applications, and implementing consistency across many Human Resources operations. Computers don't get tired, need benefits, or require an eight-hour workday with breaks.

Yet with this advancement, there are limitations and even dangers. For example, employers typically try to hire candidates that possess specific positive qualities, which tend to be subjective. Translating those quality markers into algorithms may skew the data search along the lines of subjective labels that lead to the inclusion of prejudices. Additionally, AI programs operate through the use of algorithms, which have been described as "in part, our opinions embedded in code."[54] When human bias manifests itself, either consciously or unconsciously, through the actions of an AI hiring manager, then discrimination may result.

"Employers recognize that they can't or shouldn't ask candidates about their family status or political orientation, or whether they are pregnant, straight, gay, sad, lonely, depressed, physically or mentally ill, drinking too much, abusing drugs, or sleeping too little. However, new technologies may already be able to discern many of these factors indirectly and without proper (or even any) consent."[55] For example, research predicts that face and voice reading AI will be able to determine candidates' sexual and political orientation, internal states (mood and emotion), personality elements, and even genetic attributes. The technology changes in AI are making available to companies information that they cannot currently ask candidates and that is potentially considered private.[56]

In a study where researchers used Facebook "likes" to "automatically and accurately predict highly sensitive personal attributes including: sexual orientation, ethnicity, religious and political views, personality traits, intelligence, happiness, use of addictive substances, parental separation, age, and gender," the results were astounding.[57] The model analysts used correctly distinguish between homosexual and heterosexual men in 88 percent of cases, African Americans and Caucasian Americans in 95 percent of cases, and Democrat and Republican in 85 percent of cases. The authors cautioned that the "predictability of individual attributes from digital records of behavior may have considerable negative implications, because it can easily be applied to large numbers of people without obtaining their individual consent and without them noticing."[58]

VALUE GOAL: To use Artificial Intelligence to ease the burdens associated with employee searches and hiring.

STRATEGY: Develop a strategy that would allow employers to apply Artificial Intelligence to employee job search functions while providing safeguards against discrimination.

LAW: In 2019, the State of Illinois became the first to respond to the use of artificial intelligence in hiring. See its law here: http://www.ilga.gov/legislation/publicacts/fulltext.asp?Name=101-0260. Does this law affect or alter the strategy you developed? If necessary, refine your strategy to align with the law.

ETHICS: It has been argued that one of the primary issues with using AI in employment searches is that the algorithms are biased toward the prejudices of the programmers and designers. Keeping this issue in mind, examine your strategy for ethical issues, working through these four steps of ethical decision making: (1) describe the ethical dilemma, (2) identify the stakeholders involved, (3) analyze options (including how each group of stakeholders will be affected), and (4) make a decision based on your analysis. After examining ethical issues associated with the strategy, determine whether any modifications should be made.

Check for law research materials in the Appendix: Legal Resources for Business Decisions

STRATEGY	
LAW	***Three Pillars Decision: Hopping Around the Issue***
ETHICS	

It can be difficult to control sexual harassment in a sexually-themed environment, as cases against Hooters America have demonstrated. In the following decision making analysis, we examine how the classic Playboy Club is addressing "bunny" protection in light of the #MeToo movement.

In late 2018, Playboy Club New York opened in Midtown Manhattan. The venue features fourteen thousand square feet of restaurants, speakeasies, and lounges, as well as forty-four Playboy Bunnies outfitted in the trademark black satin bunny suit with a white cotton tail. The club environment has many asking whether there is room for this type of entertainment in the #MeToo era? There are special concerns because the club builds on a tradition that was started by Playboy founder Hugh Hefner, whose organization was built on the objectification of women.

According to Valerie Golson, Senior Vice President of Playboy Enterprises: "Being a Bunny at Playboy—a lot of people maybe are like, 'Well, maybe it's not the right time because of the #MeToo movement,' . . . and I think the opposite; I think it's the perfect time for it. Because these girls are all from different backgrounds, they all look different, they have different personalities, some of them don't have service experience. But they all have one common thread, and that's the fact that they made a choice to do this. And why should we take that away from them because of the #MeToo movement? The #MeToo movement isn't about objectification. The #MeToo movement is about sexual harassment and consent. So, these girls are making a choice and they feel empowered. We should have the choice to make any choice we want, right? Why should we take that away from them?"[59]

Yet employees at workplaces like the Playboy Club are especially vulnerable to sexual harassment from co-workers, management, and guests. According to Linda Seabrook, director of the legal program at the not-for-profit group *Futures Without Violence*: "The Restaurant Opportunities Center United did this survey of hospitality restaurant workers in New York City and found astounding rates of sexual violence and harassment. The Playboy Club is fundamentally a restaurant, and then you add onto that, women in skimpy outfits—it's the perfect storm, in a way, for sexual harassment to flourish."[60]

VALUE GOAL: To prevent sexual harassment in especially vulnerable workplaces.

STRATEGY: Can sexually-themed workplaces develop a strategy that would establish infrastructure to protect workers from sexual harassment and sex discrimination, or should these workplaces be closed because they cannot avoid violation of the law?

LAW: Review the US Equal Employment Opportunity Commission's guidelines on harassment at this link: https://www.eeoc.gov/eeoc/newsroom/wysk/ harassed_at_work.cfm. Does this information affect or alter the strategy you developed? If necessary, refine your strategy to align with the law.ℰ

ETHICS: The Playboy Club and Hooters Restaurants encourage sexual banter and innuendo as a part of their brand. Keeping this objective in mind, apply ethics to the issue of continuing sexually-themed workplaces by working through these four steps of ethical decision making: (1) describe the ethical dilemma, (2) identify the stakeholders involved, (3) analyze options (including how each group of stakeholders will be affected), and (4) make a decision based on your analysis. After examining ethical issues associated with the strategy, determine whether any modifications should be made.

ℰ*Check for law research materials in the Appendix: Legal Resources for Business Decisions*

---

[1] Chubb, *Worth the Risk* (2013).

[2] Cranman and Baum, "Approach to Your Employment Law Audit," *ACC Docket*, March 2007.

[3] *Toussaint v. Blue Cross & Blue Shield* (1980).

[4] *Wagenseller v. Scottsdale Memorial Hospital* (1985).

[5] *Hill v. Buck* (1984).

[6] "A Bit of Performance Management Humor," https://www.compensationforce.com/2006/08/ some_performanc.html.

[7] Reuss, "$61 Million Awarded for Firing," *Times Tribune*, April 5, 1985.

[8] Sella, "More Big Bucks in Jury Verdicts," *ABAJ*, July 1989.

[9] Varchaver, "Turmoil at Triton," *American Lawyer*, March 1993.

[10] Chassany, "Decay of the Permanent Job as France Balks at Labour Reform," *Financial Times*, August 11, 2015.

[11] Adler and Peirce, "The Legal, Ethical, and Social Implications of the 'Reasonable Woman' Standard," *Fordham Law Review*, 1993.

[12] L'Oreal slogan.

13   Susman Godfrey, "Libel/Slander Litigation".

14   *Zechman v. Merrill Lynch* (1990).

15   *Lewis v. Equitable* (1986).

16   Dertouzos and Karoly, *Labor Market Responses to Employer Liability* (1992).

17   DuFresnes, "Honest Employee Evaluations, *World Reports*, July–September 1994.

18   https://www.entrepreneur.com/article/287521.

19   Schoenberger, "The Risk of Reviews," *Wall Street Journal*, October 26, 2015.

20   "Trust in Me," *The Economist*, December 16, 1995.

21   https://en.wikipedia.org/wiki/Me_Too_movement.

22   Fuchs, "The 8 Largest Sexual Harassment Verdicts in History," *Business Insider*, September 3, 2012.

23   Sullivan, "Sexual Harassment Matters," *In House*, December 21, 2015.

24   "Harassment," EEOC, http://www.eeoc.gov/laws/types/harassment.cfm.

25   Orrick, Herrington, and Sutcliffe, "New Definition of Sexual Harassment," http://www.lexology.com/library/detail.aspx?g=df743079-0af7-4eea-8f70-65b66826edd9.

26   "Nasty, but Rarer," November 12, 2011.

27   *Faragher v. City of Boca Raton* (1998).

28   *Id.*

29   Machlowitz and Machlowitz, "Preventing Sexual Harassment," *ABAJ*, October 1, 1987.

30   *Robinson v. Jacksonville Shipyards* (1991).

31   *Fenton v. Hisan* (1999).

32   *Thompson v. North American Stainless* (2011).

33   "Retaliation—Making It Personal," http://www.eeoc.gov/laws/types/retaliation_considerations.cfm.

34   Aronson, "Justices' Sex Harassment Decisions Spark Fears," *National Law Journal*, November 9, 1998.

35   Segal, "Getting Serious About Sexual Harassment," *Business Week*, November 2, 1992.

36   Gallucci, "90 Percent of Female Restaurant Workers Sexually Harassed," *Observer*, October 8, 2014.

37   "Stop Violence Against Women," http://www.stopvaw.org/sexual_harassment.

38   Albo, "The Percentages of Women Who Have Been Sexually Harassed in Public Are Staggering," *Good*, January 20, 2016.

39   "Sexual Harassment," http://www.eeoc.gov/eeoc/statistics/enforcement/sexual_harassment.cfm.

40   Barrier, "Sexual Harassment," *Nation's Business*, December, 1998.

41   McMorris, "Employees Face Greater Liability in Race Cases," *Wall Street Journal*, July 1, 1999.

42   *Booker v. Budget Rent-A-Car Systems* (1998).

43   *Lockard v. Pizza Hut* (1998).

44   *Pryor v. United Air Lines* (2015).

45   "Dow Recognized for Support of Lesbian, Gay, Bisexual and Transgender Rights," https://newsroom.dow.com/press-release/company-news/dow-recognized-support-lesbian-gay-bisexual-and-transgender-rights.

46   Lublin, "New Report Finds a Diversity Dividend at Work," *Wall Street Journal*, January 20, 2015.

47   Hooter's slogan.

48   https://www.ibtimes.com/walmart-employee-kristopher-oswald-fired-violating-company-policy-after-helping-assaulted-woman.

49   https://www.nbcnews.com/news/us-news/home-depot-employee-says-he-was-fired-after-trying-stop-n780531.

50   https://www.click2houston.com/news/man-claims-he-was-fired-from-ntb-after-helping-a-customer.

51   https://www.clickorlando.com/news/4-home-depot-workers-fired-after-following-shoplifter.

52   https://www.wilx.com/home/headlines/UPDATE-Meijer-Employee-Fired—236237201.html.

[53] Reference to Elon Musk's quote "I think we should be very careful about artificial intelligence. If I had to guess at what our biggest existential threat is, it's probably that. So we need to be very careful. . ... With artificial intelligence we're summoning the demon."

[54] Gideon Mann & Cathy O'Neil, Hiring Algorithms Are Not Neutral, Harv. Bus. Rev. (Dec. 9, 2016), https://hbr.org/2016/12/hiring-algorithms-are-not-neutral [https://perma.cc/AN4B-RX4B].

[55] https://www.thehrobserver.com/the-legal-and-ethical-implications-of-using-ai-in-hiring/.

[56] *Id.*

[57] https://www.pnas.org/content/110/15/5802.

[58] *Id.*

[59] https://www.elle.com/culture/career-politics/a23569483/nyc-playboy-club-me-too/.

[60] *Id.*

Use Government Regulation to Develop New Business Models

According to the McKinsey survey mentioned in Chapter 2, executives across the globe conclude that government regulators are second only to customers among the key stakeholders who have the greatest effect on a company's economic value. Another McKinsey study provides details showing why executives might reach that conclusion. According to the study, the business value from government intervention is around 30 percent of a company's earnings.[1] This translated into numbers makes a vivid impression: one European utility company discovered that its value in regulation was "€1.5 billion ($1.6 billion USD), or about €30 million ($33 million USD) for every employee involved in handling the company's regulatory affairs."[2]

The importance of understanding government extends to all business decision-makers. In a co-authored article, CEO of BP John Browne and McKinsey expert Robin Nuttall wrote that

"The logic [of understanding government] is simple and compelling. The success of a business depends on its relationships with the external world—regulators . . . activists, and legislators. Decisions made at all levels of the business, from the boardroom to the shop floor, affect that relationship."[3]

Despite this obvious logic, evidence exists that companies are failing in their attempts to work successfully with government. A global survey cited by Browne and Nuttall concluded that more than 80 percent of companies do not experience frequent success with regulatory decisions and attempts to influence government policy. Thus, companies that *are* able to work successfully with government have an opportunity to achieve sustainable competitive advantage.

This chapter opens with a legal briefing on government regulation. The focus then turns to the Law Pillar and managing regulatory risk, with emphasis on how companies can shape the law and use government regulation as a source of competitive advantage. The chapter closes by examining the overlap between the Strategy Pillar and Law Pillar and how, in some cases, the law can become the foundation for new directions in strategy.

LEGAL BRIEFING ON GOVERNMENT REGULATION

In countries around the world that adhere to the rule of law, government provides three key functions. First, a legislative body has primary responsibility for creating law in the form of legislation. Second, a judicial function is tasked with interpreting the law. Third, an executive function enforces the law.

In the United States, these three functions constitute the branches of government, and each branch has its own separate powers. Several countries follow this "separation of powers" approach to government, whereas in other countries the powers are intertwined. And even in the United States, the boundaries between the branches are permeable. For example, courts in the United States (a common law system) make law when they establish precedents that future courts follow.

One exception to the separation of powers model is especially relevant to business. Because it is difficult for legislatures to enact detailed legislation, they delegate the task of filling in the details to government agencies. This is necessary even when the legislation is already quite detailed. For example, Congress enacted the Dodd-Frank Act in response to the financial crisis that began in 2007. Although this 2,300-page law went into effect in 2010, this was not the end of the law-making story, because the law required government agencies to adopt 398 regulations relating to the Act.[4]

Called the "fourth branch" of the US government, these agencies have become a key interface between business and government. Professor Jonathan Turley of George Washington University noted that as a result of administrative regulations, "The shift of authority [from the other three branches] has been staggering. The fourth branch now has a larger practical impact on the lives of citizens than all the other branches combined." To back up this statement, he observed that "Today, we have 2,840,000 federal workers in 15 departments, 69 agencies and 383 nonmilitary sub-agencies. . . . One study found that in 2007, Congress enacted 138 public laws, while federal agencies finalized 2,926 rules, including 61 major regulations."[5]

Government agencies are especially powerful and important to business because they combine the power of all three branches of government. They make law in the form of regulations, but they also enforce the law. For example, the Federal Trade Commission (FTC) filed a complaint against Twitter alleging that Twitter deceived consumers by failing to protect private information. As evidence, the FTC alleged that despite Twitter's policy that it had adopted measures to protect users' information, hackers were able to send out false tweets from President Obama's account to more than 150,000 people offering them an opportunity to win free gasoline. In settling with the FTC in 2010, Twitter agreed to improve security and to remain on probation for twenty years.[6]

In addition to government agency enforcement of the law, judges linked to the agencies determine whether the law has been violated. As Professor Turley noted,

> As the number of federal regulations increased, however, Congress decided to relieve the judiciary of most regulatory cases and create administrative courts tied to individual agencies. The result is that a citizen is 10 times more likely to be tried by an agency than by an actual court. In a given year, federal judges conduct roughly 95,000 adjudicatory proceedings, including trials, while federal agencies complete more than 939,000.[7]

In other words, the separation of powers principle does not apply to government agencies, which make and enforce regulations and often determine, through administrative courts, whether you have violated their rules. As a result, as we will see in the next section, your interaction with these agencies in attempting to manage regulatory risk is an important aspect of legal risk management.

THE LAW PILLAR: GOVERNMENT REGULATION RISK MANAGEMENT

Two fundamental strategies can help you manage risks related to government regulation. One strategy is to attempt to shape laws and regulation. The second strategy is for you to take action after laws and regulations become effective. Managing political risks beyond the border of your own country raises special concerns that are addressed at the conclusion of this section.

Shaping Laws and Regulations

Successful companies recognize that public policy is an important element in their success. JPMorgan Chase officially operates six lines of business.[8] But CEO Jamie Dimon calls government regulation a "seventh line of business" that is important to the success of the other six lines.[9] And General Electric (GE) puts it this way: "The success of GE depends significantly on sound public policies. . . . Governments, through advancing their legitimate regulatory and political interests, affect the environment in which GE operates."[10]

We now turn to five general strategies companies can use to shape legislation, as well as a specific strategy, called the public comment process, that is useful when companies are concerned about regulations that agencies propose.

Corporate Political Strategies. In their article "Corporate Political Strategy and Legislative Decision Making," Gerald Keim and Carl Zeithaml identified five key strategies that are used by companies that are politically active.[11]

1.   *Constituency building.* Immediately after being elected to public office, one question dominates the thinking of a member of the legislature: will I be reelected? As a result, legislators are especially concerned about meeting the needs of their constituents—the voters. Your efforts to influence the legislative process should involve these constituents.

For example, let's assume that proposed legislation will affect your manufacturing facilities located in three states. You should use a three-step process to build constituent support:

a.   Identify constituents who have an interest in your company. Obvious candidates are shareholders, employees, customers, suppliers, and leaders in the community where your plants are located.

b.   Organize and educate the constituents.

c.   Develop an action plan that includes constituent contact with their elected representatives to share opinions about legislative proposals. The contact might take the form of email, letters, phone calls, and office visits.

2.   *Campaign contributions.* Running for elected office is an expensive undertaking. In 2014, the winner in the Kentucky Senate race, Republican Mitch McConnell, spent more than $30 million, whereas the loser, Democrat Alison Grimes, spent more than $18 million.[12] To fund their campaigns, elected representatives spend considerable time engaged in fundraising. This has led to what is called the "Tuesday–Thursday Club," referring to Congressional

representatives who work in Washington only on Tuesday through Thursday of each week and spend the rest of the week fundraising at home.

In the United States, organizations called Political Action Committees (PACs) are often used to raise money to support or defeat candidates for office. PACs can represent businesses (Microsoft PAC), labor (Teamsters PAC), or other interests (National Rifle Association PAC).[13] In the 2018 election cycle, the top PAC contributor was the National Beer Wholesalers Association, which contributed $3.4 million to federal candidates, both Democrats (48 percent) and Republicans (52 percent). Foreign companies can also use the PAC structure when their American subsidiaries form PACs funded by employees in the United States. In the 2018 election cycle, foreign-connected PACs made contributions totaling over $23 million.[14]

3.   *Advocacy advertising.* Companies can use advertising as a means to reach a broad audience in an attempt to influence legislators. Unlike usual corporate advertising, which promotes a service or a product, advocacy advertising focuses on public policy concerns. For example, in the 1970s, Mobil Oil Company started an advocacy campaign regarding the need for offshore oil drilling to address the energy crisis.[15]

4.   *Lobbying.* Lobbying is generally defined as an attempt to influence the decisions of government officials. Company leaders can directly engage in lobbying, or they can hire professionals.

Spending on lobbying in the United States has grown considerably over the years, from $1.56 billion in 2000 to $3.5 billion in 2018. In 2018, the top spenders were the US Chamber of Commerce ($94.8 million) and the National Association of Realtors ($72.8 million). The leading issues were the federal budget, taxes, and health issues.[16]

Growth in lobbying expenditures can parallel the success of a company. For example, in 2004, Google's lobbying expenditures totaled $180,000. By 2014, the expenditure had grown to $16.8 million.[17] During that year, Google opened its new Capitol Hill office that is roughly the size of the White House. Why? According to an article in *The Washington Post*, "Google's increasingly muscular Washington presence matches its expanded needs and ambitions as it has fended off a series of executive- and legislative-branch threats to regulate its activities and well-funded challenges by its corporate rivals."[18]

Lobbying is often seen as a self-serving activity that large companies use to increase their wealth. But this constitutionally-protected activity (falling within the Constitution's 1st Amendment rights to free speech and to petition government) can also provide a useful service to government officials by giving them information they need to make informed decisions. A lobbyist who does not provide this information in a balanced manner will quickly lose credibility. As a government official in Asia put it, "Bad lobbying is telling me something I know. Average lobbying is telling me something I did not know. Excellent lobbying is telling me something I did not know and that's useful to me."[19]

Assistance to lawmakers aligns with the Ethics Pillar when lobbying efforts are fair and transparent, ultimately contributing to the common good. According to the Markkula Center for Applied Ethics, an "obviously unethical (and illegal) practice associated with lobbying is paying a policy maker to vote in a favorable way or rewarding him or her after a vote with valuable considerations."[20] If these actions were legal, it would be unfair to individuals and companies who do not have the money to provide such incentives. But even with these restrictions, lobbying can be unfair. As Senator Kirsten Gillibrand noted, "Few lobby for food stamps, because the people who need them aren't in positions of power."[21]

Transparency is promoted by requiring lobbyists to register and file a report on the issues discussed with legislators. Issues with transparency have also arisen at the federal level with the use of "earmarks" ("pork barrelling")—spending additions to appropriation bills that focus on providing benefits to particular groups or organizations. Because these provisions are typically last-minute and often thought to be the result of too-narrow lobbyist influence, the US Senate adopted a permanent ban against this practice in 2019.

This movement away from self-promotion is a positive step that leading businesses use to their advantage in lobbying efforts. According to a McKinsey article on increasing the impact of your company's external engagement, the most successful organizations do not focus only on what would improve their own position but also concentrate on exploring underlying issues through efforts such as economic analysis and international benchmarking.[22] When a company identifies universal situations and the broader classes of stakeholders affected, it "dramatically improves the quality of engagement and can even break through seemingly deadlocked situations—for example, when a company can quickly and accurately show a regulatory proposal's negative consequences for national employment rates or tax revenues."[23]

Therefore, lobbying may be regarded as an effective process for all organizations and the public, not just businesses and private groups. Responsible business leaders frequently lobby for changes in public policy that benefit society at large. According to one of the most powerful leaders in corporate America, David E. A. Carson (former CEO of the largest bank in Connecticut):

In my career I've been involved in everything from neighborhood block watches to talking to the chief of staff of the President of the United States. . . . And everyone in between—state legislators, regulators, elected officials and bureaucrats—who can make the changes I thought would be good for our society. I've never lobbied to make more money. I've lobbied because I think the system works better if constraints are reasonable and understood.[24]

Public service in the form of lobbying beyond corporate interests is not without reward. As Carson puts it, "The people who end up with power in our society are those who get involved."

5. *Coalition building.* Coalition building is a useful tactic when you can find other businesses that share your interests. For example, Facebook's Mark Zuckerberg formed a group that was interested in education and immigration policy, and Facebook also formed a trade association with Amazon, Google, and Yahoo "to make sure policymakers do nothing to hamstring the free flow of information or overly regulate technology firms."[25] Coalitions are especially useful when members of the coalition are constituents of a legislator whom you are attempting to influence (see #1 above).

Public Comment Process. In addition to these five general strategies, businesses use a specific approach when dealing with proposed administrative regulations. As mentioned, government agencies adopt rules that complement legislation Congress has adopted. This typically involves a four-step process. First, the agency does background research and drafts a proposed rule. Second, the proposed rule is published in the *Federal Register*, an official government publication. Third, the public can comment on the proposed rule. Fourth, the agency takes action on the rule in light of the comments.

The third step is especially important to businesses because it gives them a chance to voice opinions about proposed rules. The process of submitting comments has become much easier in recent years as a result of an eRulemaking initiative. By visiting a website (http://www.regulations.gov), you can easily search for rules, comments, and other documents. For example, a search of the random term "tennis" produces information about a Department of Energy proposal to require anyone who imports certain products, such as table tennis, into the United States to provide a certificate of admissibility. The comment period for this proposed rule was set at forty-five days.

Once you identify a proposed regulation that interests you, you can immediately participate in the rulemaking process by submitting a comment. Try it out. As the website suggests, "Make a difference. Submit your comments and let your voice be heard." Here is a slightly-edited example submitted by someone from Microsoft who is discussing a proposed rule on "Improving and Expanding Training Opportunities for F-1 Nonimmigrant Students with STEM (Science, Technology, Engineering, and Mathematics) Degrees":

> Improving and expanding OPT [Optional Practical Training] for STEM students is obviously good for the US people and the US economy.
>
> 1.   In my city (Seattle), one foreign worker creates nine local jobs in service sector including restaurants, Medicare, transportation, education, sales, retail, etc. Foreign students under OPT are usually single and young, so they often contribute more than average foreign workers.
>
> 2.   In the STEM area, it is a well-known fact that there [are not] enough US graduates to fill job positions. I have never seen or heard of a US citizen who successfully earned a degree [who] is not able to find a better position in the job market than average foreigners. . . .
>
> 3.   Diversity and foreign talent of US offices have been the cutting-edge for US businesses. All nations have talents, but only the US has the advantage of importing a large number of foreign workers. Von Neumann, Cate Blanchett, Brin Sergey, Jerry Yang were all foreign-born. Marquis de Lafayette was foreign born.

As a variation on the standard comment process, regulators have developed regulatory negotiation (also called "reg-neg"). Under this variation, regulators meet with private parties in an attempt to find shared interests and to reach consensus before a rule is even proposed. For example, the US Environmental Protection Agency (EPA) used the negotiated rulemaking process to establish a rule relating to emission standards for ovens that process coal into coke. The EPA first created a committee consisting of representatives of the EPA, environmental groups, the coke and steel industry, states, and unions. The committee met every two to three weeks for four months and drafted a proposed rule that the EPA adopted fourteen months later.[26]

Post-Adoption Strategies

After a law has been adopted, there are two fundamental risk management approaches companies should consider: (1) embrace the law with vigorous compliance efforts and (2) use the court system to challenge the new law. While these two strategies might seem contradictory, the approaches can be used simultaneously to manage regulatory risk.

Embrace the law through compliance initiatives. When your lobbying and other efforts fail, there is a tendency for companies to implement the new regulatory burdens with hostility, or at least begrudging acceptance. After all, these burdens bring with them costs that will directly affect your company's bottom line. For example, after the Dodd-Frank law became effective in 2010, banks took the following actions:[27]

- Goldman Sachs reduced its balance sheet by $56 billion in one quarter in order to, in the words of the Chief Financial Officer, "proactively comply with regulatory developments";

- Morgan Stanley reduced its assets by one-third;

- Citicorp sold more than sixty businesses and cut almost $700 billion in assets; and

- Bank of America eliminated more than $70 billion in assets, including parts of its credit card and mortgage businesses.

Banks coupled this loss in assets with a hiring binge that was necessary to comply with the new law and with accompanying regulations. JPMorgan Chase, for example, expected to add thirteen thousand employees, bringing its total regulatory and compliance staff to thirty thousand.

Despite these regulatory burdens, regulation can bring opportunities for competitive advantage. For example, while most companies had a negative reaction to the reporting requirements imposed by the Sarbanes-Oxley Act of 2002 (Microsystems CEO Scott McNealy described the law as throwing "buckets of sand into the gears of the market economy")[28], a few firms recognized competitive advantage opportunities and used the law "as a leveraging tool to consolidate financial processes, eliminate redundant IT systems, broaden responsibility for financial controls, and integrate distant business units. Firms achieved significant cost savings, increased data integrity, and gained a more effective understanding of their own operations."[29]

These competitive advantage opportunities are available worldwide. For instance, in its response to the financial crisis, the European Union established a new regulatory framework that places significant burdens on investment firms. However, despite a "tough regulatory landscape" that became effective in 2017, companies that quickly adapted to the regulations had the opportunity to "gain competitive advantage by expanding core competencies, winding down unprofitable portfolios and improving client services, and leveraging implementation synergies driven by regulations. . . ."[30] These regulations provide a stimulus to strengthen internal controls and reduce risks that are under the surveillance of regulatory authorities.

In some situations, business leaders attempt to encourage strict enforcement of regulations, with an eye toward the competitive advantage their efforts will bring following the law's adoption. For example, a senior executive for a multinational corporation once related that he traveled, along with a group of executives who held similar positions at other global firms, to several less-developed countries. The purpose of the trip was to convince government officials to enforce stricter environmental laws.

Company efforts to push for stricter regulation might seem counterintuitive, but there is a compelling logic that drives the push for higher standards. In the wake of increasing uniformity of environmental regulations worldwide, global companies often adopt environmental standards that apply even in countries where environmental regulation is weak. These high standards result in additional costs that make it difficult for global companies to compete with local firms. Strengthening local environmental law levels the playing field by forcing local companies to incur environmental expenses similar to those of the multinationals.[31]

Challenge the law (and competitors). The second post-adoption strategy is to challenge new laws or regulations in court. Courts can even come into play before an agency ultimately adopts a regulation. In a legendary case, companies that produced peanut butter challenged a proposed government regulation specifying that peanut butter had to contain at least 95 percent peanut content. When this regulation was first proposed, some manufacturers were producing peanut butter that contained 20 percent to 25 percent hydrogenated oils (lard). The manufacturers fought the proposed rule because the higher peanut content would increase their costs. Through a combination of tactics that included public hearings and appeals in the court system, the regulation was delayed for twelve years. In the meantime, the rule's peanut content requirement was lowered to 90 percent.[32]

An electronic cigarette case provides an example of a court battle after a regulation is enacted. A company that imports and sells electronic cigarettes challenged a regulation the US Food and Drug Administration (FDA) adopted under a federal drug law. The FDA had decided to use the regulation to prevent the importation of the plaintiff's electronic cigarettes into the United States. The case reached a federal appellate court in 2010. The court described electronic cigarettes as follows:

> Battery powered products that allow users to inhale nicotine vapor with fire, smoke, ash, or carbon monoxide. Designed to look like a traditional cigarette, each e-cigarette consists of three parts: the nicotine cartridge, the atomizer or heating element, and the battery and electronics. . . . The atomizer vaporizes the liquid nicotine, and the battery and electronics power the atomizer and monitor air flow. When the user inhales, the electronics detect the air flow and activate the atomizer; the liquid nicotine is vaporized, and the user inhales the vapor.

With this definition in mind, the court decided that the FDA did not have authority to regulate electronic cigarettes as drugs and could regulate them only under less-restrictive tobacco laws.[33]

Even long-standing laws that restrict corporations may be challenged if believed to be unconstitutional. In the US Supreme Court case of *Tennessee Wine and Spirits Retailers Association v. Russell F. Thomas, Executive Director of the Tennessee Alcoholic Beverage Commission, et al.*, the Court struck down a Tennessee law that favored in-state residents and stymied commerce.

STRATEGY	
LAW	***Three Pillars Case: Tennessee Born and Brewed***
ETHICS	

Citation: *Tennessee Wine and Spirits Retailers Association v. Thomas*, 139 S .Ct. 2449 (U.S. 2019)

The durational-residency regulation at the heart of this action prevented Utah couple Doug and Mary Ketchum from opening a liquor store in Tennessee. The Ketchums moved to the state for a better environment and situation to support their severely disabled daughter, Stacie. This decision by the Supreme Court not only affected the State of Tennessee but also more than a dozen states with similarly-restrictive laws.

Syllabus excerpt (*prepared by the Reporter of Decisions of the Supreme Court of the United States*): The State of Tennessee imposes demanding durational-residency requirements on all individuals and businesses seeking to obtain or renew a license to operate a liquor store.

. . . Two businesses that did not meet the residency requirements (both respondents here) applied for licenses to own and operate liquor stores in Tennessee. Petitioner Tennessee Wine and Spirits Retailers Association (Association)—a trade association of in-state liquor stores—threatened to sue the

TABC if it granted the licenses, so the TABC's executive director (also a respondent) filed a declaratory judgment action in state court to settle the question of the residency requirements' constitutionality. The case was removed to Federal District Court, which found the requirements unconstitutional. The State declined to appeal, but the Association took the case to the Sixth Circuit. It affirmed, concluding that the provisions violated the Commerce Clause.

ALITO, J., delivered the opinion of the Court, in which ROBERTS, C.J., and GINSBURG, BREYER, SOTOMAYOR, KAGAN, and KAVANAUGH, JJ., joined. GORSUCH, J., filed a dissenting opinion, in which THOMAS, J., joined.

. . . To obtain an initial retail license, an individual must demonstrate that he or she has "been a bona fide resident" of the State for the previous two years. And to renew such a license—which Tennessee law requires after only one year of operation—an individual must show continuous residency in the State for a period of 10 consecutive years.

The rule for corporations is also extraordinarily restrictive. A corporation cannot get a retail license unless all of its officers, directors, and owners of capital stock satisfy the durational-residency requirements applicable to individuals. In practice, this means that no corporation whose stock is publicly traded may operate a liquor store in the State.

. . . In 2016, respondents Tennessee Fine Wines and Spirits, LLC and Affluere Investments, Inc. applied for licenses to own and operate liquor stores in Tennessee. At the time, neither Total Wine nor Affluere satisfied the durational-residency requirements. . . . [Tennessee Alcoholic Beverage Commission] TABC staff recommended approval of the applications, but petitioner Tennessee Wine and Spirits Retailers Association (the Association)—a trade association of in-state liquor stores—threatened to sue the TABC if it granted them.

. . . In support of the argument that the Tennessee scheme is constitutional, the Association. . . . claim[s] that discriminatory distribution laws, including in-state presence and residency requirements, long predate Prohibition and were adopted by many States following ratification of the Twenty-first Amendment. Indeed, the Association notes that the 2-year durational-residency requirement now before us dates back to 1939 and is consistent with durational-residency regimes adopted by several other States around the same time.

. . . Insofar as the Association's argument is based on state laws adopted prior to Prohibition, it infers too much from the existence of laws that were never tested in this Court. Had they been tested here, there is no reason to conclude that they would have been sustained.

. . . If we viewed Tennessee's durational-residency requirements as a package, it would be hard to avoid the conclusion that their overall purpose and effect is protectionist. Indeed, two of those requirements—the 10-year residency requirement for license renewal and the provision that shuts out all publicly traded corporations—are so plainly based on unalloyed protectionism that neither the Association nor the State is willing to come to their defense. The provision that the Association and the State seek to preserve—the 2-year residency requirement for initial license applicants—forms part of that scheme.

. . . In this Court, the Association has attempted to defend the 2-year residency requirement on public health and safety grounds, but this argument is implausible on its face. The Association claims that the requirement ensures that retailers are "amenable to the direct process of state courts", but the Association does not explain why this objective could not easily be achieved by ready alternatives, such as requiring a nonresident to designate an agent to receive process or to consent to suit in the Tennessee courts.

Similarly unpersuasive is the Association's claim that the 2-year requirement gives the State a better opportunity to determine an applicant's fitness to sell alcohol and guards against "undesirable nonresidents" moving into the State for the purpose of operating a liquor store. The State can thoroughly investigate applicants without requiring them to reside in the State for two years before obtaining a license. Tennessee law already calls for criminal background checks on all applicants, and more searching checks could be demanded if necessary. As the Fifth Circuit observed in a similar case, "[i]f [the State] desires to scrutinize its applicants thoroughly, as is its right, it can devise nondiscriminatory means short of saddling applicants with the 'burden' of residing" in the State.

. . . In addition to citing the State's interest in regulatory control, the Association argues that the 2-year residency requirement would promote responsible alcohol consumption. According to the Association, the requirement makes it more likely that retailers will be familiar with the communities served by their stores, and this, it is suggested, will lead to responsible sales practices. The idea, it seems, is that a responsible neighborhood proprietor will counsel or cut off sales to patrons who are known to be abusing alcohol, who manifest the effects of alcohol abuse, or who perhaps appear to be purchasing too much alcohol. No evidence has been offered that durational-residency requirements actually foster such sales practices, and in any event, the requirement now before us is very poorly designed to do so.

For one thing, it applies to those who hold a license, not to those who actually make sales. For another, it requires residence in the State, not in the community that a store serves. The Association cannot explain why a proprietor who lives in

Bristol, Virginia, will be less knowledgeable about the needs of his neighbors right across the border in Bristol, Tennessee, than someone who lives 500 miles away in Memphis. And the rationale is further undermined by other features of Tennessee law, particularly the lack of durational-residency requirements for owners of bars and other establishments that sell alcohol for on-premises consumption.

Not only is the 2-year residency requirement ill-suited to promote responsible sales and consumption practices, but there are obvious alternatives that better serve that goal without discriminating against nonresidents. State law empowers the relevant authorities to limit both the number of retail licenses and the amount of alcohol that may be sold to an individual. The State could also mandate more extensive training for managers and employees and could even demand that they demonstrate an adequate connection with and knowledge of the local community And the State of course remains free to monitor the practices of retailers and to take action against those who violate the law. . . .

The judgment of the Court of Appeals for the Sixth Circuit is affirmed.

THREE PILLARS CASE QUESTIONS

(1)   Why did the Court believe that the residency requirement was poorly designed to promote responsible alcohol consumption?

(2)   How did the Court suggest that the State of Tennessee could promote liquor regulation without discriminating against nonresidents?

(3)   The Court believed the durational-residency requirement was primarily intended to limit competition in the state's retail liquor industry. How would increased competition benefit consumers and liquor retailers in the wake of the Court's decision?

(4)   Following the Supreme Court's decision in Tennessee, a half-dozen cases were initiated to open up the possibility of interstate wine sales in jurisdictions where the practice is currently prohibited. What are benefits and drawbacks of interstate sales? What would be the benefits and drawbacks to consumers if the prohibitions were lifted?

In addition to supporting challenges to the law, as in the Tennessee case above, courts can become company allies in other ways. For example, companies can use the law and litigation as sources of competitive advantage by challenging the business practices of their competitors in court. Marketing decisions are often described in terms of the classic four "Ps": price, product, promotion, and place. The use of litigation adds a fifth "P" to the marketing mix: plaintiff.

Here is an example. For several years, Apple and Samsung have engaged in a so-called "patent war" in courts around the world. In 2014, they agreed to end litigation outside the United States, but their battle continued in US courts. For instance, in 2012, a jury awarded Apple more than $1 billion (later reduced to $400 million) on the grounds that Samsung violated Apple's patents when designing smartphones. However, that decision was appealed, and the litigation bounced around in the court system—including a short foray into the US Supreme Court in 2016—until the case was resolved in Apple's favor with a $539 million award in mid-2018.[34] In the words of Santa Clara School of Law professor Brian Love, Samsung should have emphasized to the jury that Apple "is losing marketplace share [to Samsung] and so wants to compete in the courtroom instead."[35]

The risk management strategies described thus far in this section can be effective in countries that adhere to the rule of law. But what if you decide to do business in countries where checks and balances among the branches of government are ineffective, and you are subject to the random decisions of whoever is in power? This situation calls for a political risk management strategy. As Stanford Business School professor Ken Shotts described (using as an example the risk that a government will seize your business assets),[36] there are two elements to this strategy.

First, you should determine the likelihood that the government will expropriate your assets. This depends on three key questions:

1. Does the government receive significant tax revenue from your company? If not, the chance of expropriation is higher.

2. Can the government operate your business without your expertise? If so, the chance of asset seizure is higher.

3. Will government leaders benefit politically from the expropriation? If so, the likelihood of it happening is higher.

Second, in situations where you do face the risk of expropriation, you should factor this risk into your strategic planning and implementation. For instance, you should consider measures to reduce the risk by gaining local support. These actions might include hiring local workers, offering training programs, building roads and making other infrastructure improvements, and using local sources for your production.

ALIGN STRATEGY AND LAW: USE GOVERNMENT REGULATION TO CREATE VALUE

Opportunities to create value by aligning the Strategy Pillar with the Law Pillar fall within two categories: anticipating regulation (called the "Regulatory Frontier" strategy) and using gaps in government regulation to develop new business models (called the "Regulatory Gap" strategy). Both categories bring together the Strategy Pillar and Law Pillar by focusing on stakeholder needs.

Anticipating Regulation—the Regulatory Frontier Strategy

An article in the *McKinsey Quarterly* on societal expectations of business distinguishes between issues already addressed by formal laws and regulations and issues that are "frontier expectations." The latter category includes issues such as obesity that could, over time, result in regulation. This is the way the authors put it:

> It had always been widely believed that the responsibility for avoiding [obesity] lay with individuals, who choose what they eat, not with the companies that make or sell fattening products. But the blame is shifting, much as the debate around tobacco shifted the responsibility from individuals to an industry perceived to be aggressively marketing addictive products. Food companies may not be forced to modify the fat and sugar content of their products, but the momentum on this issue could already be so great that lawmakers or regulators will step in and formalize social expectations by imposing new legal restraints.[37]

Companies that develop frontier thinking achieve two forms of competitive advantage. First, they are ahead of their competitors when regulations are eventually adopted. A company's approach to a frontier issue might even become a model for future regulation. Second, they might achieve a first-mover advantage by developing products and services that meet the consumer needs reflected by the social concern. In achieving this competitive advantage, these companies might be able to embed their corporate social responsibilities into their strategic planning initiatives.

For example, how would you react to the possibility that the FDA would adopt a regulation that requires your company to add labels to its products showing the amount of trans fats in them? PepsiCo's Frito Lay division reacted by deciding to stop using trans fats in potato chips and other products. This turned into a marketing advantage when the company obtained FDA approval to place prominent labels on these products showing that they had no trans fats.[38]

Operating on the Regulatory Frontier can produce significant cost savings for companies. For example, Siemens decided to help its customers reduce their carbon impact by developing new green products. The result: additional revenues of €32.3 billion while preventing 377 million metric tons of carbon emissions.[39]

Beyond these savings are the benefits to society that result from a focus on stakeholder interests. For example, look at what happened when Johnson & Johnson decided to invest in wellness programs for its employees. The company benefited by having a more productive workforce, coupled with healthcare savings of $250 million over a six-year period.[40] These benefits undoubtedly cascade down to employees and society at large in the form of better health and lower healthcare costs.

In the following case, beverage manufacturers and retailers challenged, on First Amendment grounds, an ordinance that required health warnings for soft drinks. The district court declined the plaintiff's request for a preliminary injunction that would delay enforcement of the ordinance, but the circuit court reversed that decision. The circumstances raise the question of what strategy the companies could adopt if they eventually lose the case.

STRATEGY
LAW   ***Three Pillars Case: It's Not Too Sweet*** [41]
ETHICS

Citation: *American Beverage Association; California Retailers Association v. City and County of San Francisco,* 916 F.3d 749 (9th Cir. 2019)

Government regulation of corporate free speech is examined in this decision, which illustrates the ability of companies to challenge regulations that might have a tremendous detrimental effect on their business operations.

GRABER, CIRCUIT JUDGE:

. . . In June 2015, Defendant enacted the Ordinance, which requires that certain SSB advertisements ("SSB Ads") include the following statement:

WARNING: Drinking beverages with added sugar(s) contributes to obesity, diabetes, and tooth decay. This is a message from the City and County of San Francisco. City & Cty. of S.F., Cal., Health Code art. 42, div. I, § 4203(a) (2015).

An "SSB Ad" covers any advertisement, including, without limitation, any logo, that identifies, promotes, or markets a Sugar-Sweetened Beverage for sale or use that is any of the following: (a) on paper, poster, or a billboard; (b) in or on a stadium, arena, transit shelter, or any other structure; (c) in or on a bus, car, train, pedicab, or any other vehicle; or (d) on a wall, or any other surface or material.

. . . The Ordinance defines "SSB" as "any Nonalcoholic Beverage sold for human consumption, including, without limitation, beverages produced from Concentrate, that has one or more added Caloric Sweeteners and contains more than 25 calories per 12 ounces of beverage." But "SSB" does not include drinks such as milk, plant-based milk alternatives, natural fruit and vegetable juices, infant formulas, and supplements. The Ordinance provides detailed instructions regarding the form, content, and placement of the warning on SSB Ads, including a requirement that the warning occupy at least 20% of the advertisement and be set off with a rectangular border.

Defendant's stated purpose in requiring the warning is, among other reasons, to "inform the public of the presence of added sugars and thus promote informed consumer choice that may result in reduced caloric intake and improved diet and health, thereby reducing illnesses to which SSBs contribute and associated economic burdens." Failure to comply with the warning requirement can result in administrative penalties imposed by San Francisco's Director of Health.

Plaintiffs [American Beverage Association, California Retailers Association, California State Outdoor Advertising Association] sued to prevent implementation of the Ordinance. The district court denied Plaintiffs' motion for a preliminary injunction. Concluding that Plaintiffs likely would not succeed on the merits of their First Amendment challenge, the district court held that the warning is not misleading, does not place an undue burden on Plaintiffs' commercial speech, and is rationally related to a substantial government interest. . . . A three-judge panel of this court reversed the district court's denial of a preliminary injunction. . . . Because Plaintiffs have a colorable First Amendment claim, they have demonstrated that they likely will suffer irreparable harm if the Ordinance takes effect. Next, "[t]he fact that [Plaintiffs] have raised serious First Amendment questions compels a finding that . . . the balance of hardships tips sharply in [Plaintiffs'] favor." Finally, we have "consistently recognized the significant public interest in upholding First Amendment principles." Indeed, "it is always in the public interest to prevent the violation of a party's constitutional rights."

. . . We begin by considering Plaintiffs' likelihood of success on the merits of their First Amendment challenge. The First Amendment provides that "Congress shall make no law . . . abridging the freedom of speech." Its protection is broad, and the Supreme Court has "been reluctant to mark off new categories of speech for diminished constitutional protection.". . . .

The *Zauderer* test . . . contains three inquiries: whether the notice is (1) purely factual, (2) noncontroversial, and (3) not unjustified or unduly burdensome. A compelled disclosure accompanying a related product or service must meet all three criteria to be constitutional. . . . [No] Supreme Court precedent requires that we apply these criteria in any particular order. . . . [The Supreme] Court's analysis began with the question whether the notice was "unjustified or unduly burdensome" . . . . [W]e find it useful to begin with that prong here.

. . . Defendant's argument that the border and 20% size requirements adhere to the best practices for health and safety warnings is unpersuasive. We recognize that some tobacco and prescription warnings must occupy at least 20% of those products' labels or advertisements. And Defendant's expert concluded that larger warnings are more effective. But the record here shows that a smaller warning— half the size—would accomplish Defendant's stated goals. . . . The Supreme Court made clear . . . that a government-compelled disclosure that imposes an undue burden fails for that reason alone. Indeed, the Court ended its own analysis with that holding. We need not, and therefore do not, decide whether the warning here is factually accurate and noncontroversial.

The remaining factors of the preliminary injunction test also favor an injunction. Because Plaintiffs have a colorable First Amendment claim, they have demonstrated that they likely will suffer irreparable harm if the Ordinance takes effect. Next, "[t]he fact that [Plaintiffs] have raised serious First Amendment questions compels a finding that . . . the balance of hardships tips sharply in [Plaintiffs'] favor." Finally, we have "consistently recognized the significant public interest in upholding First Amendment principles." Indeed, "it is always in the public interest to prevent the violation of a party's constitutional rights."

In summary, Plaintiffs have met each of the requirements for a preliminary injunction. We therefore conclude that the district court abused its discretion by denying Plaintiffs' motion.

THREE PILLARS CASE QUESTIONS

(1)   How were the plaintiffs' First Amendment rights being affected in this situation?

(2)   The 9th Circuit granted a preliminary injunction in this case, which is an order allowing the plaintiffs to avoid complying with the ordinance, at least until a formal

hearing can be held. Why do you think this type of temporary delay may be important to individuals and companies challenging such a new rule?

(3)   Why would the beverage association and retailers be against such an ordinance? How would the law potentially affect their business?

(4)   In making its decision, why did the Court not consider all three parts of the *Zauderer* test: (1) purely factual, (2) noncontroversial, and (3) not unjustified or unduly burdensome?

(5)   The defendant proposed that the purpose of the ordinance was to promote healthy habits: "The City's purpose in requiring warnings for SSBs is to inform the public of the presence of added sugars and thus promote informed consumer choice that may result in reduced caloric intake and improved diet and health, thereby reducing illnesses to which SSBs contribute and associated economic burdens." Do you believe this is an ethical ordinance? Do you believe that the beverage industry's challenge to the ordinance is ethical?

(6)   If the manufacturers' and retailers' challenge of the ordinance ultimately fails, what strategy could they develop to comply with the law and create value for their companies?

Ignoring Regulation—the Regulatory Gap Strategy

The goal of the Regulatory Gap strategy is to uncover gaps in existing regulations that enable you to serve customers in new ways. This strategy can lead to a complete overlap of the Strategy Pillar and Law Pillar when new business models are created based on the gaps you identify. For example, in 1967, Texas entrepreneur Rollin King and his lawyer Herb Kelleher incorporated an airline in Texas that they called Air Southwest. Their business model was based on the idea that by limiting their flights to Texas, they could escape federal regulation and charge cheaper fares. Competitors such as Continental Airlines sued them (the fifth "P" strategy described earlier), but Air Southwest prevailed and changed its name to Southwest Airlines.[42] Subsequent airline deregulation enabled the company to expand its operations beyond Texas.

Opportunities to use the Regulatory Gap strategy abound today with the sharing opportunities that technology creates. The so-called "sharing economy" includes business models that give consumers more control over their transactions, such as ride-sharing, room-sharing, office-sharing, meal-sharing, clothes-sharing, and solar energy-sharing.[43]

Jack Wroldsen, a former professor of legal studies at Oklahoma State University's Spears School of Business and founder of Initio Law, has observed that the disruptive innovation that accompanies these business models has changed the role of attorneys from transaction cost engineers to business disruption framers.[44] This new role requires business leaders and their lawyers to work together closely in developing strategic plans for new business models, just as King and Kelleher did when they formed Southwest Airlines.

Uber has become the poster child for the Regulatory Gap strategy. Uber's business model is based on the company's belief that taxi regulations do not cover transportation service companies that, instead of operating a fleet of cabs and hiring drivers, merely connect passengers to drivers. Uber's strategy is first to enter markets without permission from regulators and then to gather support from drivers and customers who use the service.

By 2015, five years after its launch, there were projections that Uber's value was higher than General Motors, Ford, and Honda—companies whose traditional business model Uber is disrupting.[45] Following a public offering of its stock in 2019, the company was valued at almost $70 billion. With its growth, Uber has supplemented the Regulatory Gap strategy with the traditional strategies discussed previously in this chapter—such as lobbying for changes in the law, compliance with local regulations, and adjustments in its business model. In India, for example, the company has sold its ride-sharing business for cars and is partnering with the e-bike company Yulu to promote a popular bicycle-sharing platform.[46]

KEY TAKEAWAYS

This chapter focuses on a key stakeholder in every business—government. To manage business risks and develop opportunities arising from your interaction with government, you should:

1.   **Become legally savvy about government regulation.** You should understand the three key functions of government and the important role played by administrative agencies—the "fourth branch" of government. By exercising legislative, executive, and judicial functions, administrative agencies play an important role in your business success.

2.   **Manage risks resulting from government regulation.** Risk management requires that you attempt to shape the laws and regulations that affect your business. This involves using several corporate political strategies, such as constituency building, lobbying, and coalition

building. You can also shape the law through the public comment process that administrative agencies use. After laws have been adopted, your risk management strategy should emphasize rigorous compliance and mounting challenges to rules and regulations that are harmful to your business.

3.   Create value by meeting stakeholder needs through business strategies based on government regulation. One key strategy, the Regulatory Frontier strategy, enables you to achieve competitive advantage by anticipating future regulations. With the other key strategy, the Regulatory Gap strategy, you should attempt to identify gaps in government regulation that enable you to serve customers in new ways.

STRATEGY

LAW   ***Three Pillars Decision: Muzzle on the Mills***

ETHICS

This decision analysis examines how a company can create value in a situation that can quickly turn an industry "upside down."

Puppy and kitten "mills" have been a pet protection issue in a number of jurisdictions for many years. Animal welfare and advocacy groups have highlighted the terrible conditions at some breeding facilities, and the animals supplied to pet stores from these locations are often malnourished, injured, or in poor health. As a result of these concerns, two states have banned the sale of dogs and cats at pet stores that obtain them from commercial breeders, requiring retail establishments to instead sell only pets obtained from animal shelters. A majority of pet store owners maintain that they obtain their animals from humane, licensed breeders and that the new law will negatively impact their businesses.

VALUE GOAL: To diminish the effect of new state laws limiting the sale of dogs and cats by retail pet stores.

STRATEGY: Develop a strategy that would reduce the impact on pet stores of the limitations on the sale of dogs and cats.

LAW: Research the laws of states that have adopted the commercial sale ban, such as California and Maryland. Do these provisions affect or alter the strategy you developed? If necessary, refine your strategy to align with the law.**ဆ**

The State of New York, among others, is considering a similar law banning commercial pet sales. When writing new potential laws, legislators are often sensitive to the interests of their constituents with regard to future impacts of those laws. If you were a pet store owner in New York, what would you advise your representatives about the construction of this proposed law? Is there a way to balance the interests of pet store owners and the goal of the state to protect animals?

ETHICS: This situation requires balance between the rights and protections of various groups. Apply ethics to your strategy by working through these four steps of ethical decision making: (1) describe the ethical dilemma, (2) identify the stakeholders involved, (3) analyze options (including how each group of stakeholders will be affected), and (4) make a decision based on your analysis. After examining ethical issues associated with the strategy, determine whether any modifications should be made.

℞*Check for law research materials in the Appendix: Legal Resources for Business Decisions*

STRATEGY	
LAW	***Three Pillars Decision: In Pursuit of Food Justice***
ETHICS	

Similar to the situation in the American Beverage Association case, passage of some laws intended to promote health may have detrimental effects on the companies involved and require innovative techniques to adapt.

San Francisco, California's *Healthy Food Incentive Ordinance* (Code §§ 471.1–471.9)[47] went into effect on December 1, 2011. The law was identified as the "Happy Meal Ban" because it was believed to primarily target McDonald's Corporation and its inclusion of toys in children's meals. Rationales for the ordinance included research by the Centers for Disease Control and Prevention (CDC), which demonstrated an increase in the rate of US childhood obesity, placing children at risk for chronic health problems. Lawmakers also cited the linking of toys and other incentive items to highly caloric meal packages, encouraging children (and their parents) to purchase the food items and consume an average of 770 calories in a single meal offering.

Supervisor Eric Mar, sponsor of the San Francisco ordinance, said, "We're part of a movement that is moving forward an agenda of food justice."[48] However, there has been debate over whether the law is based in consumer protection or is, instead, merely an exercise of paternalism. To date, the law has largely withstood legal challenges. Following the San Francisco enactment, other jurisdictions have passed similar laws or considered legislating on the issue.

VALUE GOAL: To adapt the selling of fast food meals packaged with toys to comply with healthy food ordinances.

STRATEGY: Develop a strategy that would allow McDonald's Happy Meal® to comply with the San Francisco ordinance.

LAW: Research the *California Healthy Food Incentive Ordinance*. How does this research affect or alter the strategy you developed? If necessary, refine your strategy to align with the law.❧

ETHICS: Apply ethics to your strategy by working through these four steps of ethical decision making: (1) describe the ethical dilemma, (2) identify the stakeholders involved, (3) analyze options (including how each group of stakeholders will be affected), and (4) make a decision based on your analysis. After examining ethical issues associated with the strategy, determine whether any modifications should be made.

❧*Check for law research materials in the Appendix: Legal Resources for Business Decisions*

STRATEGY	
LAW	***Three Pillars Decision: Climbing Conundrum***
ETHICS	

Sometimes businesses fight regulations that restrict them when it would be more advantageous for them to work with government, especially to prevent tragic situations from developing.

Between the years 1922 and 2006, there were over eleven thousand attempts to climb Mount Everest—the highest mountain on Earth above sea level.[49] While always dangerous, the Nepalese-Chinese ascent has become increasingly treacherous in the last few years, as more and more climbers set out to replicate what Edmund Hilary and Tenzing Norgay accomplished when they reached Everest's peak in 1953. "Traffic jams" have formed near the top of the mountain, where hundreds of climbers stand for hours at the pinnacle of the world. The peak, located above twenty-six thousand feet (eight thousand meters), is known as the "death zone" where "the human body is not designed to survive."[50]

Lines forming near the top of the mountain and the extended wait times to reach the top are said to be responsible for the rising death toll over the last few years—with May 2019 being the worst in recent memory. Nearly a dozen climbers, trying to reach the peak in a five-day seasonal window of favorable conditions, lost their lives on the descent from altitude sickness and exhaustion. The 2019 climbing situation was attributed to a number of factors, including excess permits issued by Nepal, unfavorable weather, inexperienced climbers, and China's reduction in issuing permits on the north side of Everest due to a buildup of more than sixty thousand pounds of trash and debris. The commercial industry that has developed around the mountain is a foundation of the Nepalese economy: Nepal charges

$11,000 to issue a permit, and climbing operators offer their services at a cost of $45,000–$130,000. The country brought in $643 million in tourism revenue in the 2017–18 fiscal year.[51]

VALUE GOAL: To reduce crowding on Mount Everest and promote safer climbing conditions.

STRATEGY: Develop a strategy for new regulations that a climbing operation could suggest to mountain regulators that would reduce crowding and promote safety on Mount Everest while still securing this very important Nepalese-Chinese industry. Then develop a strategy as a climbing operation to address the current situation if regulations remain unchanged.

LAW: Research the Nepalese Mountaineering Expedition Regulations under the Tourism Act and the Chinese regulations from the China Tibet Mountaineering Association (CTMA). Does this research affect or alter the strategy you developed? If necessary, refine your strategy to align with the law.☜

ETHICS: There is a significant ethical concern in issuing too many permits to climb the mountain, resulting in human safety issues and undesirable effects on the sensitive mountain environment. In examining this situation, apply ethics to your strategy by working through these four steps of ethical decision making: (1) describe the ethical dilemma, (2) identify the stakeholders involved, (3) analyze options (including how each group of stakeholders will be affected), and (4) make a decision based on your analysis. After examining ethical issues associated with the strategy, determine whether any modifications should be made.

☜*Check for law research materials in the Appendix: Legal Resources for Business Decisions*

STRATEGY	
LAW	***Three Pillars Decision: Don't Tread on My Hemp***
ETHICS	

As seen in the Tennessee Wine and Spirits Retailers Association case (presented earlier in this chapter), the easing of regulations can provide new opportunity.

Industrial hemp is made from non-psychoactive varieties of the plant *Cannabis sativa*—the same species that produces medicinal and recreational marijuana. Hemp, however, contains only very minute amounts of tetrahydrocannabinol (THC), the chemical that produces a "high" in those who smoke or consume it. The benefits of hemp production are considerable, resulting in thousands of useful products from the stalk and seed, including fibers, insulation, biofuel, foods, filters, and paper products. Hemp is also an attractive rotation crop for farmers because it detoxifies soil and prevents erosion as it grows. The Hemp

Industries Association (HIA) estimates that the total retail value of hemp products sold in the US is $620 million annually; however, all these products are imported from outside the country.[52]

The modern view of industrial hemp is very different from that held in early US history. In "17th Century America, farmers in Virginia, Massachusetts and Connecticut were ordered by law to grow hemp, and by the early 18th century, individuals could be sentenced to jail if they were not growing hemp on their land."[53] Yet in the twentieth century, US hemp production was prohibited following the passage of the 1937 Marijuana Tax Act, which assumed that hemp and marijuana were the same plant with the same intoxicating effects. This false assumption was propagated by leading tycoons of the time, such as William Randolph Hearst, who feared that his significant investments in timber for paper production would be devastated by the growth of renewable hemp fibers. However, recent changes in legislation have invigorated the industrial hemp industry, positioning it for expansive development.

VALUE GOAL: To take advantage of the changing landscape with regard to the domestic (US) production and sale of industrial hemp.

STRATEGY: Develop a strategy to grow and market industrial hemp in the following states that originally grew the crop in the 1600s: Virginia, Massachusetts, and Connecticut.

LAW: Research the federal law and state laws in Virginia, Massachusetts, and Connecticut related to the growth and sale of industrial hemp. How does this research affect or alter the strategy you developed? If necessary, refine your strategy to align with the law. Now research the status of industrial hemp production in South Dakota, Georgia, and Texas. What changes would you need to make to your strategy in those locations?❧

ETHICS: Apply ethics to your strategy by working through these four steps of ethical decision making: (1) describe the ethical dilemma, (2) identify the stakeholders involved, (3) analyze options (including how each group of stakeholders will be affected), and (4) make a decision based on your analysis. After examining ethical issues associated with the strategy, determine whether any modifications should be made.

❧*Check for law research materials in the Appendix: Legal Resources for Business Decisions*

STRATEGY	
LAW	***Three Pillars Decision: Home Turf Brewing***
ETHICS	

The development of new products and services is often restricted by existing laws, as illustrated by the popularity of microbreweries.

Microbreweries are typically much smaller operations than large-scale corporate beer manufacturers, and these companies pride themselves in producing limited batches of craft brews that focus on quality and diversity. In the US alone, the last thirty years have witnessed a tremendous rise in this form of beer production, increasing from less than two hundred small, independent breweries in 1988 to nearly seventy-five hundred in 2018. With more microbreweries on the landscape, however, competition is fierce to generate a public following and thereby increase market share. As a result, more and more craft breweries are focusing on methods for bypassing the distributors and restaurants they supply and selling directly to the consumer from their manufacturing sites in an effort to increase brand recognition for their little piece of the beer-boom real estate.

VALUE GOAL: To increase market share and profits for a microbrewery by selling craft beer directly to the consumer.

STRATEGY: Develop a strategy for a New York craft beer brewer to provide alcohol directly to the consumer on the site of its manufacturing facility.

LAW: Research the New York state law related to licensing for establishments that provide alcohol directly to the public. How does this research affect or alter the strategy you developed? If necessary, refine your strategy to align with the law.&

ETHICS: Apply ethics to your strategy by working through these four steps of ethical decision making: (1) describe the ethical dilemma, (2) identify the stakeholders involved, (3) analyze options (including how each group of stakeholders will be affected), and (4) make a decision based on your analysis. After examining ethical issues associated with the strategy, determine whether any modifications should be made.

&*Check for law research materials in the Appendix: Legal Resources for Business Decisions*

---

[1]   Musters, Parekh and Ramkumar, "Organizing the Government-Affairs Function for Impact," *McKinsey Quarterly*, November 2013.

2   https://www.mckinsey.com/business-functions/strategy-and-corporate-finance/our-insights/organizing-the-government-affairs-function-for-impact.

3   "Beyond Corporate Social Responsibility," http://www.mckinsey.com/insights/strategy/beyond_corporate_social_responsibility_integrated_external_engagement.

4   Wallison, "Four Years of Dodd-Frank Damage," *Wall Street Journal*, July 20, 2014.

5   "The Rise of the Fourth Branch of Government," *The Washington Post*, May 24, 2013.

6   "Twitter Settles Charges That It Failed to Protect Consumers' Personal Information," http://www.ftc.gov/news-events/press-releases/2010/06/twitter-settles-charges-it-failed-protect-consumers-personal.

7   "The Rise of the Fourth Branch of Government," *supra*.

8   JPMorgan Chase & Co., http://careers.jpmorganchase.com/career/jpmc/careers/lob.

9   Calmes and Story, "In Washington, One Bank Chief Still Holds Sway," *The New York Times*, July 18, 2009.

10 "Political Activities," http://www.gesustainability.com/enabling-progress/political-activities/.

11 *Academy of Management Review*, October 1986.

12 "Kentucky Senate Race," http://www.opensecrets.org/races/summary.php?id=KYS1&cycle=2014.

13 "What is a PAC?" http://www.opensecrets.org/pacs/pacfaq.php.

14 This data is from OpenSecrets.org, http://www.opensecrets.org/.

15 "Advocacy Advertising," http://www.allbusiness.com/barrons_dictionary/dictionary-advocacy-advertising-4950473-1.html.

16 "OpenSecrets.org," http://www.opensecrets.org/.

17 *Id.*

18 Hamburger and Gold, "Google, Once Disdainful of Lobbying, Now a Master of Washington Influence," April 12, 2014.

19 Marchi and Parekh, "How the Sharing Economy Can Make Its Case," *McKinsey Quarterly*, December 2015.

20 https://www.scu.edu/government-ethics/resources/what-is-government-ethics/lobbying-ethics/.

21 *Off the Sidelines: Raise your Voice, Change the World* (2014) by Kirsten Gillibrand.

22 https://www.mckinsey.com/business-functions/strategy-and-corporate-finance/our-insights/organizing-the-government-affairs-function-for-impact.

23 https://www.mckinsey.com/business-functions/strategy-and-corporate-finance/our-insights/organizing-the-government-affairs-function-for-impact.

24 Grimaldi, *Bow Tie Banker* (2008).

25 Newman, "Why Mark Zuckerberg is Getting Political," *US News & World Report*, March 27, 2013.

26 Adapted from Siedel, *Using the Law for Competitive Advantage* (2002).

27 McGrane and Steinberg, "Wall Street Adapts to New Regulatory Regime," *Wall Street Journal*, July 21, 2014.

28 https://www.orlandosentinel.com/news/os-xpm-2006-03-23-sarbox23-1-story.html.

29 "Rediscovering the Power of Law in Business Education," http://www.aacsb.edu/blog/2016/february/rediscovering-the-power-of-law-in-business-education.

30 Culp, Werthen, Frei and Schelling, "Turning Regulatory Challenges into Business Opportunities," December 2014.

31 Adapted from Siedel, *supra*.

32 *Id.*

33 *Sottera v. FDA* (2010).

34 https://en.wikipedia.org/wiki/Apple_Inc._v._Samsung_Electronics_Co.

35 Whitney, "Apple, Samsung to Return to Court in 2016 for Next Round of Patent War," *CNET*, September 2, 2015.

36 "How to Mitigate Political Risk," *Stanford Business*, Autumn 2015.

37 Bonini, Mendonca and Oppenheim, "When Social Issues Become Strategic," March 2006.

[38]　Bagley, et al., "Who Let the Lawyers Out?" *University of Pennsylvania Law Journal of Business Law*, forthcoming.

[39]　Bonini and Swartz, "Bringing Discipline to Your Sustainability Initiatives," August 2014.

[40]　Porter and Kramer, "Creating Shared Value," *Harvard Business Review*, January–February 2011.

[41]　Canada Dry Ginger Ale slogan.

[42]　"Southwest Airlines," http://en.wikipedia.org/wiki/Southwest_Airlines#Early_history.

[43]　Marchi and Parekh, *supra*.

[44]　"Creative Destruction Legal Conflict: Lawyers as Disruption Framers in Entrepreneurship," http://papers.ssrn.com/sol3/papers.cfm?abstract_id=2692833.

[45]　Chen, "At $68 Billion Valuation, Uber Will Be Bigger Than GM, Ford, and Honda," *Forbes*, December 4, 2015.

[46]　https://techcrunch.com/2019/05/09/uber-begins-trialing-e-bikes-and-bicycles-rides-in-india/.

[47]　http://library.amlegal.com/nxt/gateway.dll/California/health/article8foodandfoodproducts?f=templates$fn=default.htm$3.0$vid=amlegal:sanfrancisco_ca$anc=JD_471.1.

[48]　https://www.mercurynews.com/2010/11/04/hicks-s-f-s-ban-on-happy-meal-toys-strikes-at-the-heart-of-america/.

[49]　http://www.adventurestats.com/statistics.shtml.

[50]　https://www.cbsnews.com/news/mount-everest-deaths-human-traffic-jam-today-2019-05-24/.

[51]　https://www.businessinsider.com/mount-everest-expeditions-climbing-companies-6-2019?utm_source=notification&utm_medium=referral.

[52]　https://www.leafly.com/news/cannabis-101/hemp-101-what-is-hemp-whats-it-used-for-and-why-is-it-illegal.

[53]　https://www.hemp.com/hemp-history/.

Use Your Intellectual Property to Create Shareholder Value

Take a moment to examine your surroundings. Whether you are at your kitchen table at home, sitting at an office desk, or traveling by train into the countryside, your environment is saturated with intellectual property. Intangible assets are represented on the cereal box from breakfast, in the fabric design of your desk chair, and in the whistle of the train as you pull into the next station. Even when you are hiking in the remotest place in the world, intellectual property will accompany you on your journey—possibly in the form of a backpack design, your boots, a handheld GPS, or a simple printed map. You will find these embodiments of innovation not only in every place but also in every period of time throughout the history of the world.

In *Driving Innovation* (2008), author Michael Gollin calls intellectual property (IP) the "invisible infrastructure of innovation" that supports us by providing comfort, convenience, and enjoyment in our everyday lives. Intellectual property has tremendous financial value—worth trillions of dollars. According to the World Intellectual Property Organization (WIPO), global businesses, universities, research institutions, and individuals are adding to that value at an unprecedented rate.[1] This intense escalation in innovation spurs wise IP holders to protect their inventions and creations and to strategize on the best use of these assets. A properly designed strategic IP management plan will often result in increased profits, reduced liabilities, and a company's secure and successful future for investors.

To build a legal strategy for commercial intellectual property, businesses must first understand that their intangible assets—whether as simple as a candy wrapper or as complex as a cellular phone—are part of a global framework. Awareness of the interdependence of world markets is an integral part of understanding how to develop, protect, and grow the value of intellectual property assets. Intellectual property protection laws and enforcement can vary widely from country to country; therefore, it is important to be familiar with the international legal landscape. Through that global perspective, an effective strategic company plan identifies potential IP assets and selects proper protection, all within the context of mapping organizational goals and resources.

This chapter defines and examines the nature of intellectual property and the legal forms available to protect these intangible assets. The chapter also covers strategic tools to manage IP efficiently and effectively, with a special focus on how businesses can use intangible assets to create value, which is essential for attracting investors.

LEGAL BRIEFING ON
INTELLECTUAL PROPERTY

Most everyone recognizes famous inventions such as Samsung's Galaxy phones or Apple's iPads as intellectual property. But few people realize how much more of the world is comprised of intangible assets. Take the "Happy Birthday to You" song, which has been sung around candlelit birthday cakes since the nineteenth century. The simple "Happy Birthday" eight-note melody and lyrics have been protected by US copyright laws since 1893 and earned their copyright holder, Warner Music Group, an estimated $2 million per year in licensing fees. "Happy Birthday" is joined internationally by millions of existing musical creations and compositions that may be classified as intellectual property.[2]

The WIPO defines intellectual property as "creations of the mind, such as inventions; literary and artistic works; designs; and symbols, names and images used in commerce."[3] We are immersed in a sea of intellectual creativity intended to improve the quality of our lives. From the cultivation of rice—developed by the Chinese as early as 7,000 BC[4]—to the forerunner of modern computers—invented by British mathematician Charles Babbage in the mid-1800s[5]—individuals have been thinking about, creating, and expressing the "invisible infrastructure of innovation" for thousands of years.

For nearly as long as people have expressed their thoughts and visions, there have been rules and laws to protect the innovator and innovation alike. The various forms of intellectual property—trade secrets, trademarks, patents, and copyrights—provide differing rights and responsibilities, as well as distinctive laws governing their use and availability.

In the US, the initial legal basis for intellectual property protection is found in the Constitution: "To promote the Progress of Science and useful Arts, by securing for limited Times to Authors and Inventors the exclusive Right to their respective Writings and Discoveries."[6] This clause specifically directs safeguards for inventions (patents) and writings (copyright), with the purpose of providing an incentive for people to engage in these activities and ultimately benefit society as a whole. Therefore, the primary ethical argument for protecting IP is one based in fairness, with a utilitarian justification. To be equitable to the inventor or property originators, they should be rewarded for the time, effort, and money invested in their work. IP protections are also beneficial to society, as they incentivize innovation.[7]

Other laws protecting IP are also native to the United States, such as the US Uniform Trade Secrets Act, which has been adopted in some form by almost all American states. Still other laws are international, such as the World Trade Organization's Agreement on Trade-Related Aspects of Intellectual Property Rights (TRIPS), which requires each member country to establish specific IP protection and enforcement procedures. IP protection may also be strengthened through agreements between individual countries, such as the recent US-Mexico-Canada Agreement (USMCA) which, in 2018, replaced the North American Free Trade Agreement (NAFTA). The USMCA features forward-looking elements, including a "10-year term of regulatory protection for biologics, more effective trade secret protection (with criminal sanctions), and stronger enforcement mechanisms against counterfeit goods."[8]

Significant challenges in securing intellectual property rights have also been at the center of global trade disputes between the US and China. The hope is that provisions to improve IP protection will be seriously considered in future agreements between the two largest economies in the world. Effective intellectual property statutes and rules in every country should be designed to provide IP owners with some benefit from their creative efforts while concurrently encouraging continued innovation.

It is said that 9/10ths of an iceberg is hidden below the surface of the sea; therefore, the majority of its nature is largely unknown. The same can be said of intellectual property, where business managers must understand the entire potential IP landscape for their company. Identifying intellectual property assets, classifying them, and understanding the laws that protect these assets are among the key steps in creating and maximizing IP value. Once the "iceberg" is unveiled, a strategic plan to fully use and integrate IP assets can be set in motion.

A company's wealth is based on its assets, which may be defined as the resources the company owns that have value or expected value. The primary accounting categories of assets include working capital, fixed assets, and intangible assets. Several decades ago, an estimated 75 percent of a company's holdings were fixed assets, such as buildings, machinery, equipment, and computers. Today, business portfolios hold, on average, 70 percent intangible assets, including goodwill and intellectual property.[9] Due to this tremendous shift in what constitutes the value of a company, it is increasingly important for business owners and managers to understand intellectual property assets and their associated rights.

Although international IP rights and laws vary, there are common features as well. The following sections summarize the various categories of IP rights—trade secrets, patents, trademarks, and copyrights—and also include specific examples from different countries.

Trade Secrets

A trade secret is a formula, practice, process, design, instrument, pattern, or compilation of information that has independent economic value in being not generally known or reasonably ascertainable (that is, the secret gives the owner some actual or potential competitive advantage).[10] A trade secret is fairly easy to create: identify undisclosed information that has some actual or potential value and then take reasonable means to protect its secrecy. Some examples of intangible assets protected by trade secrets include recipes, customer lists, marketing strategies, and manufacturing techniques.

The greatest advantage of a trade secret is that it may potentially remain a secret forever. In most countries, to have the protection of trade secret laws, a company must take certain steps to ensure the security of the secret. These steps include physical and computer security measures and confidentiality and nondisclosure agreements. Confidentiality agreements are especially important in licensing, where one company may be processing and manufacturing another company's trade secret products. Once a trade secret is exposed to the world and becomes part of the public domain, trade secret protection ends.

Perhaps the most famous trade secret in the world is the soft drink formula for *Coca-Cola*®, which has been continuously protected since around 1880. In addition to its global fame, *Coca-Cola*® might be the most valuable product known to mankind, generating more than $11 billion in sales annually and possessing a brand value of $74 billion.[11] The Coca-Cola Company takes several precautions to protect this profitable intellectual property, including keeping the formula in a locked bank vault that can only be opened by resolution of the company's board of directors. In addition, it has been reported that only two living Coca-Cola executives know the formula at the same time, and these individuals are not allowed to travel together. In the 1970s, when a food safety government official in India requested the ingredient list for *Coca-Cola®*, the company refused and stopped exporting the product to India. Other examples of trade secrets in the United States include the Kentucky Fried Chicken recipe (which, like *Coca-Cola®*, only two living executives know at any given time), the *Farmer's Almanac®* weather-predicting formula, and the methodology used to select books for *The New York Times®* Best-Seller List.[12]

Trade secrets in the United States are protected in nearly every state by the Uniform Trade Secrets Act (UTSA). At the core of the UTSA legislation is an understanding of the commercial value and competitive advantage inherent in trade secrets. The UTSA provides several remedies for the misappropriation of trade secrets, including injunctions (which prevent further use of the trade secret), financial compensation, and sometimes even punitive damages (intended to punish the wrongdoer and deter others) and/or attorney fees.

The UTSA provides valuable protection because, when a company has a very famous product protected by trade secret, there is considerable nefarious activity around trying to profit from it. For example, a significant case occurred in 2006 involving rivals Coca-Cola Company and PepsiCo., when three Coca-Cola employees—Ibrahim Dimson, Joya Williams, and Edmund Duhaney—attempted to sell their company's trade secrets to Pepsi. Court documents demonstrate that the employees conspired together and contacted Pepsi directly, using Coca-Cola letterhead and envelopes and offering highly confidential information and beverage samples. Shortly after receiving the letter, Pepsi faxed a copy to Coca-Cola executives, who went to the FBI, initiating an undercover investigation.

Over the course of several months, the employees, thinking they were conversing with PepsiCo., divulged trade secret documents, samples, and other materials to FBI agents posing as Pepsi employees. Dimson told agents, "I can even provide actual products and packaging of certain products, that no eye has seen, outside of maybe five top execs. . . . I need to know today if I have a serious partner or not." According to US Attorney David E. Nahmias, the conspiring trio hoped to be paid $1.5 million for the stolen secrets. The employees were convicted under 18 US Code § 1832 (Theft of Trade Secrets). Following the trial, Attorney Nahmias commented, "As the market becomes more global, the need to protect intellectual property becomes even more vital to protecting American companies and our economic growth."[13]

As noted at the US Library of Congress website,[14] other countries also recognize and protect the rights in a trade secret. In Brazil, a violation of trade secret law is considered a crime of unfair competition, and the violator must make reparations to fix the damage caused to the intellectual property owner. Labor law in Brazil also allows employers to terminate employees for trade secret violations.

In India, unlike the United States, there are no specific trade secret laws. However, undisclosed information and secrets can be protected through breach of contract or breach of confidence actions. If there is a confidentiality agreement between two parties, for example, and one party discloses information that violates the contract, the other side is entitled to a remedy similar to those available in the United States: injunctions, monetary compensation, and return of the confidential information.[15]

China, like India, also does not have a unified trade secrets law. However, numerous Chinese laws provide trade secret protection, such as the Anti-Unfair Competition Law (AUCL), which was amended in 2019 to add additional protections for trade secret rights-holders.[16] This statute defines a trade secret as "technology information" or "business information" that is unknown to the public, valuable, and protected from disclosure by the rights-holder. New provisions in AUCL shift the burden to the defendant to prove they have not misappropriated the plaintiff's trade secret—a significant departure from the prior version of the law—as well as provide for enhanced punitive damages.[17] In addition to the AUCL, China has labor, contract, and criminal laws that include trade secret-related provisions.[18]

A trade secret is the best protection when nondisclosure has great value. Contrast the trade secret with the patent. Patents require public disclosure, and the protection provided is for a limited duration. The formula for *Coca-Cola®*, for example, would now be in the public domain if protected only under patent laws. Trade secrets are also a good choice for intellectual property that may not be patentable subject matter, such as customer lists. It is also necessary to consider a trade secret if your intellectual property is related to a fast-moving field, as it would be unwise to invest significant funds in patenting an invention that may be obsolete even before the patent issues.

One of the disadvantages of the trade secret is that you have no protection against someone who independently discovers it. For example, if competitors of the Kentucky Fried Chicken franchise discover the Colonel's secret recipe by experimenting on their own, they are fully entitled to use their discovery without restriction.

In the following case, the court decided that a chocolate chip cookie recipe was a legitimate trade secret and that the company took appropriate, albeit simple, measures to keep it safe.

STRATEGY
LAW   ***Three Pillars Case: The Chocolate Chip Cookie Caper***
ETHICS

Citation: *Peggy Lawton Kitchens, INC. v. Terence M. Hogan*, 18 Mass. App. Ct. 937 (1984)

The case of the "miraculous" chocolate chip cookie is one that demonstrates the importance that trade secret holders must ascribe to reasonable measures against non-discovery.

Nothing is sacred. We have before us a case of theft of a recipe for baking chocolate chip cookies. The issue is whether the plaintiff, Peggy Lawton Kitchens, Inc. (Kitchens), possessed a protected trade secret.

A Superior Court judge found that Kitchens first added chocolate chip cookies to its line of prepackaged bakery products in 1960. They were an indifferent success. In 1963, Lawton Wolf, a principal officer of Kitchens, mixed the chaff from Walnuts ("nut dust" he called it) in his chocolate chip cookie batter. This, as the judge found, "produced a distinctive flavor. It was an immediate commercial success." Lawton Wolf, in his testimony, described what nut dust did for his cookies in rhapsodic terms: "Miraculous." Sales, he said "took off immediately. It did to the cookies what butter does to popcorn or salt to a pretzel. It really made the flavor sing."

The judge found that, from the beginning of its use, Kitchens carefully guarded the cookie recipe. One copy of the recipe was locked in an office safe. A duplicate was secured in the desk of William Wolf, Lawton's son. To satisfied customers who asked for the recipe, Kitchens wrote that the formula was a trade secret. For work day use, Kitchens broke down the formula into baking ingredients, small ingredients (e.g., the nut dust), and bulk ingredients. The three components were kept on separate cards which contained gross weights. Even though those cards concealed the true proportions of the ingredients, access to the cards was limited to long-time trusted employees. The defendant Terence Hogan, whose responsibilities at Kitchens were plant and equipment maintenance and safety, was not among those entrusted with the ingredients cards. Hogan, the judge found, had gained access to the cards through a pretext, and after Hogan left Kitchens' employ, a master key, which could open the vault and the office in which William Wolf's desk was located, was found in Hogan's desk.

Hogan and his wife organized a bakery business to sell prepackaged bakery products under the trade name Hogie Bear. Among the first products Hogie Bear made was a chocolate chip cookie. It had the same recipe, including the miraculous nut dust. The judge found that about forty brands of chocolate chip cookies were sold in New England. Except for those made by Kitchens and Hogie Bear, no two are alike. The judge found Hogie Bear's cookie "similar in appearance, color, cell construction, texture, flavor and taste. They are 'formulated' in a similar fashion. They are the same."

As to damages, the judge described the evidence as too vague and speculative to support a finding. A judgment was entered enjoining the defendants from making, baking, and selling chocolate chip cookies which use the plaintiff's formula. . . .

1.   Was there a trade secret? No doubt, the basic ingredients, flour, sugar, shortening, chocolate chips, eggs, and salt, would be common to any chocolate chip cookie. The combination in which those ingredients are used, the diameter and thickness of the cookie, and the degree to which it is baked would, however, constitute a formula which its proprietor could protect from infringement by an employee who either gains access to the formula in confidence or by improper means. In any event, the insertion of the nut dust into the mix served to add that modicum of originality which separates a process from the everyday and so characterizes a trade secret. Lawton Wolf's testimony that "sales took off immediately" supports a determination that the improved recipe had competitive value so far as Kitchens was concerned.

2.   Conduct of the defendants. Once information qualifies as a trade secret, determination of whether the trade secret has been misused steers the inquiry to examining the conduct of the defendant, and the legal character of that conduct, in turn, is much affected by the steps taken by the proprietor of the trade secret to protect it. Here, as we have seen, the holder of the secret took reasonable steps to maintain its mystery and to narrow the circle of those privy to its essentials. We do not think that the absence of admonitions about secrecy or the failure to emphasize secrecy in employment contracts (if there were any in this relatively small business) is fatal to the plaintiff. That Hogan brought no experience in volume baking to his employment with Kitchens and that he employed a ruse to examine the ingredients cards and may have helped himself to a look at the formula tucked away in Kitchens' safe or William Wolf's desk are relevant factors. Listing of nut meal on the plaintiff's label does not constitute publication of the recipe because it discloses nothing about the proportions in which the ingredients are used, nor does it say what kind of nuts or what part of the nuts imparted special zing to Kitchens' cookies.

3.   The length and breadth of the injunction. The injunction against use of the plaintiff's recipe was permanent and without limit as to area. Injunctions of that length and breadth are unusual, but not without precedent. We do not think the judge was bound to calibrate a more precise area and duration for an injunction

as limited as the one imposed. It does not drive Hogan or Hogie Bear Snacks, Inc., out of the cookie business; the injunction forbids only use of Kitchens' precise formula. Other recipes — and the evidence included many — are available to Hogie Bear. There is no limitation on Hogie Bear's packaging or marketing methods.

. . . Judgment affirmed.

THREE PILLARS CASE QUESTIONS

(1)   How did Peggy Lawton Kitchens protect its chocolate chip cookie recipe?

(2)   What evidence did the court use to determine that Hogan had taken the plaintiff's trade secret?

(3)   Describe the remedy that the court awarded to Peggy Lawton Kitchens. Why didn't the court just award money damages to the plaintiff?

(4)   What other steps could Peggy Lawton Kitchens take in the future to prevent a repeat of this event?

Patents

A patent is an exclusive right granted for an invention, which is a product or a process that provides a new way of doing something or that offers a new technical solution to a problem.[19] The government issues the patent to the inventor or the inventor's assignee and usually excludes others from making, using, or selling the invention for a limited time in exchange for public disclosure of the invention. Patents are, in essence, time-restricted legal monopolies. In most countries, to qualify for patent protection, an invention must be novel (new), non-obvious to a person with ordinary skill in the art of the invention, and useful.

Patentable subject matter covers a broad range of inventions—from genetically modified mice (Harvard's OncoMouse)[20] to a cow urine and antibiotic mixture (Indian Gomutra).[21] But many categories are not protectable, such as natural phenomena (even if you discover it), printed matter (look to copyright instead), abstract ideas, and scientific principles. In 2013, the US Supreme Court decided that isolating a genetic DNA sequence is not entitled to protection, calling into question the validity of many previously issued patents.[22] However, for non-patentable subject matter, there is still the possibility of legal protection through copyrights, trademarks, and trade secrets.

A common misconception about patent protection is that the grant is an exclusive right for the inventor to use the invention. A patent is actually not a right of the inventor to use, but a right to exclude others from use. Patent holders have a protected right to prevent others from using, making and selling the invention. You may wonder—"what's the value in a patent then, if it's not a right for inventors to use their own invention?" The answer is that the right to exclude allows the patent holder to control the marketplace by keeping others out; it is a powerful tool to create value for an organization. Take for example the multiple patents (in excess of 6,000) owned by CEO Mark Zuckerberg's Facebook; the nimble use of these rights to exclude competitors has allowed the half-a-trillion dollar company to dominate the market of social networking.[23]

A similar misconception relates to the words "patent pending"—a term that you may occasionally see on products. It is important to know that a patent filing per se doesn't offer any protection, but it does serve as a warning to competitors that if the patent issues, their use will potentially be infringement. Marking an item as patent pending is, therefore, a good strategy to limit competition from other companies.

There are many famous patents worldwide—the bread toaster, the smartphone, the aerosol spray can. From Whitney's cotton gin to Intel's microprocessors, protected inventions revolutionize our way of life and provide their creators with benefits. This system of encouraging innovation through the grant of a "patent"—like other intellectual property protection—is believed to be thousands of years old.

According to Kenneth W. Dobyns in *The Patent Office Pony: A History of the Early Patent Office* (1997) protecting innovation was seen for the first time around 500 BC in a Greek colony known as Sybaris. The Sybarites, who

> enjoyed living in luxury, made a law that if any confectioner or cook should invent any peculiar and excellent dish, no other artist was allowed to make this dish for one year. He who invented it was entitled to all the profit to be derived from the manufacture of it for that time. This was done in order that others might be induced to labor at excelling in such pursuits.

In addition to encouraging creativity, this culinary patent was a clever business strategy in that it attracted curious and wealthy visitors looking to experience the luxurious Sybarite culture.

In the United States, three types of patents may be granted to an inventor: (1) utility patent, (2) design patent, and (3) plant patent. The utility patent may be issued for a new and useful machine, process, article of manufacture, or composition of matter (or improvement). The term of this form of patent is twenty years from the filing date. Utility patents make up the majority of the approximately eight million patents that have been issued by the US Patent and Trademark Office. The patentable subject matter included in this protection is quite broad. Examples include the popular board game *Monopoly*, Alexander Graham Bell's telephone (thought to be the most valuable patent in history), and Clarence Birdseye's process for packaging frozen food.[24]

The design patent may be granted for a new, original, and ornamental design for an article of manufacture. The term of this form of patent is fourteen years from the date of issuance (fifteen years for filings after May 13, 2015). Design patents protect the way an article looks. They have been issued for the Lamborghini Murciélago car design, the Rolex diving watch, and even for the shape of Frito-Lay's Wavy Lays potato chips.[25]

The plant patent may be issued for any distinct or new variety of plant generated through asexual reproductive methods. Sexually reproduced plants are not "made by man" and, for that reason, cannot be the subject of a patent. The term of this form of patent is twenty years from the filing date. This type is the rarest form of patent protection issued by the patent office, accounting for less than a third of 1 percent of patents granted annually. Some plant patents include the Bridal Pink™ Rose, *Royal Tioga* cherry tree, and the hundreds of seed patents owned by US corporations such as Monsanto.[26]

In the United States, there is rigorous patent enforcement and protection of the inventor's right to exclude. US patent laws trace their origin to Article I, section 8, clause 8 of the Constitution, intending to "promote the Progress of Science and useful Arts, by securing for limited Times to Authors and Inventors the exclusive Right to their respective Writings and Discoveries." Title 35 of the US Code is the modern statute that protects American inventors. The United States Patent and Trademark Office (USPTO) grants patents, and these patent rights extend only throughout the United States. Because US patents have no effect in a foreign country, inventors interested in extending their invention protection in other countries must apply for a patent in each of the desired countries or in regional patent offices.

Internationally, the World Trade Organization's (WTO) 1994 Agreement on Trade-Related Aspects of Intellectual Property Rights (TRIPS) sets minimum standards for member countries with respect to the availability, scope, and use of intellectual property rights, including patent rights. All member countries—those that have signed the TRIPS agreement—are required to establish and enforce the minimum standards, although each country can institute more stringent requirements. Through the TRIPS agreement, the WTO recognizes the importance of consistency in protecting and enforcing intellectual property in our globally-connected world.[27]

The application of TRIPS has helped build uniformity in worldwide patenting. For example, the majority of countries that issue patents now adhere to the twenty-year term of protection. And, in 2013, the United States moved closer to a long-standing international standard by transitioning from a "first to invent" to a "first inventor to file" system.

Under the old first-to-invent system, inventors could gain priority over competing patent applications by proving that they were the first to develop an invention. When there were conflicting claims between inventors, the patent office would declare an "interference" and hold a hearing. A famous American interference in the early 1880s involved a claim by inventors William E. Sawyer and Albon Man against Thomas Edison, all creators of the incandescent lamp. After much legal wrangling, US Patent 317,676 was granted to Sawyer and Man in 1883.[28] But in the recently-adopted first-to-file process, the first of competing inventors to file a patent application on the same invention usually receives priority.

Patenting is increasing globally at a phenomenal rate, with millions of patent applications filed worldwide every year. The process of obtaining a patent is known as "patent prosecution" and begins with filing an application that describes the invention in great detail. Inventors disclose not only how to make and use their inventions but also, in some countries, any related or similar types of inventions that may already exist—known as "prior art." The United States is among the small number of countries that require an affirmative duty of disclosure. For example, there was a US patent (No. 147,119) issued in 1874 for a combined eating utensil improvement—which later came to be known as a "spork"—and the prior art disclosed for this invention included the spoon, fork, and knife.[29]

The patent office receiving the application reviews the claims the inventor makes and, if the invention meets the statutory requirements, will grant the patent. Due to the complexity of patenting, it is wise to seek the help of a patent attorney. The United Kingdom patenting office estimates that only one in twenty inventors is able to succeed in obtaining a patent without an attorney's assistance. While the patent prosecution process can be lengthy and tedious, the average twenty years of protection for an invention can be advantageous.[30]

Patent protection, as opposed to trade secret protection, is best for inventions that can be "reverse-engineered" or otherwise easily discovered by others. Reverse engineering refers to the process by which you take apart an invention and figure out how it is made and operates. A patent discloses all the information that would be obtained through the reverse-engineering process and prevents the potential reverse engineer from making or using the invention for a limited time.

The idea behind a patent is an equitable one—to give inventors time to profit from their work before others may do the same. However, the public disclosure requirement of patenting is a double-edged sword. Indeed, when everyone knows how to make your invention, someone will inevitably try to use or sell it before your protection ends. While the risk of possible infringement of your patent is one of the disadvantages of this form of protection over a trade secret, the patent does provide recourse against these interlopers. Accordingly, patent protection is also best for inventions in which infringement of the patent is readily detectable.

In the following case, the rival booksellers participated in what was, according to media reports, "the highest profile patent dispute on the internet."[31] Amazon's patent on the one-click ordering system had many questioning the fairness of granting exclusivity for a seemingly standard use of technology.

STRATEGY	
LAW	***Three Pillars Case: One-Click Wonder***
ETHICS	

Citation: *Amazon.com, Inc. v. Barnesandnoble.com, Inc.*, 239 F.3d 1343 (U.S. Ct. Appl. 2001)

Infringement actions are common between companies that are major competitors. In this case the relatively simple technology featured in the "one-click" purchasing mechanism resulted in significant online chatter about Amazon having an unfair monopoly.

CLEVENGER, CIRCUIT JUDGE.

This is a patent infringement suit brought by Amazon.com, Inc. ("Amazon") against barnesandnoble.com ("BN"). Amazon moved for a preliminary injunction to prohibit BN's use of a feature of its web site called "Express Lane." BN resisted the preliminary injunction on several grounds, including that its Express Lane feature did not infringe the claims of Amazon's patent, and that substantial questions exist as to the validity of Amazon's patent. The United States District Court for the Western District of Washington rejected BN's contentions.

. . . After careful review of the district court's opinion, the record, and the arguments advanced by the parties, we conclude that BN has mounted a substantial challenge to the validity of the patent in suit.

. . . This case involves United States Patent No. 5,960,411 ("the '411 patent"), which issued on September 28, 1999, and is assigned to Amazon. On October 21, 1999, Amazon brought suit against BN alleging infringement of the patent and seeking a preliminary injunction.

The '411 patent describes a method and system in which a consumer can complete a purchase order for an item via an electronic network using only a "single action," such as the click of a computer mouse button on the client computer system. Amazon developed the patent to cope with what it considered to be frustrations presented by what is known as the "shopping cart model" purchase system for electronic commerce purchasing events. . . . The '411 patent sought to reduce the number of actions required from a consumer to effect a placed order.

BN's short-cut ordering system, called "Express Lane" . . . also presents the person with a description of a single action that can be taken to complete a purchase order for the item. If the single action described is taken, for example by a mouse click, the person will have effected a purchase order using BN's Express Lane feature. . . . Because only a single action need be taken to complete the purchase order once the product page is displayed, the district court concluded that Amazon had made a showing of likelihood of success on its allegation of patent infringement.

. . . Irreparable harm is presumed when a clear showing of patent validity and infringement has been made. . . . After full review of the record before us, we conclude that under a proper claim interpretation, Amazon has made the showing that it is likely to succeed at trial on its infringement case. . . . The question remaining, however, is whether the district court correctly determined that BN failed to mount a substantial challenge to the validity of the claims in the '411 patent.

. . . In this case, we find that the district court committed clear error by misreading the factual content of the prior art references cited by BN and by failing to recognize that BN had raised a substantial question of invalidity of the asserted claims in view of these prior art references.

. . . One of the references cited by BN was the "CompuServe Trend System." The undisputed evidence indicates that in the mid-1990s, CompuServe offered a service called "Trend" whereby CompuServe subscribers could obtain stock charts for a surcharge of 50 cents per chart. Before the district court, BN argued that this system anticipated claim 11 of the '411 patent. The district court failed to recognize the substantial question of invalidity raised by BN in citing the CompuServe Trend reference, in that this system appears to have used "single action ordering technology" within the scope of the claims in the '411 patent.

. . . In its brief, Amazon argues that this feature of the CompuServe Trend system amounts to an additional "confirmation step necessary to complete the ordering process," and that the CompuServe Trend system therefore does not use "single action" technology within the scope of the claims in the '411 patent. However, all of the claims only require sending a request to order an item in response to performance of only a single action.

In addition to the CompuServe Trend system, other prior art references were cited by BN, but ultimately rejected by the district court. For example, BN's expert, Dr. Lockwood, testified that he developed an on-line ordering system called "Web Basket" in or around August 1996. . . . The district court concluded that the Web Basket system was "inconsistent with the single-action requirements of the '411 patent" because "it requires a multiple-step ordering process from the time that an item to be purchased is displayed." However . . . the undisputed evidence demonstrates that the accused BN Express Lane feature also requires a multiple-step ordering process (i.e., at least two "clicks") from the time that an item to be purchased is first displayed on the menu page, yet the district court concluded that BN's Express Lane feature infringed all of the asserted claims of the '411 patent. The district court's failure to recognize the inconsistency in these two conclusions was erroneous.

. . . Another reference cited by BN, a print-out from a web page describing the "Oliver's Market" ordering system, generally describes a prior art multi-step shopping cart model. The reference begins with an intriguing sentence: *A single click on its picture is all it takes to order an item.*

. . . The district court failed to recognize that a reasonable jury could find that this sentence provides a motivation to modify a shopping cart model to implement "single-click" ordering as claimed in the '411 patent. In addition, the district court failed to recognize that other passages from this reference could be construed by a reasonable jury as anticipating and/or rendering obvious the allegedly novel "single action ordering technology" of the '411 patent.

. . . VACATED AND REMANDED

THREE PILLARS CASE QUESTIONS

(1)   What was the court's rationale for allowing Barnes & Noble another chance to prove its case?

(2)   How does demonstrating that a patent is invalid help a defendant accused of infringement?

(3)   This case has been suggested as representative of unfairness in the patent system. Do you believe the issuing of patents is an unfair monopoly? Why?

(4)   In response to the Amazon suit and an initial injunction, Barnes & Noble eliminated its one-click system. Later, even though the company won the repeal of that injunction (as stated above), the company never returned to the one-click method. Some analysts have suggested that Amazon brought lawsuits over the '411 patent to stifle competition. The patent's use was estimated to bring Amazon about $2.4 billion in additional revenue annually. Although this use of legal action is common in business, was Apple's lawsuit strategy ethical?

(5)   Amazon and Barnes & Noble settled their dispute in 2002, and Amazon's one-click patent protection expired in 2017. Soon after the patent term ended, Apple, Facebook, American Express, Google, and other companies began working on adding a one-click standard. Ironically, while the patent was still active in 2000, Amazon's CEO Jeff Bezos began calling on the government to reduce patent terms for software and Internet business systems (like *one-click*) from the existing twenty years to three to five years. What do you think was Bezos' strategy in making this request?

———————

Trademarks

A trademark is a word, phrase, symbol, or design, or a combination thereof, that identifies and distinguishes the source of the goods of one party from those of others.[32] The name "Google," for example, is a trademark and is considered to be the most valuable in the world, with an estimated value of more than $100 billion.[33] In the US, trademarks may be protected under state common law or supplemental state trademark laws and/or registered federally under the Lanham Act. Federal registration acts as nationwide constructive notice to others of the registrant's ownership of the mark.[34]

In addition to trademarks for goods, other forms of marks also exist, including service marks, which distinguish the source of a service rather than goods. The golden arches of McDonald's restaurants are an example of a service mark. There are also collective marks, which are used to identify members of an organization, such as the Girl Scouts of America, and certification marks, which identify products or services as meeting certain standards.[35]

A common international certification mark is the CE mark, which indicates that a product complies with safety, health, or environmental requirements set by the European Commission. (CE stands for Communauté Européenne, which is French for "European Community.") The CE mark is mandatory on certain products sold within the European Economic Area ("EEA"). The EEA comprises the twenty-eight member states of the European Union, the four member states of the European Free Trade Association (Iceland, Liechtenstein, Norway, and Switzerland), and Turkey.[36]

Even sounds can be trademarked (called "sound marks"). Famous sound marks include Apple's start-up chime for Mac computers, Tarzan's yell, and Duracell Battery's three-note "coppertop" audio logo.[37] In 1994, the American motorcycle manufacturer Harley-Davidson tried to obtain a sound mark for its classic crankpin V-twin engine exhaust sound. This trademark application caused considerable concern among other manufacturers that their V-twin motorcycles might infringe on such a mark. After years of dogged pursuit in court, Harley-Davidson finally withdrew its application.[38]

Trademarks are often among the most valuable assets of a business. Trademarked symbols, logos, words, stylized letters, colors, sounds, motions, textures, and even scents allow a business to build brand recognition in the marketplace. Therefore, to be valid, a trademark must be distinctive. The mark must allow consumers and other users to identify goods or services as being provided by a particular source.

The "Swoosh" of Nike® athletic shoes and products, for example, is considered the most recognizable branding trademark in the world. The swoosh was created by a graphic arts student in 1971, who was paid thirty-five dollars for the design. At the time the mark was adopted, Nike cofounder Phil Knight said about the swoosh, "I don't love it, but I think it will grow on me."[39] The Nike company created value by "associating its trademark with a lifestyle and way of doing things that provided consumers with something meaningful to identify with," as the swoosh "stands for athleticism, power, fitness."[40] The swoosh features prominently in the one hundred dollars per second that the company spends on advertising each year. With more than $35 billion in annual sales, it is clear the company's trademark strategies have contributed greatly to Nike's success.[41]

The all-important distinctiveness requirement for trademarks separates marks into four categories: (1) fanciful (coined), (2) arbitrary, (3) suggestive, and (4) descriptive. Fanciful marks are considered to be the most distinctive and provide the trademark owner with the strongest protection. These marks are combinations of symbols or words that do not signify anything outside of the goods or services they are being used to identify. Xerox®, Kodak®, and Google® are examples of fanciful or coined marks. These types of marks provide the best protection because they are so distinctive. In the event of infringement or cybersquatting, owners will be in a strong position to argue the integrity of their mark.

Google® was originally named "Backrub," presumably because the underlying algorithm counts backlinks. If Google founders Larry Page and Sergey Brin had decided to keep the name Backrub, it would likely be characterized as an arbitrary mark and would not provide the same level of protection as the fanciful Google®.[42,43] Arbitrary marks typically have a common meaning, but that meaning is not connected with the goods or services they represent. Arbitrary marks do not offer the same level of protection as the fanciful mark because they are not as distinctive.

The Apple® trademark is a good example of an arbitrary mark that has created some legal and use problems for the company. For nearly forty years, Apple Corps (the Beatles-founded record label and holding company) and Apple, Inc. (Apple computers) have been fighting over the use of the "Apple" trademark. Apple Corps has sued Apple, Inc. multiple times for trademark infringement based on the association of the word "Apple" with music-related materials. The most recent lawsuit focused on iTunes and iPod music and was settled in 2007 when the companies agreed that Apple, Inc. would own all the trademarks related to "Apple" and license the trademark back to the Beatles's Apple Corps. The Apple saga illustrates the concerns that arbitrary marks can create for holders.[44,45]

Suggestive marks contain some attribute or benefit of the goods or services they represent but do not describe the products themselves. For example, Microsoft® represents software for microcomputers, and Greyhound® is a bus transportation service.[46] Courts have said that a mark is suggestive if it requires imagination, thought, and perception to determine what the trademark represents.

An example of the protection, or lack thereof, afforded a suggestive mark is the 2002 case of *Thane International v. Trek Bicycle*. When the litigation began, Trek Bicycles had long used the trademark TREK and had associated the mark with more than a thousand products. When Thane began to use the trademark Orbitrek on its stationary bikes, Trek sued for infringement. The court found in favor of Thane:

> TREK is a suggestive mark because trek means a long journey, and one can undertake a long journey on a bicycle. As a suggestive mark, TREK has more distinctiveness than a merely descriptive mark and deserves some trademark protection. However, it does not belong to the highest category of distinctiveness, that reserved for arbitrary and fanciful marks, and thus does not deserve as much protection.

In most countries, descriptive marks are usually not protectable unless the public has come to recognize them as trademarks. These marks are said to have "acquired distinctiveness" or "secondary meaning." For example, the word "Sharp" is associated with televisions as a suggestive trademark. Yet even with secondary meaning, the descriptive mark is a weak mark with very narrow protection. This type of mark's lack of distinctiveness is frequently the source of disagreements between company marketing professionals and their legal departments. While marketers try to convey information about products and services by using descriptive terms, from the perspective of a legal strategy these types of marks are difficult to enforce. Therefore, businesses should focus on the use of fanciful and arbitrary marks, which ensure the best trademark protection.

The trademarking of quotes and slogans is another source of intellectual property revenue for a company or individual. For instance, the phrase "Let's Get Ready to Rumble" is a registered trademark of American boxing and wrestling ring announcer Michael Buffer. Buffer, who began using the slogan in 1984, obtained a trademark for it in 1992 and has licensed it in music recordings, video games, and commercials, earning over $400 million.[47] There are limits to this process, however; the USPTO is very rigorous in its review of slogan trademark applications. According to the site *SecureYourTrademark.com*, the trademark office rejected nine applications for the phrase "Boston Strong" following the 2013 Boston Marathon bombing event. In its rejection, the USPTO wrote, "consumers are accustomed to seeing this slogan or motto commonly used in everyday speech by many different sources."[48]

Another type of trademark protection that businesses may consider is known as "trade dress." This category is defined by the International Trademark Association in its fact sheet as "the overall commercial image (look and feel) of a product that indicates or identifies the source of the product and distinguishes it from those of others." Trade dress may include product packaging, ornamental aspects, and even physical décor and environment that complement the "total visual image" of a company's products and/or services.

In 1992, there was a case of trade dress infringement before the US Supreme Court.[49] The restaurant chain Taco Cabana sued a similar eatery group, Two Pesos, for the latter's copycat use of bright colors, patio areas, and building paint schemes. The Court found in favor of Taco Cabana, stating that the restaurant's trade dress was inherently distinctive and entitled to protection. In the year following the decision, for which Taco Cabana received $3.7 million in damages, the twenty-nine existing Two Pesos restaurants were sold to Taco Cabana and promptly liquidated.[50]

Trademark rights are typically established through use in commerce or by a registration process. In legal systems based primarily on English common law, such as the United States, the United Kingdom, Hong Kong, and India, simply using a mark can establish rights. In some of these common law countries, the unregistered trademark may be enforced against an infringer through the tort of "passing off." This common law tort prevents one business from portraying its goods or services as being the goods and services of another business in a manner creating confusion in consumer markets.

An interesting defense that may be used by the party accused of "passing off" is the "moron in a hurry" test. This test was first used by British Justice Foster in a 1978 case in which the publishers of the *Morning Star*, a British Communist Party newspaper, sought to prevent Express Newspapers from launching a new tabloid, the *Daily Star*. The judge ruled against the *Morning Star*, noting that "If one puts the two papers side by side, I for myself would find that the two papers are so different in every way that only a moron in a hurry would be misled."[51] Interestingly enough, Apple, Inc. used the "moron in a hurry" defense in one of the Beatles's Apple Corps lawsuits. Apple Inc.'s lawyers argued that "even a moron in a hurry could not be mistaken about" the difference between iTunes and the Beatles's Apple record label.[52]

Under a trademark registration system, a company may apply for more formal protection of trademarks used in commerce through a country's governmental trademark agency. In the United States, trademark registration begins with an application to the Patent and Trademark Office. The application provides evidence that the mark has been used in commerce or will be used within six months after the filing.

The initial trademark term is ten years, but the owner may renew the mark indefinitely provided it is still in use (although continued use is not required for renewal in every country). Some of the oldest registered trademarks include the Bass Brewery label in the United Kingdom (1876), the Samson Rope Technologies mark in the United States (1884), and the Krupp Steel Company mark in Germany

(1875).[53] Provisions under TRIPS also set the international standard of a ten-year registration.

Certain symbols, such as ®, Reg., TM, and SM, are often attached to marks to show registration status. The symbols ® or Reg. may be associated with registration in one or more countries, while TM and SM are used for unregistered trademarks and service marks to indicate either protection under common law or pending formal registration. Other symbols include "Marca Registrada" or MR in some countries where Spanish is the dominant language, and "Marque Déposée" ("Marque de Commerce") or their abbreviations (MD and MC) in some countries where French is the dominant language.[54] Trademark registration symbols serve to place others on notice that there is a recognized right in the trademark—a right that the trademark holder is potentially ready to enforce.

The greatest advantage of trademark protection is the company's opportunity to safeguard its brand and reputation from potential counterfeiters and infringers. While misuse of trademarks may result in small lost profits, misuse can also ruin the trademark holder's reputation and cause business failure. One disadvantage of the trademark is the relatively weak nature of mark protection. This drawback should encourage businesses to concentrate on mark distinctiveness, which affords better protection than marks classified as fanciful or arbitrary.

While a company has the responsibility to rigorously protect its trademark, there are times when the public views these actions as a form of bullying by big corporations against the "little guy." We examine this perception in the next case, where Federal Express Corporation filed suit against a small coffee purveyor in New York State.

STRATEGY	
LAW	***Three Pillars Case: Freedom of Espresso***
ETHICS	

Citation: *Federal Express Corporation v. Federal Espresso, Inc.*, 201 F.3d 168 (U.S. Ct. Appl. 2000)

Companies have a responsibility to take action against suspected trademark infringers in the marketplace, or else they might lose some of their power to enforce the protections of this form of intellectual property.

KEARSE, CIRCUIT JUDGE.

. . . Federal Express, incorporated in 1972, invented the overnight shipping business. It has used the name "Federal Express" since 1973. In 1984, it also registered the mark "FedEx"; and in 1994 it introduced a new corporate logo that included both names. Federal Express currently has 140,000 employees, ships 2.9 million packages per day, and has annual revenues of more than $11 billion.

Federal Express provides service in at least 210 countries and has registrations of, or pending applications to register, the name "Federal Express" in some 175 countries. Federal Express spends $35,000 to $40,000 a month to file, prosecute, and maintain its trademarks. Various stylings of the "Federal Express" mark are registered as trademarks and service marks with respect to a variety of uses, both for those integral to Federal Express's shipping operations, such as pick-up, transportation, storage, tracing, and delivery of documents, packages, and cargo, and for those that are farther removed from Federal Express's core business, such as beach towels, beverage bottles, and clothing. Those marks that are not black-and-white use the colors orange and purple.

. . . In March 1994, defendants Anna Dobbs ("Dobbs") and David J. Ruston, her brother, formed a business called New York Espresso in Syracuse, New York, for the wholesale distribution of commercial espresso machines. In April 1994, Dobbs, her husband defendant John Dobbs, and Ruston decided to change the name of the business from New York Espresso to "Federal Espresso."

. . . [I]n November 1995, Dobbs opened a coffee shop. . . . The sign over the entrance displayed the name "FEDERAL ESPRESSO" in bright yellow capitals on a dark blue background. Dobbs stated that she chose typeface and colors that were different from the Federal Express typeface and colors in order to avoid confusion. The company fashioned a circular logo consisting of a stylized lion's head inside of three rings: an outer ring formed by repetitions of the letters "OWTU," a middle ring depicting cups poised to catch falling coffee beans, and an inner ring reading "FEDERAL ESPRESSO YOUR LOCAL ROASTER." The logo was used in various color combinations for various purposes. For example, a combination of yellow, green, navy blue, brown and white were used on a sign in the shop; silver and purple were used on coffee bags; and beige and purple were used on frequent-customer discount cards.

In 1996, defendants applied to the Patent and Trademark Office ("PTO") for registration of "Federal Espresso" as a service mark. Federal Express formally opposed the application and sent defendants a cease-and-desist letter. In April 1997, Federal Express and Federal Espresso entered into a settlement agreement before the PTO Trademark Trial and Appeal Board, in which defendants withdrew their application and agreed to cease, on or before June 1, 1997, all use of "Federal Espresso." Federal Express waived its rights to seek monetary damages from defendants unless defendants subsequently breached the agreement.

In June 1997, defendants changed the name of their store to "Ex Federal Espresso." They bought yellow letters "E" and "X" and placed them at a 45-degree angle to the left of "Federal Espresso" on signs at the Pearl Street store. Dobbs testified that defendants chose that alteration because it would be inexpensive. Defendants retained supplies bearing the name "Federal Espresso," but they handwrote "EX" on most of them before using them. Some items were used without the addition of "EX"; some store signs still read "Federal Espresso" in November 1997; and the corporation's name was not changed until December 1997.

Having learned that defendants continued after June 1, 1997, to use the mark "Federal Espresso" and were using "Ex Federal Espresso," Federal Express commenced the present action in August 1997. It principally asserted claims of service mark infringement, trademark infringement, and unfair competition . . . and claims of dilution of the distinctive quality of its famous mark . . . and it moved for a preliminary injunction, which was denied.

. . . As to the infringement claims, the court analyzed the evidence before it in light of . . . eight factors[:] 1) the strength of the plaintiff's mark; 2) the similarity of plaintiff's and defendant's marks; 3) the competitive proximity of the products; 4) the likelihood that plaintiff will "bridge the gap" and offer a product like defendant's; 5) actual confusion between products; 6) good faith on the defendant's part; 7) the quality of defendant's product; and 8) the sophistication of buyers.

The court concluded that only the first factor, the strength of the Federal Express mark, favored Federal Express. As to the second factor, the court found that although the words FEDERAL ESPRESSO and FEDERAL EXPRESS are somewhat similar in content and sound, those similarities are far outweighed by the dissimilarities evident in the parties' use of the marks. The words are entirely different in meaning, they are different in pronunciation, and they appear different in use. The marks appear in different typefaces and colors, and as part of distinctly different logos. In addition, defendants' use of their mark is always accompanied by other indicia of origin, such as a logo, pictures of coffee cups, or words like "coffee," that prevent any confusion as to the source of their products. Because the marks are not sufficiently similar to cause confusion, this factor favors defendants.

As to . . . factors three through eight, the court found that there was little similarity between the overnight shipping business and the sale of coffee and espresso machines, no intent by Federal Express to enter the coffee business, no evidence that defendants' coffee or machines were of inferior quality, no actual confusion between products, and no apparent lack of sophistication on the part of consumers such as would cause confusion in buying; and it found insufficient evidence that defendants chose the Federal Espresso name in bad faith.

. . . We also note that, although there apparently was no delay by Federal Express in bringing the present action, this Court may take into account whether or not a plaintiff has been assiduous in pursuing the litigation once started. At the oral argument of this appeal, which took place nearly a year after the district court denied the preliminary injunction motion, Federal Express informed us that nothing had been done in the district court to speed the proceedings toward an ultimate resolution of the merits. The seeming lack of urgency on the part of a plaintiff who has been denied interim relief tends to confirm the view that irreparable harm was not imminent.

. . . Having considered all of Federal Express's contentions on this appeal and having found in them no merit except as indicated above, we see no basis for reversal. The order of the district court denying a preliminary injunction is affirmed.

THREE PILLARS CASE QUESTIONS

(1)   What was the court's rationale for affirming Federal Express's preliminary injunction denial?

(2)   When interviewed, co-owner Ann Dobbs said of the coffee shop Federal Espresso: "No one has ever tried to ship a package from here."[55] Which of the eight factors presented in the case would this statement potentially be used as evidence to support?

(3)   How did the coffee shop try to distinguish itself from the overnight shipper? Did these actions benefit Federal Espresso in this case? What other strategies could the coffee shop have used to avoid litigation?

(4)   After about three years of legal proceedings, Federal Espresso changed its name to "Freedom of Espresso." In 2002, the Center for Justice and Democracy (CJ&D) called out Federal Express as hypocritical for promoting tort reform while suing small businesses such Federal Espresso:

> Many corporate supporters of [tort reform] enjoy unfettered use of the courts to recoup financial losses resulting from a host of troubles, from trademark violations, contract breaches, patent infringements and other unfair competition claims, to property damage, lost goods, unpaid bills or, ironically, fraud. While calling consumers' lawyers "greedy" and insensitive to the importance of keeping companies "litigation-free," their own

corporate lawyers sue at the smallest provocation, targeting not only competitors but also tiny businesses that are sued into submission.[56]

Do you agree with CJ&D on this issue? Do you think there can be a balance between large and small businesses on the trademark enforcement and infringement issues?

Copyrights

A copyright is a form of protection granted by law for original works of authorship fixed in a tangible medium of expression. Copyright covers both published and unpublished works and includes materials such as computer programs, musical compositions, broadcasts, sound recordings, films, and writings.[57]

Many people do not realize that a copyright instantly attaches to a work once it is expressed in a tangible medium. In many countries, you do not need to register a copyright unless you intend to seek damages for copyright infringement. The exclusive rights under a copyright typically include making copies of the work, distributing copies, controlling derivative works, and the right to attribution (being credited as the work's creator).

The duration of a copyright varies depending on the jurisdiction, but for most works it usually includes the life of the author plus fifty to one hundred years. For example, the current copyright terms in Mexico, the United States, India, and China are, respectively, the author's life plus one hundred, seventy, sixty, and fifty years. If a country is a signatory to either the Berne Convention or the WTO's TRIPS agreement, the copyright term is a minimum of the author's life plus fifty years. Country member candidates for entrance into the European Union are required to set a term of life plus seventy years.[58]

After the copyright term expires, the work falls into the public domain, which means that anyone can copy, distribute, or otherwise use it. Recall the once-copyrighted "Happy Birthday to You" song mentioned earlier. Prior to September 2015, it was fine to sing the Happy Birthday song to a loved one in your dining room but illegal to post a video of the song on YouTube or sing it at a restaurant unless a fee was paid to either the American Society of Composers, Authors and Publishers (ASCAP) or the copyright holder. (ASCAP collects fees for public performances of many copyrighted works.)

Although holders (music publisher Warner/Chappell) of the copyright to the Happy Birthday song have collected around $50 million in licensing fees, a lawsuit filed in 2013 claimed the song is in the public domain. Although Warner/Chappell had expected to hold the copyright until the year 2030, a federal judge ruled on

September 22, 2015, that there was no evidence that a copyright claim to the Happy Birthday song was valid.[59] In February 2016, Warner/Chappell proposed a settlement which declares the song to be in the public domain. So, for anyone celebrating an upcoming birthday, feel free to sing away in the venue of your choosing, compliments of lawsuit filer Jennifer Nelson and the US District Court for the Central District of California.

Copyright infringement situations are common. Of all the forms of intellectual property, copyright might be the most difficult to monitor and enforce against unauthorized use, due primarily to the vast number of protected works. From the millions of songs available, for example, a music digital download can be purchased and then multiple illegal copies produced from that single copy.

One of the most famous cases of copyright infringement involved the music industry in a 2001 case, *A&M Records v. Napster*. Around the year 2000, peer-to-peer (P2P) file-sharing increased at a phenomenal rate. A company known as Napster began an Internet website with technology that allowed people to share MP3 files with others very easily. At its peak, the group had eighty million registered users.[60]

In 2000, after several major musicians experienced unauthorized pre-release circulation of their music, bands and recording companies sued Napster for copyright infringement. Unable to prevail in court, Napster ceased operations in 2001 and declared bankruptcy in 2002. The company's assets were acquired initially by Roxio, then later by the online music subscription service Rhapsody. Although just one of many infringement cases in the music industry, the highly-publicized *Napster* case was one of the first to drive home the point that much of P2P sharing violated the law.[61]

Defenses to copyright infringement in the United States include the First Sale Doctrine and Fair Use rule. Under the First Sale Doctrine, the owner of a legally-obtained copy of a work is entitled to sell that copy. The doctrine does not, however, allow the legal owner to make and sell copies of the owned copy—or even to give them away. In limited circumstances, copyright law will allow a legal owner to make archival copies for personal use. For example, the law permits you to make a single copy of a legally-obtained computer software program in case the original is lost or damaged. But that back-up copy must be destroyed or transferred if you ever sell the original copy.

The Fair Use rule is a part of copyright law that allows for the limited use of copyrighted material without permission from the rights holder. Examples include the use of copyrighted material for commentary, parody, research, criticism, and teaching. Fair use may also apply to news reporting. In 2014, a US court confirmed that the news organization Bloomberg did not infringe copyright when it published a corporate earnings report phone call transcript and recording. The court said that because the publication had a newsworthy purpose, it qualified for a copyright exception under fair use.[62]

An example application of the fair use infringement defense is the case of *Whitmill v. Warner Brothers* involving the film "The Hangover Part II." In the movie, one of the characters has a facial tattoo that resembles the Maori design of boxing champion Mike Tyson's facial tattoo. Tyson played a role in the film. Tyson's tattoo artist, S. Victor Whitmill, sued Warner Brothers for violating his copyright in the design. Warner Brothers claimed that the depiction fell under the fair use exception as a parody, but before a full hearing could be scheduled, the case settled and the film was released. Another issue in the case was whether Whitmill himself committed a copyright violation by stealing an original Maori design.[63]

If the fair use is for educational purposes, there is also a bit of leeway to use copyrighted material, although this is not a free pass to use such material without discretion. Even educators and librarians are cautioned to seek permission if there is extensive or prolonged use of copyrighted material. Not every country has a fair use exception to copyright. China has no equivalent to the exception, but Indian court decisions and British law allow limited fair use—termed "fair dealing"—for research, private study, criticism, and review.[64]

An additional defense to copyright infringement is the demonstration that material was developed in a "clean room." This is a process, often used by software companies, where individuals work independently without access to outside or third-party sources. Developments in the clean room are not considered to be infringing on copyrighted material, even if substantially similar to existing sources.

One advantage of copyright protection is that it is the least expensive form of protection for eligible intellectual property. A benefit of a registered copyright is the ability to sue infringers and potentially collect significant damages, including profits earned and attorney fees. In 2010, a US District Court jury awarded the software company Oracle a record $1.3 billion in copyright infringement damages from the technical support service group SAP.[65] Although the amount of the monetary award was later reduced, without registered copyright protection Oracle would have had difficulty obtaining a remedy for SAP's infringement. Given the minimal time, fees, and effort required to file for a copyright, you should strongly consider using this form of IP protection.

In the following court of appeals decision, plaintiff photographer Art Rogers sued artist Jeff Koons for copyright infringement after Koons created a sculpture based on one of Rogers's images. Koons claimed that the sculpture of two individuals holding a string of puppies qualified for a fair use exception as a parody and social commentary.

STRATEGY LAW ETHICS	*Three Pillars Case: Photographs, Puppies, and Parody*

Citation: *Rogers v. Koons*, 960 F.2d 301 (2d Cir. 1992)

Artist Jeff Koons created his sculpture "String of Puppies" based on a photograph taken by Art Rogers. This case includes a good example of what qualifies as a fair use exception to copyright infringement—and what doesn't.

CARDAMONE, CIRCUIT JUDGE.

The key to this copyright infringement suit, brought by a plaintiff photographer against a defendant sculptor and the gallery representing him, is defendants' borrowing of plaintiff's expression of a typical American scene—a smiling husband and wife holding a litter of charming puppies. The copying was so deliberate as to suggest that defendants resolved so long as they were significant players in the art business, and the copies they produced bettered the price of the copied work by a thousand to one, their piracy of a less well-known artist's work would escape being sullied by an accusation of plagiarism.

. . . Plaintiff, Art Rogers, a 43-year-old professional artist-photographer, has a studio and home at Point Reyes, California, where he makes his living by creating, exhibiting, publishing and otherwise making use of his rights in his photographic works. . . . In 1980 an acquaintance, Jim Scanlon, commissioned Rogers to photograph his eight new German Shepherd puppies. When Rogers went to his home on September 21, 1980 he decided that taking a picture of the puppies alone would not work successfully, and chose instead to include Scanlon and his wife holding them. Substantial creative effort went into both the composition and production of "Puppies," a black and white photograph.

. . . Defendant Jeff Koons is a 37-year-old artist and sculptor residing in New York City. . . . His works sell at very substantial prices, over $100,000. He is a controversial artist hailed by some as a "modern Michelangelo," while others find his art "truly offensive." A New York Times critic complained that "Koons is pushing the relationship between art and money so far that everyone involved comes out looking slightly absurd."

Koons acknowledges that the source for "String of Puppies" [sculpture] was a Museum Graphics notecard of "Puppies" which he purchased in a "very commercial, tourist-like card shop" in 1987. After buying the card, he tore off that portion showing Rogers' copyright of "Puppies." . . . [H]e viewed the picture as part of the mass culture—"resting in the collective sub-consciousness of people regardless of whether the card had actually ever been seen by such people."

. . . Appellant gave his artisans one of Rogers' notecards and told them to copy it. . . . When it was finished, "String of Puppies" was displayed at the Sonnabend Gallery, which opened the Banality Show on November 19, 1988. Three of the four copies made were sold to collectors for a total of $367,000; the fourth or artist's copy was kept by Koons. Defendant Koons' use of "Puppies" to create "String of Puppies" was not authorized by plaintiff. Rogers learned of Koons' unauthorized use of his work through Jim Scanlon, the man who had commissioned Rogers to create "Puppies." A friend of Scanlon's, who was familiar with the photograph, called to tell him that what she took to be a "colorized" version of "Puppies" was on the front page of the calendar section of the May 7, 1989 Sunday Los Angeles Times. In fact, as she and Scanlon later learned, the newspaper actually depicted Koons' "String of Puppies" in connection with an article about its exhibition at the Los Angeles Museum of Contemporary Art.

. . . Defendant Koons . . . defends his use of Rogers' work "Puppies" to craft "String of Puppies" under a claim of a privilege of "fair use." This equitable doctrine permits other people to use copyrighted material without the owner's consent in a reasonable manner for certain purposes.

. . . Knowing exploitation of a copyrighted work for personal gain militates against a finding of fair use. And—because it is an equitable doctrine—wrongful denial of exploitative conduct towards the work of another may bar an otherwise legitimate fair use claim. Relevant to this issue is Koons' conduct, especially his action in tearing the copyright mark off of a Rogers notecard prior to sending it to the Italian artisans. This action suggests bad faith in defendant's use of plaintiff's work, and militates against a finding of fair use.

. . . [C]omment on or criticism of a copyrighted work may be a valid use under the fair use doctrine. We must analyze therefore whether "String of Puppies" is properly considered a comment on or criticism of the photograph "Puppies." Koons argues that his sculpture is a satire or parody of society at large. He insists that "String of Puppies" is a fair social criticism and asserts to support that proposition that he belongs to the school of American artists who believe the mass production of commodities and media images has caused a deterioration in the quality of society, and this artistic tradition of which he is a member proposes through incorporating these images into works of art to comment critically both on the incorporated object and the political and economic system that created it.

... Parody or satire, as we understand it, is when one artist, for comic effect or social commentary, closely imitates the style of another artist and in so doing creates a new art work that makes ridiculous the style and expression of the original. Under our cases parody and satire are valued forms of criticism, encouraged because this sort of criticism itself fosters the creativity protected by the copyright law. . . . The problem in the instant case is that even given that "String of Puppies" is a satirical critique of our materialistic society, it is difficult to discern any parody of the photograph "Puppies" itself. We conclude therefore that this first factor of the fair use doctrine cuts against a finding of fair use. The circumstances of this case indicate that Koons' copying of the photograph "Puppies" was done in bad faith, primarily for profit-making motives, and did not constitute a parody of the original work.

... Accordingly, the judgment of the district court is affirmed in all respects.

THREE PILLARS CASE QUESTIONS

(1)   What is the purpose of the "fair use" exception to copyright protection?

(2)   What did the court cite as factors that argued against Koons' fair use of Rogers's photograph?

(3)   In order to prove copyright infringement, there must be substantial similarity between the works in question. Examine the two images, which may be accessed at https://www.designobserver.com/feature/art-rogers-vs-jeff-koons/6467. How are the artworks alike? How are they different? If you had to argue against substantial similarity, what would be your argument? If you had to argue for substantial similarity, what would be your argument?

(4)   What is a strategy that Jeff Koons could have employed to avoid litigation in this case?

THE LAW PILLAR: INTELLECTUAL PROPERTY RISK MANAGEMENT

You might be familiar with the American chocolate wafer and cream cookie once called *Hydrox*™ that is rumored to have evolved into the Nabisco brand Oreo®. The *Hydrox*™ cookie was marketed beginning in 1908 but then withdrawn from the market in 2008. Leaf Brands, a company that revives disappeared food items, decided to bring *Hydrox*™ back. However, there was an obstacle—the US-based company Kellogg owned the cookie's trademark.

Leaf Brands knew that if a company is not using a trademark, you can in essence "steal" it by asking the USPTO for permission to use it. The only caveat is that you must provide the trademark office evidence that the current trademark owner is not using the trademark and has no future plans to use it. So, Leaf Brands cleverly wrote to Kellogg's consumer affairs office, explaining that it was a fan of the cookie and asking, "Do you have any plans to bring it back?" Kellogg replied, "Sorry—no plans to ever revive the *Hydrox*™ brand." Shortly thereafter, Leaf Brands received permission from the USPTO to use the *Hydrox*™ trademark.[66]

The Leaf Brands example illustrates the need to protect your company's intellectual property. What follows are both general and specific legal strategies for safeguarding IP assets.

General Strategies

The best general IP protection strategies focus on strong offensive and defensive approaches. Two possibilities are described in Michael Gollin's book *Driving Innovation* (2008) on international IP strategies: the Burning Stick strategy and the Suit of Armor and Shield strategy.

The offensive Burning Stick strategy is especially relevant to small-sized and medium-sized enterprises that are organizing their IP portfolios amid an eat-or-be-eaten competitive jungle. These organizations need to build a campfire to ward off "wild animals"—competitors and others who might hinder their success. Gollin notes that the fire doesn't need to be big, but it should be strong—including vigorous protection of key assets that companies identify as vital to their goals. Also important is to protect not only what is valuable to your company but what may be important to other companies as well. You should apply for patents quickly to hold your place in the first-to-file system, and you should mark products as "patent-pending." You should fortify trade secret protections with restricted access—for example, the only-two-executives rule of Coca-Cola and Kentucky Fried Chicken. Airtight confidentiality agreements should accompany even the smallest disclosure of proprietary information.

All copyrightable materials—company newsletters, advertising materials, training manuals—should be noted as such. Important copyrights should be registered and marked with a © symbol or the word "Copyright." Even though using the copyright symbol is no longer required to enforce your rights under the

Berne Convention (an international treaty), it still serves to warn potential infringers. All valuable trademarks, especially those associated with key assets, should be registered and marked on all literature, packaging, and websites.

Any infringement should be addressed through a cease-and-desist letter, which is usually enough to discourage further violations. If the infringement persists, the company may threaten litigation—but it is wise to seek more conservative avenues first, such as licensing arrangements. Although this highly vigilant strategy appears aggressive, it will place the company in a strong position to move forward in creating value for its IP assets.

The second possible strategy, Suit of Armor and Shield, adds a defensive component to the Burning Stick approach. The company in this scenario suits up like a warrior in battle to face the army of IP-holding competitors. As Sun Tzu said in *The Art of War*, "Victorious warriors win first and then go to war, while defeated warriors go to war first and then seek to win."

Preparation is the key to this strategy. Conduct Freedom to Operate Analyses (FTOs) on your key assets, which is the process of determining whether an action, such as commercializing a product, will infringe on the IP rights of others. This information serves as a risk management tool to minimize and plan around potential infringing activities. You can reduce costs by starting with your own IP searches, such as looking for patents at USPTO.gov or patents.google.com. Also note that there are many services that will conduct these studies for you, and for very important assets, you may secure an FTO opinion from an experienced patent attorney.

Although the FTO opinion might be costly, it can support your defense in an infringement suit. The FTO is especially important for company products or services that are entering a highly-competitive market dominated by big industry players (with deep pockets to support infringement litigation). Knowing what the competition is doing will also help identify infringement on *your* company's holdings. Even if you do not act on competitor infringement immediately, you should keep the FTO in reserve to form the basis for counterclaims, in case you are sued at a later date. The stickier the situation becomes, the more likely all parties will settle through low-key negotiation or mediation, as opposed to expensive litigation.

Specific Strategies: Trade Secrets

The key to trade secret success is maintaining strict confidentiality in the IP asset. Because trade secret protection can be lost when companies fail to take reasonable efforts to maintain secrecy, a company's conduct is at the core of this IP form. The first reasonable effort a company can take is to educate employees about the importance and nature of trade secret protection and to require each individual to sign an agreement that addresses confidentiality and IP ownership. Customers, independent contractors, consultants, and even volunteers and interns should also sign agreements outlining permissible use of proprietary information. Physical and computer security measures should be rigorous. Online postings should be scrutinized carefully so that confidential information is not inadvertently exposed—because once the trade secret is disclosed, whether accidental or otherwise, the protection for that asset ends and can never be revived.

One of the limitations of trade secret protection is the potential for reverse engineering. If an asset can be reversed engineered easily, a patent may be the wiser form of protection. Google's mix of invention trade secrets and patents illustrates this strategy well. For example, the PageRank link analysis algorithm process is patented, while PageRank manipulation tools are trade secrets.[67]

Another strategy for protecting the trade secret is to employ technical obstructions, such as black-box components, to prevent reverse engineering. This strategy depends on the design and scope of the material being protected and can offer some obstacles on the road to independent discovery.

Specific Strategies: Patents

Patenting is a very strong form of protection for inventions. In addition to encouraging creativity (US President Abraham Lincoln said the patent "added the fuel of interest to the fire of genius"[68]), the enforcement system has spurred specific strategies that take full advantage of patenting logistics.

For example, International Business Machines (IBM) ranks as one of the most innovative organizations in the world, reflected in the thousands of patents the company receives every year. In 2018 alone, IBM was granted 9,100 patents—nearly twice that of the next company on the list, Samsung Electronics (5,850) and a four-fold increase over Apple, Inc., which registered 2,160.[69] Like all the big tech players, IBM patents core technologies and rigorously protects its inventions. But the company also uses strategies designed to extend their protection well beyond the essential focus of the primary patent.

One of these strategies is known as the "Picket Fence." In the usual picket fence approach, a company patents all of the incremental innovations surrounding the main invention. This ancillary protection forms a fence or blanket around the core technology and prevents other companies from building IP that can compete with the protected asset.

But IBM's picket fence strategy has a twist. Instead of patenting all the peripheral inventions, the company publishes them. Once available to the public, these small associated features of the core patent become "prior art" (recall the spork invention) and cannot be patented. So, in addition to saving the cost of non-core patenting, IBM prevents competitors from patenting around their primary innovation.[70]

Modern and historic patent infringement litigation is a serious issue. In recent years, Samsung and Apple were engaged in a patent infringement war over their respective smartphones. Both companies dominate the mobile phone market and are responsible for more than half the phones sold worldwide. At issue were claims of infringement of both companies' utility and design patents, trademarks, and other intellectual property. Fifty lawsuits had been filed in ten countries in the Samsung-Apple conflict. But the litigation on smartphone technology is not limited to Samsung and Apple, as Google, HTC, HUAWEI, Microsoft, Motorola, Nokia, and Sony have also either sued or been sued in smartphone and tablet patent skirmishes.[71]

WIPO estimates that the average patent infringement case in the United States costs a company between $3 million and $10 million and takes two to three years to litigate. Such conflicts are unfortunately not new. For example, by the year 1896 there were more than three hundred patent suits pending between early radio broadcasting giants General Electric and Westinghouse.[72]

There are some specific strategies companies can use to avoid this type of combat. For example, they can seek a licensing or cross-licensing arrangement for the IP that is at the center of the controversy. This strategy benefits the parties by both ending the expense of litigation and creating the potential to generate profits.

Similarity in products/IP portfolios might also form a basis for merger and acquisition activity. In the late 1990s, two American companies, TV Guide and Gemstar, were close competitors and the only providers of interactive programming guides for dominant digital formats. After long-term patent litigation between them, these companies made the decision to merge. The result was a new company and a $14.2 billion stock deal. This pleased shareholders much more than the continued expense of litigation.[73] So, while some strategies may begin in adversity, there is always room at the negotiating table for a favorable settlement.

Specific Strategies: Trademarks

Patents and trade secrets are like the internal, unseen bones of a company's intellectual property, whereas trademarks are the face of the company that is making the actual connection with the user and consumer. Branding is, therefore, a critical strategy for growing a company and gaining recognition in the marketplace. A great advantage of the trademark, mentioned earlier, is indefinite registration renewal. Like a trade secret, trademark protection can theoretically extend for eternity.

Before adopting a new mark, the company should search trademark databases (that's TESS in the United States—Trademark Electronic Search System) and be certain that the mark is available. Lack of knowledge is normally not a defense to trademark infringement, and it is also better to avoid wasting your investment if the trademark is already registered.

Some companies focus on a trademark strategy that registers multiple related marks, forming a trademark cluster. The National Football League (NFL), for example, has created a trademark cluster around the phrase "Super Bowl®." The League has registered the Super Bowl® phrase for television broadcasting services, promotional materials, clothing, entertainment services, and Super Bowl® concerts. This cluster allows the NFL to control virtually every commercial aspect of the trademark in every venue.[74]

A trademark portfolio may also include registered domain names that can extend a company's brand throughout the online community. While most generic top-level domain names are relatively inexpensive, there are a few that have garnered top dollar such as insurance.com, which sold for over $35 million in 2010.[75]

The most effective strategies for trademarks are prompt registration, use of trademark symbols, and monitoring renewals. Failure to renew trademarks and pay fees can potentially result in losing trademark protection. To ensure maximum legal protection, do not forget the importance of "distinctiveness" as it relates to the four trademark categories.

Specific Strategies: Copyright

Like trademarks, prompt copyright registration is important if your business plans to enforce the rights in infringement actions. All transfers of copyright ownership must be in writing; oral transfers are not valid. Therefore, any outside consultants your company hires—website designers, copywriters, advertising professionals—should sign written copyright assignments. Clear and documented understanding of who owns the various rights in the copyright bundle should be a priority for all companies.

Copyright may be provided to the many writings important to a company, including annual public company reports, computer software programs (make sure to keep the copyright of an outside programmer's work in the name of the company), customer and mailing lists stored on a computer, product drawings and technical schematics, instructional manuals, promotional materials, and logos. As with any intellectual property, copyrights should be monitored carefully for infringement, especially in light of the ease in which violations occur via the Internet.

As mentioned, companies should keep in mind defenses to infringement, such as fair use and the clean room strategy. Documentation is the key to supporting authorized use in case the company is challenged in its use of copyrighted material.

Companies should be aware that there are different ways to both own and share copyright. Depending on what a company hopes to accomplish with its most valuable copyrights, it may decide to commit some rights to outlets such as Shareware or the Creative Commons. The copyright owner decides what rights, if any, are offered to these sources and may require attribution or place limitations on use. Tim O'Reilly of O'Reilly Media wrote that "Obscurity is a far greater threat to authors and creative artists than piracy,"[76] and this sentiment often holds true for other corporate copyrighted material as well. While there might not be a direct profit from sharing copyright with open sources, benefits can be garnered indirectly through enhanced distribution and marketing.

It is also important for a company to think outside the box and consider nontraditional forms of expression that can be protected. For example, you can take as many photographs as you like of Paris' Eiffel Tower in the daytime and post them online. The nighttime lighting of the tower, however, is copyrighted, and anyone posting these images is expected to remit a licensing fee to the French government.[77]

ALIGN STRATEGY AND LAW: USE INTELLECTUAL PROPERTY TO CREATE VALUE

In the American film *The Matrix*, the character Morpheus offers newcomer Neo a choice between two pills—one blue, one red. The blue pill offers a continued, but comfortable, lack of awareness, and the red pill offers a gateway to a new reality. "The Matrix is everywhere. It is all around us. Even now in this very room; you can see it when you look out the window, or turn on the television . . ." Neo takes the red pill and soon comes to better understand the Matrix, with all its associated risks and rewards.

Developing and maintaining intellectual property is like taking the red pill. Once you begin to become aware of assets that are both unique to your business and protectable as intellectual property, a whole new world emerges. Whereas safeguarded intellectual property assets range from the mundane to the spectacular, nearly each and every one will provide an advantage to companies that hold them. And although identifying, protecting, and monitoring intellectual property assets might be costly and risky, the costs and risks of doing nothing are often much greater.

Designing the Intellectual Property Management Plan

Once you are familiar with the forms of intellectual property and their associated responsibilities, it is time to form a strategic plan within your company to maximize IP asset use and create value for your investors. One of the best routes to create a strategy is to take the following steps: (1) review existing goals, (2) identify assets, (3) evaluate the competition, and (4) develop a plan.[78]

Review Existing Goals. You cannot plan a trip well if you do not know where you are going. Preparing an IP strategy for a company requires understanding what the business seeks to do, or where it hopes to be, in the future. For example, one of Google's long-term goals is to be the best and most user-friendly search engine available on the Internet. To achieve this objective, Google works continuously on its search engine technology. The company makes around five-to-six-hundred improvements to its patents and trade secrets every year.[79] But before founders of Google protected any inventions, researched what their competitors were doing, or developed a strategy, they wisely established the strategic goal of being the greatest search engine in existence.[80] Once you know where your company is headed, you can identify the IP assets that will take you there.

Identify Assets. Many businesses believe that only big industry players, such as Samsung and Apple, hold valuable intellectual property. This myth keeps small-sized and medium-sized enterprises from evaluating their IP inventories. This, in turn, prevents these companies from developing strategies to create value. Some IP assets are "hidden in plain sight" around you. That's why the next step in building an IP strategy is to identify these assets. They might include obvious ones among the main categories we have already discussed: trademarks, patents, copyrights, and trade secrets. They also might include less-recognized assets such as custom software, formulations, training manuals, and other publications, licenses, branding, distribution contracts, client lists, product certifications, franchise agreements, drawings, promotional literature, raw material networks, know-how—and the list can go on and on.

An initial IP audit will be akin to Dorothy stepping from black and white film into the Technicolor wonderland of MGM's 1939 film *The Wizard of Oz*—things will never be the same. Various publications can provide a company with intellectual property assessment instruments; information about each asset should include aspects such as product life, extent of use, importance, and estimated value. You should inventory policies already in place, as well as the human resources needed to support existing assets. Very important assets can benefit from IP valuation.

Evaluate the Competition. Once you have surveyed the intellectual property landscape, you are ready to assess competition. Assessing other companies' rights and how they have protected and exercised those rights is important to understanding your internal IP prospects. For example, firms in the biotechnology field struggle with a "patent thicket" of overlapping rights that tends to result in what is known as the stacking of licensing royalties.

Because biotech research involves so many closely-related methods and processes that there are often multiple patent licenses and other rights that need to be secured before a new invention investigation can move forward. In this situation, a freedom to operate analysis, where the protected intellectual property of competitors is evaluated, is useful in preventing potential infringement. If a blocking protected right is discovered, options include assessing whether the competitor's IP is valid and, if so, cross-licensing or inventing around the existing property.

Awareness of competitor IP portfolios can also be a form of benchmarking. In *Driving Innovation*, author Michael Gollin provides the example of a brewing company with a vast array of trademarks but few patents in its portfolio compared to other brewers. Based on this information, the brewer can decide whether to increase its own patenting activities, seek to purchase existing patents, or choose other ways to strengthen its position within the industry. Awareness of competitors' IP and how they are using it helps you organize your holdings, avoid infringement, and gain a competitive edge in the marketplace.

Develop a Plan. Once a company is aware of its intellectual property and has evaluated and cataloged its portfolio, the next step is to develop a plan to maximize IP protection, use, and value in line with organizational goals. This step is accomplished by examining the company's individual assets and developing a strategy for each. Some of the plans and strategies will be simple, such as copyrighting and marking blog entries or promotional literature. Other plans will be more complex, and potentially expensive, combining multiple forms of protection and vigilant infringement monitoring.

Forming an IP strategy has tremendous benefits. When a plan is formulated and implemented, managers can look forward to increased revenues, growing brand recognition, and added attention from investors. Companies can employ numerous strategies, some of which were covered earlier in this chapter, to set the IP management plan in motion and create value in the identified assets. Managers should consider the nature of their company's assets and select strategies that align with organizational goals.

One example of a successful concentrated IP plan involves the NFL's trademark of the words Super Bowl®, mentioned earlier. The Super Bowl® event marks the season end of one of America's most popular sports. The NFL first began using the term in 1969 and has held the trademark for many years. Throughout its ownership period, the football league has been aggressive in enforcing the Super Bowl® trademark. A team of attorneys monitors every use of the mark for infringement and unauthorized use. NFL enforcers even closed down a church's game-viewing party because congregants used the Super Bowl® trademark in advertising the event.

This "super" vigilance is related to two factors. First, trademark holders must pursue infringers to maximize their damage recovery in court actions. Second, the Super Bowl® trademark is especially valuable. With sponsors paying tens of millions of dollars for the privilege of using the football league's intellectual property, the NFL's well-planned and executed protection of the Super Bowl® trademark is essential.[81]

Patents, like trademarks, can be a significant source of value for patent holders, although there might be gaps in the protection they offer. Not every company resorts to IBM's picket fence around their inventions, due primarily to time and cost. A lack of broad protection can allow others to employ an "invent around" strategy. By studying a patent or a published patent application's technology, you might be able to identify weaknesses or areas where an improvement can be developed. This approach can be as simple as changing just one element in the claims supporting a patent. Although the strategy can be tricky because you risk infringement, it can also be advantageous because much of the research and development heavy lifting is already completed. Author Gollin terms these invent-around strategies patent "jiu-jitsu" because the process involves elements of good timing, skill, and agility.

Among the most critical strategies to create value from patents is licensing. The annual revenue attributed to licensing agreements in the United States is more than $500 billion.[82] Cross-licensing between companies of their IP holdings is common. Some entities will patent or otherwise protect IP that they would not otherwise use so that these assets are available as bargaining chips for negotiating licenses on assets others hold.

This strategy should not be confused with the actions of holding companies known as the pejorative "patent trolls." As Non-Practicing Entities/Patent Assertion Entities (NPEs/PAEs), these companies acquire patents but rarely license the invention, manufacture products, or supply services related to the patents they own. Instead, the NPE/PAE subsists by exploiting invention protections through infringement suits against others for violations of their patent holdings. In the United States, more than half the states have enacted anti-trolling laws, and federal legislation that places some limitations on patent trolling has been proposed.

Licensing strategies can also enable parties to avoid litigation, as illustrated by an IP dispute between the nation of Ethiopia and the coffee company Starbucks. According to the WIPO, coffee is the second most traded commodity after oil, and global citizens drink more than four hundred billion cups each year. In 2004, the Ethiopian Intellectual Property Office attempted to register three trademarks on coffee beans in key market countries. Trademark registration would provide the Ethiopian government "with greater and more effective control over the distribution of its product, which [would] ultimately increase revenues by exporting more goods, enabling a rise in prices and benefits to farmers."[83]

The trademark applications were quickly opposed by the USPTO and by the National Coffee Association (including member Starbucks) as being too "generic" to qualify for registration. Starbucks tried to steer Ethiopia toward obtaining certification marks and foregoing trademarks, but the country held its position. "You have to understand the situation in Ethiopia," Director General Getachew Mengistie of the Ethiopian Intellectual Property Office (EIPO) explained. "Our coffee is grown on four million very small plots of land. Setting up a certification system would have been impracticable and too expensive. Trademarking was more appropriate to our needs. It was a more direct route offering more control."[84]

What began in an adversarial stance, however, ended in an alliance, due in part to Ethiopia's strategy of offering royalty-free licenses to foreign coffee distributors. The free licenses were intended to encourage large foreign coffee agents to promote and build recognition for Ethiopian products. Ethiopia's strategy of providing incentives and working cooperatively to accomplish its objectives created a win-win situation for all involved.[85]

Intellectual property holders can also cooperate by forming a patent pool. A patent pool is a grouping of intellectual property rights with the intent of cross-licensing. Patent pools have been formed to end legal wrangling (sewing machines, the movie industry), simplify manufacturing (Davoplane/Pullman folding beds), facilitate information gathering (railroads), fuel war efforts (aircraft manufacturers), seek global industry domination (radio), and protect/promote standards bodies (MPEG-2, DVD technology).[86] These patent rights consortiums have also been considered for computer software and biotechnology with the intent of eliminating or minimizing the cumulative effect of patent thickets.

A well-organized and administered patent pool can be advantageous for all participants by reducing litigation (think Samsung-Apple) and transaction costs, and by enabling companies that contribute to the pool to increase profits. Provided the pools do not become anticompetitive, they are a viable collective strategy for modern businesses.

Pools also provide a method by which the welfare of society may be accommodated by providing access to much-needed protected IP, such as patents related to medicines and food products. A great deal of ethical tension has focused on the exclusivity of rights in protected inventions and whether allowing a temporary monopoly is wholly beneficial to society, especially when people in need of the innovation may be actually or constructively barred from it. A good example of a cooperative set up to bridge this ethical divide is the Medicines Patent Pool (MPP) in Geneva, Switzerland. The MPP, administered by the United Nations-supported organization Unitaid, licenses medicines to treat HIV, Hepatitis C, and tuberculosis from patent holders. Through the pool, Unitaid permits lower-cost manufacturers to produce and distribute patented medicines in developing countries.[87] Pharmaceutical companies contributing patents to the pool receive royalties on the licensing arrangements, and millions of lives have been saved as a result.

The patent term is relatively short when compared to other forms of IP protection. But there are a few strategies to extend the life of a patent even after the specified term ends. One method is by "evergreening," which pharmaceutical companies commonly use to prolong their presence in the market. Evergreening involves patenting minor improvements or associated discoveries and then associating the changes with established brand names already in the marketplace. A related strategy is transitioning patent protection to an emphasis on trademarks through intense advertising and marketing close to the time of patent expiration. The goal is to encourage consumers to continue buying products associated with the established "name" even when competing products are available.

Strategies for the Future

Michael Gollin notes in *Driving Innovation* that "the IP system is global in reach, and local in impact," requiring a balance between exclusive rights and access. There's no doubt that the world of intellectual property is complex and rapidly changing. Imbalance will exist, yet so will continued efforts to bring IP to sustainability. The company that takes steps to determine its goals, identify and protect its assets, evaluate competition, and develop a strategic plan for managing intangible assets will be in the best position as the modern age advances. Microsoft founder Bill Gates once said that "intellectual property has the shelf life of a banana."[88] But in a world of strategically-managed IP, a few days on the shelf may be all the time you need.

KEY TAKEAWAYS

In a world where 70 percent of business assets are intangible, a company's ability to create, protect, and use intellectual property is the key to creating value and attracting investors. Value creation requires that you should:

1. **Become legally savvy about intellectual property law.** At a minimum, you should understand the four key categories of IP rights described in this chapter: trade secrets, patents, trademarks, and copyrights. You should also understand basic variations in these rights from country to country.

2. **Manage intellectual property risks.** You should consider general strategies such as the offensive Burning Stick and the defensive Suit of Armor and Shield strategies. You should also use strategies that relate to specific types of intellectual property. To protect your trade secrets, for example, you should educate employees about the nature of trade secret protection and require them to sign confidentiality agreements.

3. **Use intellectual property law to create value, which will attract investment to your company.** An IP management plan is key to creating value for your company. As part of your plan, you should

review existing goals, identify IP assets, evaluate your competitors' IP, and align your IP strategy with your company's strategic goals.

STRATEGY

LAW   ***Three Pillars Decision: Secrets of Steamboat Willie***

ETHICS

This decision scenario considers the need to strategize when IP protection time limitations are endangering valuable assets.

On January 1, 2024, the very first Mickey Mouse cartoon, *Steamboat Willie,* will pass into the public domain when its 1928 copyright expires. This means that after the January date, anyone can make copies of this most famous Walt Disney film. It is also possible that the character of Mickey Mouse—as well as other *Steamboat* cartoon stars such as Minnie Mouse and Peg Leg Pete—may also lose their copyright protection.[89]

In the United States, the constitutional requirement that copyrights only exist for a limited time is set out by Article I, Section 8, Clause 8 and was agreed-to unanimously at the Constitutional Convention in 1787. The duration of US copyright has changed over time, but as a general rule for works created after January 1, 1978, copyright protection lasts for the life of the author plus seventy years. The "seventy years"—an extension over the fifty years established by the Copyright Act of 1976—was included in the 1998 Sonny Bono Copyright Term Extension Act, which added twenty years to the protection term.

The 1998 Act was also known derisively as the *Mickey Mouse Protection Act* due to the reputed considerable sums spent by the Walt Disney Company to gain passage of the bill through lobbying efforts in Congress. According to the source *Priceonomics,*

> Watchdog records show that the Disney Political Action Committee (PAC) paid out a total of $149,612 in direct campaign contributions to those considering the Copyright Term Extension bill. Of the bill's 25 sponsors (12 in the Senate, and 13 in the House), 19 received money directly from Disney's then CEO, Michael Eisner.[90]

These efforts make sense when considering that Mickey Mouse—described by *Forbes* as the world's "richest fictional billionaire"—is worth an estimated $5.8 billion.

VALUE GOAL: To extend protection to valuable intellectual property that is vulnerable to copyright expiration.

STRATEGY: Develop a strategy that would allow Walt Disney Company to continue to protect its famous characters, such as Mickey Mouse, and other intellectual property subject to copyright.

LAW: Research the four primary types of intellectual property protection (copyright, trade secret, patent, and trademark) and the current related federal laws that are designed to prevent infringement. How does this research affect or alter the strategy you developed? If necessary, refine your strategy to align with the law.ℝ

ETHICS: Apply ethics to your strategy by working through these four steps of ethical decision making: (1) describe the ethical dilemma, (2) identify the stakeholders involved, (3) analyze options (including how each group of stakeholders will be affected), and (4) make a decision based on your analysis. After examining ethical issues associated with the strategy, determine whether any modifications should be made.

ℝ*Check for law research materials in the Appendix: Legal Resources for Business Decisions*

STRATEGY LAW ETHICS	*Three Pillars Decision: "Betcha Can't Eat Just One"* [91]

Balancing rights protection can be like walking a tightrope in certain situations, as illustrated by PepsiCo's dilemma.

PepsiCo recently brought a patent infringement suit against potato farmers in Gujarat, a state located on the western coast of India. The case alleges that these farmers grew their crops from a protected seed known as FL2027, which is used to produce potato chips for PepsiCo's subsidiary Frito-Lay. PepsiCo was seeking damages of 10 million rupees ($143,000) from each of the farmers, who only grow potatoes on a few acres each.[92] According to the farmers, they received their seeds from a local trader. PepsiCo only supplies the seed either directly or through a third-party supplier in a contract farming arrangement. As an offer of settlement, PepsiCo stated that it would drop the suit if the farmers joined their authorized cultivation program—"either join us or grow other potatoes," said a company spokesperson.[93]

Observers of the situation have criticized PepsiCo, stating that the company has a responsibility to protect its plant varieties from being supplied by unauthorized entities. "The fact that the FL2027 seed has reached the hands of a local trader in large quantities shows that PepsiCo failed to guard its seed variety from infringement," stated Economics Professor Sthanu Nair. Professor Nair also criticized the company for moving against the weakest involved parties—the farmers—as opposed to the local trader, or other potentially responsible individuals.

> It may be the case that the seeds used by the farmers were obtained from PepsiCo's third-party input supplier or they were of a spurious variety supplied by unorganised players. This brings to our attention a major pain point in India's plant variety regulatory mechanism—the large presence of spurious seeds in the market, which affects all stakeholders.[94]

VALUE GOAL: To protect patented seed varieties for the benefit of all stakeholders.

STRATEGY: Design a strategy that would protect PepsiCo's patents while also protecting the rights of Indian farmers.

LAW: Research the 2001 Protection of Plant Varieties and Farmers' Rights Act (PPVFR) of India. Does this statute have any effect on the strategy you developed? If necessary, refine your strategy to align with the law.☞

ETHICS: There are many stakeholders involved in this issue: PepsiCo and its subsidiaries, Indian farmers, suppliers, and governmental/regulatory agencies. In your ethics analysis, keep these groups in mind as you work through these four steps of ethical decision making: (1) describe the ethical dilemma, (2) identify the stakeholders involved, (3) analyze options (including how each group of stakeholders will be affected), and (4) make a decision based on your analysis. After examining ethical issues associated with the strategy, determine whether any modifications should be made.

☞*Check for law research materials in the Appendix: Legal Resources for Business Decisions*

STRATEGY LAW ETHICS	***Three Pillars Decision: FaceTime with Trolls***

This next decision scenario examines how to strategize when faced with nefarious litigation. VirnetX is a publicly-traded internet technology company that allegedly primarily earns its income by filing lawsuits against other entities for patent infringement. This business approach of being a Non-Practicing/Patent Assertion Entity (NPE/PAE) or "patent troll" has expanded considerably in recent years; more than ten thousand companies have been sued by NPE/PAEs, and patent trolls file 84 percent of high-tech patent lawsuits each year.[95]

Patent protection was originally designed by the US Congress to safeguard inventors by preventing others from using, making, or selling their inventions; it was instituted to be a reward for innovation. NPE/PAEs rarely actually use or license the invention patents they hold. Instead, their approach is to identify companies that are potentially using the patented invention and bring a lawsuit against that entity.

Patent troll companies operate in this space because it can be lucrative. Many businesses, especially Small and Medium Enterprises (SMEs), choose to settle quickly rather than be drawn into expensive litigation. Larger companies fight the good fight but don't always win. In 2019, Apple appealed a damage award of nearly $1 billion awarded against it in multiple actions filed by VirnetX for infringement of FaceTime, iPhone, iPad, iPod, and Macintosh computer-related patents.[96]

VALUE GOAL: To protect SMEs against the practice of Non-Practicing Entities/Patent Assertion Entities (NPE/PAE).

STRATEGY: Design an SME strategy for protection from and response to the actions of NPE/PAEs.

LAW: Massachusetts is one of the most recent states to propose a law related to NPE/PAEs. Access the patent troll legislation in Massachusetts at https://malegislature.gov/Bills/191/H229. After studying this legislation (or you could use proposed legislation or laws in a state of your choice), decide whether the language of the proposal/law affects your strategy.[97] If necessary, refine your strategy to align with the law.ᐤ

ETHICS: Many have suggested that NPE/PAE actions are unethical and violate the intent of the original creators of the Constitution. In your ethics analysis, keep this key factor in mind as you work through these four steps of ethical decision making: (1) describe the ethical dilemma, (2) identify the stakeholders involved, (3) analyze options (including how each group of stakeholders will be affected), and (4) make a decision based on your analysis. After examining ethical issues associated with the strategy, determine whether any modifications should be made.

ᐤ*Check for law research materials in the Appendix: Legal Resources for Business Decisions*

STRATEGY	
LAW	***Three Pillars Decision: Mutiny in Cyberspace***
ETHICS	

With the rise of Internet domain names, the World Intellectual Property Organization (WIPO) established a Domain Name Dispute Resolution process that largely mirrors ADR procedures for resolving disputes quickly and fairly. One of the first applications of this system involved the taking of the domain name registered to tiny Pitcairn Island, ancestral home of the HMS Bounty Mutineers.

The story of the Pitcairners is unique. In 1788, the HMS Bounty sailed to Tahiti to collect valuable breadfruit trees to bring to England. After the plants were prepped for the return trip Master Mate Fletcher Christian and some of the Bounty crew became restless. Many of the men were unhappy to end relationships with Tahitian women slated to be left behind, and several sailors were additionally disillusioned by Commander William Bligh's rigorous discipline and order. The dissension escalated on April 28, 1789, when eighteen members of the Bounty crew committed mutiny, setting Bligh and his eighteen loyal crew members afloat in the ship's skiff.

Bligh and his men, after an arduous journey, arrived many months later in England and reported the mutiny. In September 1789, Fletcher Christian, along with eight other crewmen, six Tahitian men, and eleven women, one with a baby, set sail from Tahiti in Bounty hoping to elude the British Royal Navy. They landed and made their new home on tiny Pitcairn Island, only two miles wide and at the time uninhabited. Soon after their arrival, they burned the HMS Bounty just off the island shore in what is now known as "Bounty Bay."[98]

Over two hundred years later, about fifty descendants of Fletcher Christian and the other mutineers continue to live and work on Pitcairn Island, but maintenance of the Pitcairners' revered island lifestyle has been problematic. The Pitcairn economy, largely based on the sale of coins, stamps, and Bounty souvenirs, has often failed to keep pace with the rising costs of modern conveniences in such an isolated location.[99] Other avenues of earning revenue were investigated and implemented, especially throughout the 1990s, including bee-keeping and tourism. But it was a somewhat odd source of economic support—the creation of an internet domain address—that would involve the Pitcairners in their own modern "mutiny."[100]

Tom Christian, direct descendant of mutineer mastermind Fletcher Christian, began negotiating in the late 1990s with Nigel Roberts, a computer consultant associated with the now-dissolved British organization Orichalk Ltd. After convincing Mr. Christian that the company could best administer a domain name address for Pitcairn Island, the Internet Assigned Numbers Authority (IANA) approved a request for initial delegation of the top-level domain (TDL) .pn on July 10, 1997. The .pn TDL ("pn" for Pitcairn) was subsequently used predominantly for registration of domain names to entities not affiliated with the territory, in exchange for a fee collected by Orichalk.[101]

Even though Tom Christian was the designated administrator for the island domain, Pitcairn had no Internet connection and, therefore, no method by which Christian could monitor either the registrations or collection of fees for use of the address. Shortly after Orichalk began selling the Pitcairn TDL, Pitcairners realized that they had no control over the domain name, its marketing, nor the value received in exchange for its use—they had been subjected to a type of "cybersquatting." The history of Pitcairn Island, the Pitcairners' knowledge of events, and the Pitcairners themselves—the commodity behind the domain name value—had been misappropriated and exploited.

VALUE GOAL: To protect domain names and designations against misappropriation.

STRATEGY: Design a strategy that protects a company's or organization's domain name.

LAW: Research the ways to legally protect a domain name at GigaLaw's website: https://giga.law/blog/2015/06/02/8-easy-ways-to-protect-your-domain-name. Align your strategy with the law if necessary.℘

ETHICS: Cybersquatting is a serious issue related to domain names. This is the practice of registering names, especially those for potential use by well-known companies, with the hopes of selling them at an enormous profit. Some have argued that cybersquatting is just smart business, and cybersquatters will often sell the URL for less than the cost of litigation. This situation is similar to that of the non-practicing entities discussed previously. Consider the question of cybersquatting and whether this practice should be allowed through an ethical analysis: (1) describe the ethical dilemma, (2) identify the stakeholders involved, (3) analyze options (including how each group of stakeholders will be affected), and (4) make a decision based on your analysis. After examining ethical issues associated with the strategy, determine whether any modifications should be made.

℘*Check for law research materials in the Appendix: Legal Resources for Business Decisions*

1   World Intellectual Property Organization (WIPO) website, http://www.wipo.int/portal/en/index. html.

2   Mai-Duc, "All the 'Happy Birthday' Song Copyright Claims Are Invalid, Federal Judge Rules," *Los Angeles Times*, September 22, 2015.

3   WIPO Website, http://www.wipo.int/about-ip/en/.

4   History of Rice Cultivation at Ricepedia, http://ricepedia.org/culture/history-of-rice-cultivation.

5   Encyclopaedia Britannica, "Charles Babbage, British Inventor and Mathematician," http://www. britannica.com/biography/Charles-Babbage.

6   US Constitution Article 1, Section 8, Clause 8.

7   https://philosophia.uncg.edu/phi361-matteson/module-6-privacy-property-and-technology/ property-and-intellectual-property/.

8   https://www.osler.com/en/resources/cross-border/2018/a-need-to-know-guide-on-ip-in-the-u-s-mexico-canada-agreement.

9   Kaplan, R.S. and Norton, D.P. (2004), "Strategy Maps – Converting Intangible Assets into Tangible Outcomes", Harvard Business School Press, Boston, MA.

10   Sailo, "Decoding the Value of Intellectual Property," *iRunway*, January 28, 2015.

11   https://brandongaille.com/24-great-coca-cola-sales-statistics/.

12   Lin, "Executive Trade Secrets," *Notre Dame Law Review*, 2012.

13   https://www.naturalnews.com/022092_Coca-Cola_conspiracy_Pepsi.html.

14   Library of Congress Website, http://www.loc.gov/law/help/tradesecrets/.

15   *Id.*

16   https://www.globalpolicywatch.com/2019/04/china-amends-trade-secret-law-to-further-favor-rights-holders/.

17   *Id.*

18   Library of Congress Website, http://www.loc.gov/law/help/tradesecrets/.

19   WIPO Website, http://www.wipo.int/patents/en/.

20   WIPO Magazine, "Bioethics and Patent Law: The Case of the Oncomouse," June 2006.

21   "Pharmaceutical Composition Containing, Cow Urine Distillate and an Antibiotic," http://www. google.com/patents/US6410059.

22   *Association for Molecular Pathology v. Myriad Genetics* (2013).

23   Sean Dennison, "How Much Is Facebook Worth?" (September 28, 2018), accessed at https://www. gobankingrates.com/making-money/business/how-much-is-facebook-worth/.

24   WIPO Website, http://www.wipo.int/patents/en/faq_patents.html.

25   PatentaDesign.com Website, http://www.patentadesign.com/knowledge/understanding-design-patents.html.

26   Swanson, "The Growing Allure of Plant Patenting for Brand Differentiation," *Earth and Table Law Reporter*, July 9, 2012.

27   World Trade Organization (WTO) Website, TRIPS Agreement, http://www.wto.org/english/ tratop_e/trips_e/t_agm0_e.htm.

28   The Thomas Edison Papers, Rutgers University, Patent Interference Files—Sawyer and Man v. Edison.

29   "Improvement in Combined Knives, Forks, and Spoons," http://www.google.com/ patents/US147119?dq=147119&hl=en&sa=X&ved=0ahUKEwju1M3zkLTKAhUBEGMKHUSRBy4Q6A EIHTAA.

30   WIPO Website, http://www.wipo.int/patents/en/faq_patents.html.

31   https://www.pinsentmasons.com/out-law/news/amazoncom-and-barnes--noblecom-settle-1-click-patent-lawsuit.

[32] USPTO Website, http://www.uspto.gov/trademarks-getting-started/trademark-basics/trademark-patent-or-copyright.

[33] Goldman, "Google Successfully Defends Its Most Valuable Asset in Court," *Forbes*, September 15, 2014.

[34] Kurt M. Saunders, Intellectual Property Law.

[35] International Trademark Association, Trademark Basics, http://www.inta.org/Media/Documents/2012_TMBasicsBusiness.pdf.

[36] *Id.*

[37] United States Patent and Trademark Office (USPTO), http://www.uspto.gov/trademark/soundmarks/trademark-sound-mark-examples.

[38] O'Dell, "Harley-Davidson Quits Trying to Hog Sound," *Los Angeles Times*, June 21, 2000.

[39] "Swoosh," http://en.wikipedia.org/wiki/Swoosh.

[40] ConceptDrop, "How Nike Redefined the Power of Brand Image," October 23, 2013.

[41] Brettman, "Nike Hits $30 Billion in Revenue For Fiscal Year 2015," *The Oregonian*, June 25, 2015.

[42] International Trademark Association, Trademark Basics, http://www.inta.org/Media/Documents/2012_TMBasicsBusiness.pdf.

[43] Novack, "Google Was Originally Called BackRub," *Gizmodo*, July 15, 2014.

[44] International Trademark Association, Trademark Basics, http://www.inta.org/Media/Documents/2012_TMBasicsBusiness.pdf.

[45] "Apple Corps v. Apple Computer," http://en.wikipedia.org/wiki/Apple_Corps_v_Apple_Computer.

[46] International Trademark Association, Trademark Basics, http://www.inta.org/Media/Documents/2012_TMBasicsBusiness.pdf.

[47] https://en.wikipedia.org/wiki/Michael_Buffer.

[48] https://secureyourtrademark.com/can-you-trademark/common-words-phrases/.

[49] *Two Pesos, Inc. v. Taco Cabana, Inc.* (1992).

[50] *"Two Pesos, Inc. v. Taco Cabana, Inc.,"* https://en.wikipedia.org/wiki/Two_Pesos,_Inc._v._Taco_Cabana,_Inc.

[51] Miller, *Where There's Life, There's Lawsuits* (2003).

[52] "A Moron in a Hurry," http://en.wikipedia.org/wiki/A_moron_in_a_hurry.

[53] "Trademark," http://en.wikipedia.org/wiki/Trademark.

[54] International Trademark Association, Trademark Basics, http://www.inta.org/Media/Documents/2012_TMBasicsBusiness.pdf.

[55] https://www.deseret.com/2000/1/9/19484686/fedex-fails-in-bid-against-ex-federal-espresso.

[56] Emily Gottlieb and Joanne Doroshow, Not in My Backyard II: The High-Tech Hypocrites of Tort Reform, Center for Justice and Democracy, No. 6 April 2001.

[57] US Copyright Office, "Copyright Basics," May 2012.

[58] "List of Countries' Copyright Lengths," http://en.wikipedia.org/wiki/List_of_countries'_copyright_lengths.

[59] *Rupa Marya, et al. v. Warner/Chappell Music, Inc., et al.* (2015).

[60] "Napster," http://en.wikipedia.org/wiki/Napster.

[61] Kumar, "Well-Known Cases of Copyright Infringement," *Bright Hub*, March 17, 2011.

[62] *Swatch Group v. Bloomberg* (2014).

[63] Tenuto, "Warner Bros. Settles Tyson Tattoo Case over Hangover II," *Article3*, June 21, 2011.

[64] "Fair Dealing," http://en.wikipedia.org/wiki/Fair_dealing.

[65] *"Oracle Corp. v. SAP AG,"* http://en.wikipedia.org/wiki/Oracle_Corp._v._SAP_AG.

[66] Kestenbaum, "One Man's Mission to Bring Back Hydrox Cookies," *NPR News Report*, September 24, 2015.

[67] "PageRank," http://en.wikipedia.org/wiki/PageRank.

68 Lincoln, "Lecture on Discoveries and Inventions," April 6, 1858, Abraham Lincoln Online, http://www.abrahamlincolnonline.org/lincoln/speeches/discoveries.htm.

69 https://www.statista.com/statistics/227230/worlds-most-innovative-companies/.

70 Arndt, "IBM's Crafty Intellectual Property Strategy," *Business Week*, December 8, 2008.

71 "Smartphone Patent Wars," http://en.wikipedia.org/wiki/Smartphone_patent_wars.

72 Scott, "The Radio Inventor/Entrepreneurs," http://www.westga.edu/~bquest/2001/radio.htm.

73 "Gemstar-TV Guide International," http://en.wikipedia.org/wiki/Gemstar-TV_Guide_International.

74 Gollin, *Driving Innovation: Intellectual Property Strategies for a Dynamic World* (2008).

75 "Shop Names," http://shop.com.co.domains.blog.ir/1391/10/02/.COM.

76 O'Reilly, "Piracy is Progressive Taxation, and Other Thoughts on the Evolution of Online Distribution," openp2p.com, December 11, 2002.

77 Schlackman, "Do Night Photos of the Eiffel Tower Violate Copyright?" *Art Law Journal*, November 16, 2014.

78 Gollin, *supra*.

79 "How Google Makes Improvements to Its Search Algorithm," http://www.youtube.com/watch?v=J5RZOU6vK4Q.

80 *Id.*

81 Alter, "God vs. Gridiron," *Wall Street Journal*, February 2, 2008.

82 Gray, "A New Era in IP Licensing," *The Licensing Journal*, Volume 28 No.10, November/December 2008.

83 https://www.wipo.int/ipadvantage/en/details.jsp?id=2621.

84 *Id.*

85 WIPO Website, "The Coffee War," http://www.wipo.int/ipadvantage/en/details.jsp?id=2621.

86 "Patent Pool," http://en.wikipedia.org/wiki/Patent_pool.

87 https://en.wikipedia.org/wiki/Medicines_Patent_Pool.

88 Munger, "A Dozen Things I've Learned about Business from Bill Gates," *25iq*, July 2014.

89 http://copyright.nova.edu/mickey-public-domain/#note-676-1.

90 https://priceonomics.com/how-mickey-mouse-evades-the-public-domain/.

91 Frito-Lay's potato chip advertising slogan (1963) by Young & Rubicam.

92 https://www.cnn.com/2019/04/25/business/pepsico-india-potato-farmer-lawsuit/index.html.

93 *Id.*

94 http://www.newindianexpress.com/opinions/2019/jun/08/lessons-from-pepsicos-farmer-lawsuit-1987474.html.

95 https://techcrunch.com/2017/05/04/why-we-stepped-up-to-the-patent-troll-problem/.

96 https://seekingalpha.com/filing/4484631#FORM10Q_HTM_LEGALPRO.

97 https://www.gandb.com/2019/05/legislative-update-massachusetts-proposes-patent-troll-act/.

98 Caroline Alexander, The Bounty: The True Story of the Mutiny on the Bounty. ISBN 0006532462.

99 Foreign and Commonwealth Office, Profile on Pitcairn Islands, British Overseas Territory, 11 February 2010.

100 News Release, Internet Suffix is returned to Pitcairn, Pitcairn Islands Study Center, February 21, 2000.

101 IANA Report on Request for Re-delegation of the .pn Top-Level Domain (February 11, 2000).

Develop Contracts That Create Value for Both Sides

Earlier chapters of this book link key stakeholders with the most important legal risks affecting business: customers and product liability (Chapter 4), employees and employment law (Chapter 5), government and regulatory law (Chapter 6), and investors and intellectual property (Chapter 7). We now turn to the two remaining top legal risks that recent surveys have identified: contracts (in this chapter) and dispute resolution (in Chapter 9). These risks involve processes that affect all stakeholders.

Any business, whether a startup or a major international corporation, relies on a web of contracts with stakeholders that include creditors, customers, employees, investors, and suppliers. As a result, business leaders must understand the fundamentals of contract law that are covered in the next section. The chapter will then turn to the Law Pillar and managing contract risks. The final section of the chapter aligns the Strategy Pillar with the Law Pillar by examining lean contracting and contract visualization.

LEGAL BRIEFING ON CONTRACTS

Perspectives on Contract Law

In essence, a contract is an agreement that is enforceable by law. We all enter into many agreements that are not legally enforceable. For example, you and I can strongly agree that a certain movie is the worst one we have ever seen, but our agreement is not enforceable in court. Contract law provides a framework for determining which of our agreements are enforceable.

Three perspectives are useful when thinking about contract law. First, there is a global perspective. In the global world of business, the rule of law is critically important when making business decisions. No legal rules are more important than contract law because contracts establish your rights and duties in business deals. Your first question when making investments in any country should be: will my contract rights be respected and enforced in this country?

Second, from a company perspective, contracts are the key to business success. All other company activities—accounting, marketing, finance, strategy, and so on—are futile if your contracts are not profitable. Within companies, value is created during contract negotiations. And companies can fail when these negotiations do not produce successful results.

Third, from a personal perspective, contracts (both written and unwritten) permeate our daily lives. Whether these contracts involve the simple purchase of a meal or more complex transactions such as buying a house, they represent an important aspect of our interactions with other humans.

Because contracts are so common in our business and personal lives, we need a fundamental understanding of the sources of contract law and the four key elements that determine whether a contract has been formed. We now turn to those topics.

Understand the Sources of Contract Law

When you are involved in a negotiation and a contract law question arises, where can you find the answer? Two key questions determine the source of contract law. First, are you in civil law country or common law country? Second, what type of contract are you negotiating?

Type of Legal System. Although contract law in a globalized economy has become increasingly similar from country to country, differences still exist. The industrialized world is split between countries that have a civil law system and those with a common law system. Before beginning any contract negotiation, you should know which system governs your contract.

Generally, civil law countries include continental European countries and the former colonies of those countries. In civil law countries, the principles of law are found primarily in a "code"—in effect, an encyclopedia of law. In contrast, common law countries (generally England and its former colonies) rely more heavily on previously-decided cases—that is, "precedents"—as a source of law.

The distinction between civil law and common law countries is especially important because the legal requirements for a valid contract differ in some ways between the systems. For example, civil law does not include the consideration requirement discussed in the next section.

Apart from differences in legal requirements, some practitioners have observed that common law contracts are lengthier because lawyers attempt to anticipate every possible scenario that might arise when a contract is performed. Civil law contracts, in contrast, are shorter because the contracts can simply refer to provisions from the code. Even in civil law countries, however, there is a trend toward longer contracts because the two systems often blend together when negotiations cross national borders.

Type of Contract. The second variable relating to the source of contract law requires understanding the type of contract you are negotiating. For example, let's assume that you manufacture golf equipment. I am negotiating with you the purchase of one hundred putters, which I want to sell in my store. We reach an agreement on all the details except the price. Do we have a contract?

Under traditional common law, which governs the sale of real estate and services, price was a key element in forming a contract. However, our contract involves what lawyers call the sale of "goods." In the United States, the Uniform Commercial Code or, as it is commonly called in business negotiations, the UCC, governs the sale of goods. The UCC has modernized contract law. For example, if you intend to form a contract but have not said anything about price, the UCC provides that "the price is a reasonable price at the time of delivery" of the putters.

The situation becomes more complicated if you are negotiating an international contract. The good news is that ninety-two countries, including the United States, have ratified a treaty called the United Nations Convention on Contracts for the International Sale of Goods (known in business circles as the CISG). A uniform international sales law is a tremendous achievement that facilitates international trade.

The bad news is that some of the rules in the CISG differ from the UCC. For example, some experts have concluded that under the CISG the price must be stated or the contract must include a provision for determining the price.[1]

Use a Four-Part Contract Checklist

We now turn to the four key elements necessary to create a legally-enforceable contract. These elements represent a checklist for you to use in your future contract negotiations.

1.   **Reach an Agreement.** The requirement that parties reach an agreement is fairly straightforward. One party makes an offer; the other party accepts the offer. The offer should demonstrate serious intent, include specific terms, and be

communicated to a party who can accept the offer. In essence, the offer creates the power of acceptance in the person to whom the offer is made.

In the case below, business student John Leonard was in a situation that illustrates what constitutes a legitimate offer that creates a power of acceptance and how important this concept is to the formation of an enforceable contract.

STRATEGY	
LAW	***Three Pillars Case: The Pepsi Generation Gets Serious***
ETHICS	

Citation: *Leonard v. Pepsico, Inc.*, 88 F.Supp.2d 116 (1999)

The beverage company Pepsico started a promotional campaign in the mid-1990s that allowed customers purchasing Pepsi products to earn points toward the purchase of merchandise. A Pepsi commercial showing a teenager flying a Harrier jet—supposedly obtained through Pepsi points— spurred twenty-one-year-old John Leonard to gather points, capital, and investors to make a claim for the aircraft, valued at about $33 million.

This case arises out of a promotional campaign conducted by defendant, the producer and distributor of the soft drinks Pepsi and Diet Pepsi. The promotion, entitled "Pepsi Stuff," encouraged consumers to collect "Pepsi Points" from specially marked packages of Pepsi or Diet Pepsi and redeem these points for merchandise featuring the Pepsi logo. Before introducing the promotion nationally, defendant conducted a test of the promotion in the Pacific Northwest from October 1995 to March 1996. . . . While living in Seattle, plaintiff saw the Pepsi Stuff commercial he contends constituted an offer of a Harrier Jet.

. . . The commercial opens upon an idyllic, suburban morning, where the chirping of birds in sun-dappled trees welcomes a paperboy on his morning route. As the newspaper hits the stoop of a conventional two-story house, the tattoo of a military drum introduces the subtitle, "MONDAY 7:58 AM." The stirring strains of a martial air mark the appearance of a well-coiffed teenager preparing to leave for school, dressed in a shirt emblazoned with the Pepsi logo, a red-white-and-blue ball. While the teenager confidently preens, the military drumroll again sounds as the subtitle "T-SHIRT 75 PEPSI POINTS" scrolls across the screen. Bursting from his room, the teenager strides down the hallway wearing a leather jacket. The drumroll sounds again, as the subtitle "LEATHER JACKET 1450 PEPSI POINTS" appears. The teenager opens the door of his house and, unfazed by the glare of the early morning sunshine, puts on a pair of sunglasses. The drumroll then accompanies the subtitle "SHADES 175 PEPSI POINTS." A voiceover then intones, "Introducing the new Pepsi Stuff catalog," as the camera focuses on the cover of the catalog.

The scene then shifts to three young boys sitting in front of a high school building. The boy in the middle is intent on his Pepsi Stuff Catalog, while the boys on either side are each drinking Pepsi. The three boys gaze in awe at an object rushing overhead, as the military march builds to a crescendo. The Harrier Jet is not yet visible, but the observer senses the presence of a mighty plane as the extreme winds generated by its flight create a paper maelstrom in a classroom devoted to an otherwise dull physics lesson. Finally, the Harrier Jet swings into view and lands by the side of the school building, next to a bicycle rack. Several students run for cover, and the velocity of the wind strips one hapless faculty member down to his underwear. While the faculty member is being deprived of his dignity, the voiceover announces: "Now the more Pepsi you drink, the more great stuff you're gonna get."

The teenager opens the cockpit of the fighter and can be seen, helmetless, holding a Pepsi. "[L]ooking very pleased with himself," the teenager exclaims, "Sure beats the bus," and chortles. The military drumroll sounds a final time, as the following words appear: "HARRIER FIGHTER 7,000,000 PEPSI POINTS." A few seconds later, the following appears in more stylized script: "Drink Pepsi — Get Stuff." With that message, the music and the commercial end with a triumphant flourish.

Inspired by this commercial, plaintiff set out to obtain a Harrier Jet. Plaintiff explains that he is "typical of the 'Pepsi Generation'. . . [H]e is young, has an adventurous spirit, and the notion of obtaining a Harrier Jet appealed to him enormously." Plaintiff consulted the Pepsi Stuff Catalog. . . . The Catalog specifies the number of Pepsi Points required to obtain promotional merchandise. The Catalog includes an Order Form which lists, on one side, fifty-three items of Pepsi Stuff merchandise redeemable for Pepsi Points. Conspicuously absent from the Order Form is any entry or description of a Harrier Jet.

The rear foldout pages of the Catalog contain directions for redeeming Pepsi Points for merchandise. . . . The Catalog notes that in the event that a consumer lacks enough Pepsi Points to obtain a desired item, additional Pepsi Points may be purchased for ten cents each; however, at least fifteen original Pepsi Points must accompany each order.

. . . On or about March 27, 1996, plaintiff submitted an Order Form, fifteen original Pepsi Points, and a check for $700,008.50. . . . At the bottom of the Order

Form, plaintiff wrote in "1 Harrier Jet" in the "Item" column and "7,000,000" in the "Total Points" column.

On or about May 7, 1996, defendant's fulfillment house rejected plaintiff's submission and returned the check, explaining that: *The item that you have requested is not part of the Pepsi Stuff collection. It is not included in the catalogue or on the order form, and only catalogue merchandise can be redeemed under this program. The Harrier jet in the Pepsi commercial is fanciful and is simply included to create a humorous and entertaining ad. We apologize for any misunderstanding or confusion that you may have experienced and are enclosing some free product coupons for your use.*

Plaintiff . . . responded on or about May 14, 1996, as follows: *Your letter of May 7, 1996 is totally unacceptable. We have reviewed the video tape of the Pepsi Stuff commercial . . . and it clearly offers the new Harrier jet for 7,000,000 Pepsi Points. . . .*

. . . Plaintiff's understanding of the commercial as an offer must . . . be rejected because the Court finds that no objective person could reasonably have concluded that the commercial actually offered consumers a Harrier Jet.

. . . If it is clear that an offer was not serious, then no offer has been made: What kind of act creates a power of acceptance and is therefore an offer? It must be an expression of will or intention. It must be an act that leads the offeree reasonably to conclude that a power to create a contract is conferred. This applies to the content of the power as well as to the fact of its existence. It is on this ground that we must exclude invitations to deal or acts of mere preliminary negotiation, and acts evidently done in jest or without intent to create legal relations. An obvious joke, of course, would not give rise to a contract.

. . . Plaintiff's insistence that the commercial appears to be a serious offer requires the Court to explain why the commercial is funny. Explaining why a joke is funny is a daunting task; as the essayist E.B. White has remarked, "Humor can be dissected, as a frog can, but the thing dies in the process. . . ." The commercial is the embodiment of what defendant appropriately characterizes as "zany humor."

First, the commercial suggests, as commercials often do, that use of the advertised product will transform what, for most youth, can be a fairly routine and ordinary experience. . . . The implication of the commercial is that Pepsi Stuff merchandise will inject drama and moment into hitherto unexceptional lives. The commercial in this case thus makes the exaggerated claims similar to those of many television advertisements: that by consuming the featured clothing, car, beer, or potato chips, one will become attractive, stylish, desirable, and admired by all. A reasonable viewer would understand such advertisements as mere puffery, not as statements of fact.

. . . Second, the callow youth featured in the commercial is a highly improbable pilot, one who could barely be trusted with the keys to his parents' car, much less the prize aircraft of the United States Marine Corps.

. . . Third, the notion of traveling to school in a Harrier Jet is an exaggerated adolescent fantasy.

. . . Fourth, the primary mission of a Harrier Jet, according to the United States Marine Corps, is to "attack and destroy surface targets under day and night visual conditions." In light of the Harrier Jet's well-documented function in attacking and destroying surface and air targets, armed reconnaissance and air interdiction, and offensive and defensive anti-aircraft warfare, depiction of such a jet as a way to get to school in the morning is clearly not serious even if, as plaintiff contends, the jet is capable of being acquired "in a form that eliminates [its] potential for military use."

. . . Fifth, the number of Pepsi Points the commercial mentions as required to "purchase" the jet is 7,000,000. To amass that number of points, one would have to drink 7,000,000 Pepsis (or roughly 190 Pepsis a day for the next hundred years — an unlikely possibility), or one would have to purchase approximately $700,000 worth of Pepsi Points. The cost of a Harrier Jet is roughly $23 million dollars, a fact of which plaintiff was aware when he set out to gather the amount he believed necessary to accept the alleged offer. Even if an objective, reasonable person were not aware of this fact, he would conclude that purchasing a fighter plane for $700,000 is a deal too good to be true.

. . . For the reasons stated above, the Court grants defendant's motion for summary judgment.

THREE PILLARS CASE QUESTIONS

(1)   The advertising company that designed the commercial replied to John Leonard in this way:

> *I find it hard to believe that you are of the opinion that the Pepsi Stuff commercial really offers a new Harrier Jet. The use of the Jet was clearly a joke that was meant to make the Commercial more humorous and entertaining. In my opinion, no reasonable person would agree with your analysis of the Commercial.*[2]

Do you agree with the advertising agency or John Leonard?

(2)   The requirements of an offer are: serious intent, specific terms, and communication to the offeree. We know that the court stated there was no serious

intent. What about the other elements—specific terms and communication? Do you believe these elements were present?

(3)   After the Leonard lawsuit was filed, Pepsi changed the number of points advertised for the Harrier jet from seven million to seven hundred million. What do you believe was their intent in making the change?

(4)   Do you agree with Pepsi's advertising strategy? While Pepsi avoided legal liability, is its strategy ethical?

———————

In many cases, common sense dictates whether a contract has been formed, as illustrated by facts adapted from a case in China. Let's assume that on Monday, a store sent an offer to purchase televisions to a manufacturer, with delivery to be made to the store. On Wednesday, the manufacturer sent a reply accepting the offer but added that the store had to pick up the televisions at the factory. On Friday, the store agreed to this change. When the price of televisions dropped, the store claimed that there was no contract. Is there a contract?

A common-sense analysis is that the store made an offer on Monday, but the manufacturer's so-called "acceptance" was not a legal acceptance because it revised the terms of the offer by changing the place of delivery. This made the manufacturer's communication a counteroffer, which legally is a rejection of the offer. The store accepted the counteroffer on Friday, which created a contract. (For reasons too complicated to address here, under the UCC, acceptance possibly occurred on Wednesday. But in any event, there is a contract.)

Preliminary documents. Negotiators often use a preliminary document during contract negotiations. This type of document (often called a memorandum of understanding, a memorandum of agreement, a letter of intent, or an agreement in principle) is a useful negotiating tool in complex negotiations when the two sides have difficulty reducing their negotiated agreement into writing. Even in a simple negotiation, such as renting an apartment, a preprinted lease is a useful tool for converting a negotiation into a legal agreement.

Using preliminary documents carries a major risk, however, in that a court might conclude that the documents have morphed into a binding contract as they became more detailed. A simple way to designate that the contract has not been finalized is to imprint the word "DRAFT" at some location on each page; many word processing programs provide access to a watermark for this purpose.

This risk might also affect third parties. For example, several years ago, Pennzoil negotiated a memorandum of agreement to acquire Getty Oil. When Texaco later entered into a separate contract to purchase Getty Oil, Pennzoil claimed that its memorandum of agreement was actually a binding contract and that Texaco's actions interfered with Pennzoil's contract rights. In a subsequent trial, the jury agreed with Pennzoil in deciding that Texaco owed $10.5 billion in damages.

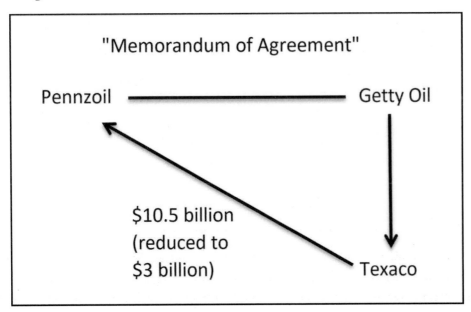

This was the largest verdict ever to be upheld on appeal. When this judgment drove Texaco into bankruptcy, the two companies reached a settlement agreement whereby Texaco paid Pennzoil "only" $3 billion. The Pennzoil attorney later recounted: "We celebrated that night [after winning the case] at my house by eating hamburgers and drinking beer. I've still got the $3 billion deposit slip on my wall."[3]

2.   Give up Something as Consideration. Consideration is a requirement under common law. While consideration has a technical legal definition, in everyday language it means that for a deal to be legally binding, both sides must give up something of value. For example, if a graduate promises to donate $20 million to her university in a written, signed agreement, the agreement is generally not binding unless the university promises to give up something in return. The "something" of value does not need to be significant; you may have noticed legal notices in the newspaper listing the conveyance of property—worth a considerable sum of money—for a single dollar. The sale is often to a family member and is intended to do nothing more than add consideration to the contract, making it legally enforceable.

In most business transactions, consideration is not a concern because both sides promise to give up something of value. One side promises to provide a service or a product, and the other side promises to make payment.

However, the risk of not meeting the consideration requirement increases when a contract is modified. Let's assume that you, as a contractor, promise to remodel a building for a customer by a certain date and the customer promises to pay you $30,000. The two promises represent your mutual consideration.

At your request, the customer promises in writing to give you a one-month extension, but you do not give the customer anything in exchange for this extension. Technically, the customer's promise is not binding unless you provide additional consideration for the one-month extension.

What constitutes consideration was established long ago in some early contract cases, such as the classic case that follows.

STRATEGY LAW ETHICS	***Three Pillars Case: Promises, Promises***

Citation: *Hamer v. Sidway*, 79 Sickels 538 (1891)

In this case, young Willie Story was asked by his uncle to refrain from drinking, smoking, swearing, and gambling in exchange for the sum of $5,000 to be paid when he turned twenty-

one years old. The trial court determined that no contract was formed between the parties, and the money was merely an undelivered "gift." While we often think of legal consideration in classic terms of money or property, this case was one of the first to introduce a novel form of consideration.

PARKER, J.

The question which provoked the most discussion by counsel on this appeal, and which lies at the foundation of plaintiff's asserted right of recovery, is whether by virtue of a contract defendant's testator, William E. Story, became indebted to his nephew, William E. Story, 2d, on his twenty-first birthday in the sum of $5,000. The trial court found as a fact that 'on the 20th day of March, 1869. . . . William E. Story agreed to and with William E. Story, 2d, that if he would refrain from drinking liquor using tobacco, swearing, and playing cards or billiards for money until should become twenty-one years of age, then he, the said William E. Story, would at that time pay him, the said William E. Story, 2d, the sum of $5,000 for such refraining, to which the said William E. Story, 2d, agreed,' and that he 'in all things fully performed his part of said agreement.' The defendant contends that the contract was without consideration to support it, and therefore invalid. He asserts that the promisee, by refraining from the use of liquor and tobacco, was not harmed, but benefited; that that which he did was best for him to do, independently of his uncle's promise,—and insists that it follows that, unless the promisor was benefited, the contract was without consideration,—a contention which, if well founded, would seem to leave open for controversy in many cases whether that which the promisee did or omitted to do was in fact of such benefit to him as to leave no consideration to support the enforcement of the promisor's agreement.

. . . The exchequer chamber in 1875 defined 'consideration' as follows: 'A valuable consideration, in the sense of the law, may consist either in some right, interest, profit, or benefit accruing to the one party, or some forbearance, detriment, loss, or responsibility given, suffered, or undertaken by the other.'

. . . 'Consideration' means not so much that one party is profiting as that the other abandons some legal right in the present, or limits his legal freedom of action in the future, as an inducement for the promise of the first.' Now, applying this rule to the facts before us, the promisee used tobacco, occasionally drank liquor, and he had a legal right to do so. That right he abandoned for a period of years upon the strength of the promise of the testator that for such forbearance he would give him $5,000. We need not speculate on the effort which may have been required to give up the use of those stimulants. It is sufficient that he restricted his lawful freedom of action within certain prescribed limits upon the faith of his uncle's agreement, and now, having fully performed the conditions imposed, it is of no moment whether such performance actually proved a benefit to the promisor, and the court will not inquire into it; but, were it a proper subject of inquiry, we see nothing in this record that would permit a determination that the uncle was not benefited in a legal sense.

. . . The order appealed from should be reversed, and the judgment of the special term affirmed, with costs payable out of the estate. All concur.

THREE PILLARS CASE QUESTIONS

(1) After agreeing to pay his nephew the $5,000, Mr. Story died, and the money went into his estate. Why did the executor of the Story estate refuse to pay the nephew?

(2) Examine the definition of "consideration" in this decision. How does the nephew's conduct match this definition? Explain.

(3) The contract between Mr. Story and his nephew was an oral contract, reinforced by letters the two exchanged. Write up a simple contract between William E. Story (Uncle) and William E. Story II (Nephew) for the payment of $5,000 in exchange for refraining from the behavior detailed in the case. Remember to include all the details that might be important to enforcing the contract, including the consideration for *both* sides.

(4) You are the president of a university. You have developed a fundraising strategy in which you will ask the ten richest alumni to make gifts of over $1 million each. Based on the definition of consideration in this case, what could you add to your agreements with the alumni to make their gift promises legally binding on them? Is this addition to the agreements ethical?

––––––––––

3. Stay Within the Law. A contract that calls for violating a law is not enforceable. In many cases—for example, a contract to sell illegal drugs—this element is uncomplicated and easy to understand. In other situations, when a public policy might be violated, the law is more complex.

For example, your company might decide to protect confidential information by adopting a policy that requires current employees to sign so-called non-compete agreements. These agreements state that the employees cannot work for a competitor within three years after leaving your company.

States differ on the legality, and therefore the enforceability, of these non-compete agreements. In some states, these agreements might be illegal because they restrict the ability of your employees to obtain employment elsewhere because they are overly burdensome with respect to length of time or geographic scope. Even where the agreement is legal, in common law countries, the consideration element would require your company to give something to current employees in exchange for requiring them to sign the non-compete agreement.

4.   **Put Your Agreement in Writing.** Writing requirements raise important and complex concerns during negotiations. Both civil law and common law countries have rules providing that certain contracts must be in writing. Here are some typical examples of contracts that must be in writing under US law:

- Contracts for the sale of real estate

- Promises to pay the debts of others

- Agreements by an executor or administrator of an estate

- Promises made in exchange for a promise to marry

- Agreements that cannot be performed within one year

- Sales of goods for $500 or more

These rules carry a huge financial risk when you make an incorrect assumption about whether your agreement must be in writing. For example, you might miss a business opportunity because you thought that your oral agreement was binding when, in fact, the law requires a written contract. Or you might create an unintended liability because you thought that your oral agreement was not binding in a situation where the contract did not legally have to be in writing.

As a result, you should never enter into contract negotiations without understanding the rules about whether writing is required. Your understanding of the law should be supplemented by a practical strategy: when negotiating important contracts, make it clear that you are not bound until a written agreement is completed. This commitment to a writing also ensures that your contracts will align with your ethical obligations in contracting, as detailed in Codex #3 (Chapter 3): *Be faithful to your word and follow through on promises, agreements, and other voluntary undertakings, whether or not embodied in legally-enforceable contracts.* Although clarity in intentions is not 100 percent guaranteed by reduction to written form, the writing saves significant time and effort later if there is a disagreement or dispute.

There are two other reasons for this writing recommendation. First, by putting your agreement in writing you will not have to worry about the complex legal rules that determine whether the agreement must be written. Second, and perhaps more importantly, you will avoid the consequences of memory failure. Even when the law allows oral contracts, the two sides to a contract will often have different recollections of the details of their negotiation and agreement. Their views might differ about when the agreement starts, how long it continues, how it can be terminated, and so on. These memory problems are avoided when you sign a written agreement. Be guided by a Chinese proverb: "Even the palest ink is better than the best memory."

Parol Evidence Rule. A separate risk arises after you reduce your agreement to writing. To illustrate this risk, assume that you have just been hired by a company in a city distant from your own. During negotiations, the company promises to pay for your moving costs, but when the agreement is put into writing, this promise is not included. Are you legally entitled to moving costs, assuming that the company admits it made the promise?

Although the law varies from country to country, under the law of the United States and many other countries, the Parol Evidence Rule states that once you put your agreement into writing, evidence of prior or contemporaneous agreements (such as the company's promise to pay your moving costs) cannot be used as evidence if you decide to sue the company.

This rule makes sense because, when negotiating a contract, both sides might make many agreements that they later cast aside and don't intend to include in the final contract. If they were allowed to bring evidence of these agreements into court, courts would forever be reviewing and attempting to untangle the details of what happened during the negotiations.

Even when you negotiate a contract under the laws of a country that has not adopted the Parol Evidence Rule, it is likely that your contract will include a provision stating that the rule applies. These provisions appear under a variety of headings—for example, merger clause, integration clause, or entire agreement clause.

It is good practice to include one of these provisions, even when negotiating in countries that have adopted the Parol Evidence Rule, because the rule might not apply in all situations. For example, as mentioned, the United States has adopted the CISG, which does not include the rule. Therefore, if you enter into a contract for the international sale of goods governed by the CISG, evidence of prior agreements might be admissible in court unless you include a merger clause clearly stating that evidence outside the written contract is not admissible.

Here is an example of a typical contract provision (from the US Securities and Exchange Commission archives). In January 2012, Facebook founder Mark Zuckerberg signed a contract amending an earlier employment agreement naming him president and chief executive officer of the company. The agreement contained the following standard provisions:

1.   *Compensation.* Base wage of $500,000, along with a bonus provision. [This consideration was probably inconsequential to Zuckerberg. By 2020 Zuckerberg was worth an estimated $75 billion and was the 5th richest person in the world. When the contract was signed, he owned approximately 28 percent of Facebook stock.]

2.   *Employee benefits.* Up to 21 days of paid time off per year.

3.   *Confidentiality agreement.* Relates to a separate confidentiality and invention assignment agreement.

4.   *No conflicting obligations.* Prohibits oral or written agreements that conflict with company policy.

5.   *Outside activities.* No other business activity without the company's consent.

6.   *Zuckerberg's general obligations.* Includes honesty, integrity, loyalty, and professionalism.

7.   *At-will employment.* Can be fired at any time.

8.   *Withholdings.* Compensation is paid after subtracting withholding payments.

The contract concluded with this sentence: "This letter agreement supersedes and replaces any prior understandings or agreements, whether oral, written or implied, between you and the Company regarding the matters described in this letter."[4] Through this statement, Zuckerberg and Facebook have affirmed the Parol Evidence Rule.

Form of the writing. Contracts do not have to be printed in a formal document that says "Contract" at the top. Any writing will usually suffice—but this can be a trap. For example, two individuals were having some drinks at a restaurant. One of them, Lucy, offered to buy Zehmer's 472-acre farm for $50,000. Zehmer accepted the offer and wrote on a restaurant order form: "We hereby agree to sell to W.O. Lucy the Ferguson Farm complete for $50,000, title satisfactory to buyer." Zehmer and his wife signed the document.

Zehmer later reneged on the agreement, claiming that he thought Lucy was kidding. He also argued that he "was as high as a Georgia pine" and that the negotiation was between "two doggoned drunks bluffing to see who could talk the biggest." In deciding that Zehmer had to give up his farm because this was a valid contract, the court emphasized several factors that indicated that this was intended to be a serious business transaction, including the appearance and completeness of the contract.[5]

Implied terms. Whether or not your agreement is written, there might be additional terms implied by the law. For example, assume that you recently moved to the United States. Some friends want you to be the catcher on their baseball team. They tell you that the pitcher on the team throws a knuckleball pitch. You have never played baseball and have no idea what that means.

A local high school baseball coach is holding a garage sale and is selling some baseball gear. You visit the sale knowing that the seller is a baseball coach and tell him that you need a catcher's mitt that will catch knuckleballs. The coach points to a mitt while stating that it is the only catcher's mitt for sale. You then negotiate a price. After buying the mitt, you discover that it is much too small to catch knuckleballs. Can you sue the coach for breach of contract?

Although you never discussed it during the negotiation, the UCC (the law governing the sale of goods) provides that in these circumstances, a seller like the coach gives you an implied warranty that the item sold is fit for the particular purpose for which you need the product—in this case, catching knuckleballs. The coach is thus in breach of this implied warranty.

Another type of implied warranty is the implied warranty of merchantability, which is a very important rule for businesses because it can be involved in just about any transaction involving the sale of "goods"—that is, products. A good example is the next case, *Williams v. O'Charley's, Inc.*, where a chicken dinner was the merchandise.

STRATEGY
LAW   ***Three Pillars Case: Tastes Like Chicken***
ETHICS

Citation: *Williams v. O'Charley's, Inc.*, No. COA11-1467 (2012)

In this case, a patron of an O'Charley's restaurant in North Carolina suffered food poisoning after consuming dinner the night before. This case demonstrates that, whether written or verbal, contracts between a business and its customers may contain terms implied by law.

Court of Appeals of North Carolina

Michael Williams (plaintiff) ate dinner at an O'Charley's restaurant (defendant) in Concord on 18 March 2008. At about 8:15 p.m., plaintiff ordered grilled chicken, rice, and a baked potato. The food arrived about 45 minutes later. The chicken had a bad aftertaste, stuck to the plate, and was dry. No other member of plaintiff's dining party ate chicken. By 8 a.m. the next morning, plaintiff was suffering from severe diarrhea and vomiting. Plaintiff did not eat any other food on 18 March 2008. He was admitted to Rowan Regional Medical Center on 21 March 2008. Plaintiff was hospitalized for seven days under the treatment of Dr. Christopher McIltrot.

Plaintiff brought this action seeking monetary damages for negligence and breach of an implied warranty of merchantability on 22 July 2009. A jury returned a verdict in favor of defendant on the negligence claim, but in favor of plaintiff on the claim for breach of an implied warranty of merchantability, and awarded $140,000 in damages for personal injuries.

. . . "[A] warranty that goods shall be merchantable is implied in a contract for their sale if the seller is a merchant with respect to goods of that kind." N.C. Gen.Stat. § 25–2–314(1) (2011). To be merchantable, goods must be "fit for the ordinary purposes for which such goods are used." N.C. Gen.Stat. § 25–2–314(2)(c) (2011).

To prove a breach of implied warranty of merchantability, a plaintiff must show (1) that the goods in question were subject to an implied warranty of merchantability; (2) that the goods were defective at the time of the sale and as such did not comply with the warranty; (3) that the resulting injury was due to the defective nature of the goods; and (4) that damages were suffered.

. . . Because of the dearth of North Carolina cases concerning food poisoning and the implied warranty of merchantability, we examine precedent from other jurisdictions.

In Sneed v. Beaverson . . . (Okla.1964), the plaintiff testified that she ate a steak at the defendant's grill, became ill, and was in the hospital for two days. Her doctor testified that "assuming the correctness of the [plaintiff's] history," it was his opinion, with reasonable certainty, that her injury came from the meat she ate.

. . . In Snead v. Waite . . . (Ky.1948), the plaintiff purchased barbecued mutton from the defendant and ate it with bread. By the next day, the plaintiff and his family were violently ill, suffering from nausea, vomiting, cramping, and diarrhea. Id. The Court of Appeals of Kentucky held that the evidence "amply proved all of the elements of an implied warranty."

In Johnson v. Kanavos . . . (Mass.1937), the plaintiffs noticed a peculiar taste in the frankfurter sandwiches they purchased from the defendant. All of the plaintiffs became sick within four hours. The Supreme Judicial Court of Massachusetts held that the evidence was adequate to support a finding in favor of the plaintiffs. "Evidence of the presence of a peculiar taste in food has some probative significance on the issue whether the food was unwholesome and the cause of a subsequent illness of a person eating it."

In Barringer v. Ocean S.S. Co. . . . (Mass.1922), the plaintiff alleged that food served on the defendant's vessel caused the plaintiff to suffer vomiting and cramps. The plaintiff ate some cold meat that did not "taste very good" to him. The Supreme Judicial Court of Massachusetts held that the evidence "was very meager; but the credibility of the witnesses was for the trial judge, and if he believed them he could find that the plaintiff's case was proved."

We hold the legal reasoning of these cases to be persuasive.

In the instant case, plaintiff testified that the chicken had a bad aftertaste, stuck to the plate, and was dry as though it had been under a heat lamp. Plaintiff got sick within several hours after eating the chicken. Plaintiff did not eat any other food on 18 March 2008. Dr. McIltrot testified that the chicken was likely the cause of his symptoms. Dr. McIltrot testified that he eliminated other possible causes of the injury by performing medical tests and procedures, including a laparoscopy.

Plaintiff suffered from no pre-existing conditions that would account for these symptoms. Plaintiff ate the chicken at approximately 9:00 p.m. on 18 March 2008, and ate nothing else that night. Plaintiff began suffering from severe vomiting and diarrhea at 8:00 a.m. the next day. Taking all of the evidence in the light most favorable to the plaintiff, sufficient circumstantial evidence was presented of a defect in the chicken to warrant submission of the case to the jury.

. . . AFFIRMED.

THREE PILLARS CASE QUESTIONS

(1)   What elements are required for a plaintiff to prove a violation of implied warranty? What evidence can you locate within the decision that supports each element in Mr. Williams' case?

(2)   In addition to the court-ordered damages that O'Charley's must remit to the plaintiff, what other actions could or should the company take with regard to the plaintiff and other patrons following this incident?

(3)   What strategic and legal steps could the company take to avoid a future breach of warranty?

THE LAW PILLAR:
CONTRACT RISK MANAGEMENT

Business contracts are defined as value-creating agreements enforceable by law. For example, when you enter into a contract with a supplier, you anticipate that the supplier's product will enable you to increase the value of your own products, which in turn is passed on to your customers.

Traditionally, lawyers have focused on the "enforceable by law" part of the contract definition. Their goal is to construct legally-perfect, enforceable agreements that minimize legal risk. The lawyers' orientation is not surprising, given their mindset. Lawyers are trained to look at contracts through the eyes of a judge who might eventually rule on a contract dispute.[6] Thus, a good contract, from the lawyers' perspective, is one that minimizes the client's risk and is enforceable in court.

In meeting their risk management goals, lawyers focus on contract provisions designed to protect their clients. A leading international association of contract negotiators, the International Association for Contract and Commercial Management (IACCM), conducts an annual survey of thousands of its members (from both common law and civil law countries) to determine the contract terms that are most negotiated. In its latest survey, the two most negotiated terms both relate to risk management: limitation of liability and indemnification clauses. Limitation of liability clauses limit the damages a party to a contract can recover for actions by the other side that cause harm.[7] Here is an example of a clause that a design professional might want to include in a contract:

> The Design Professional, and its consultants, partners, agents and employees, shall not be liable to the Owner, whether jointly, severally or individually, in excess of the compensation paid to the Design Professional under this Agreement, or in excess of the sum of $[ ], whichever is greater, as a result of any act or omission not amounting to a willful or intentional wrong.[8]

Indemnification clauses are agreements to accept responsibility for certain acts. For example, if you license your software to a licensee, you would want to include in the contract a clause such as the following, which requires the licensee to cover you for losses resulting from using the software.

> Licensee shall hold harmless and indemnify Board, System, University, its Regents, officers, employees and agents from and against any claims, demands, or causes of action whatsoever, including without limitation those arising on account of any injury or death of persons or damage to property caused by, or arising out of, or resulting from, the exercise or practice of the license granted hereunder by Licensee, its Subsidiaries or their officers, employees, agents, or representatives.[9]

For examples of other types of risk management clauses, review the Facebook provisions in the contract with Mark Zuckerberg that was summarized earlier. They include confidentiality, inventions, conflicts of interest, outside activities, and employment-at-will.

ALIGN STRATEGY AND LAW: USE CONTRACTS TO CREATE VALUE

As noted in the previous section, business contracts are value-creating agreements that are enforceable by law. While "enforceable by law" is important and cannot be ignored, legal risk management must be balanced with the "value-creating agreement" part of the definition. In other words, while you want your agreements to be enforceable, you also want contracts that enable you to achieve your business goals. As law professors Ian Macneil and Paul Gudel note in their book *Contracts: Exchange Transactions and Relations* (2002), "only lawyers and other trouble-oriented folk look on contracts primarily as a source of trouble and disputation, rather than a way of getting things done."

This section explains two approaches you can use to reconcile the tension between the Strategy Pillar (with its emphasis on value creation) and Law Pillar (with its emphasis on risk management): (1) a lean contracting strategy that reshapes the content of contracts and (2) visualization, which is designed to make legal concepts more understandable.

Simplify Your Contracts Through Lean Contracting

A lean contracting strategy might enable you to focus on creating value while minimizing legal complexity. This strategy applies lean production concepts to the "manufacture" of contracts by asking whether company contracts can be simplified by considering the costs and benefits of various contract clauses.

For example, the in-house legal team at the brewing company Scottish & Newcastle sensed that company resources were being wasted in the contract negotiation process. Their work in developing what they call the *Pathclearer* approach to commercial contracting—a form of lean contracting—illustrates the potential benefits of reorienting contracting strategy. Unless otherwise noted, the quotations in this chapter regarding this approach are from a highly-recommended article by Weatherley titled "Pathclearer—A more commercial approach to drafting commercial contracts."[10]

Purpose of a contract. The Scottish & Newcastle lawyers initially asked three fundamental questions. First, what is the purpose of a contract? In answering this question, they used a traditional definition of a legal contract:

> [T]he only purpose of a contract... is to ensure that rights and obligations which the parties agree to can be enforced in court (or arbitration). Put even more bluntly, the essence of a contract is the ability to force someone else to do something they don't want to do, or to obtain compensation for their failure.

With this definition in mind, they realized that certain terms, such as product specifications, should always be in writing and that certain types of deals, such as "share purchases, loan agreements, and guarantees," require detailed written contracts.

But they also realized that many other scenarios—for example, a long-term relationship between a customer and supplier—call for a "much lighter legal touch." They recognized that in these situations, the consequences of forcing contractual obligations on an unwilling partner through "begrudging performance" or litigation are not attractive.

They concluded that leaving long-term relationships to "free market economics [is better than an] attempt to place continuing contractual obligations on each other." In other words, freedom of the market should dominate the traditional freedom of contract philosophy that has led to detailed written contracts.[11]

Drawbacks of traditional detailed contracts. The second of the lawyers' three fundamental questions focused on the risks associated with traditional, law-oriented contracts: "What are the drawbacks of detailed written contracts?" In answering this question, the in-house lawyers reached six insightful conclusions.

1. *Illusory and costly attempts to reach certainty.* "The apparent certainty and protection of a detailed written contract. . . [are] often illusory" and wasteful as companies pay their lawyers, first for drafting contracts that only the lawyers understand, and second for interpreting what the contracts mean.

The in-house legal team witnessed "bizarre attempts" by lawyers attempting to reach certainty. For example, external lawyers spent "hours drafting and debating the precise legal definition of beer for insertion in a simple beer supply agreement." The legal team also recognized the futility of trying to predict the future.

2. *Dispute resolution.* Detailed contracts can result in legalistic dispute resolution. As the lawyers observed:

> Without a detailed contract, business people who become involved in a dispute will generally discuss the issue and reach a sensible agreement on how to resolve it. . . . However, where a detailed contract exists, the same parties will feel obliged to consult their lawyers.

3. *Complexity.* The complexity of contracts causes confusion and creates a risk that the parties will be unable to focus on key terms; indeed, it becomes "difficult to see the wood for the trees."

4. *Unnecessary terms.* The general law of contracts provides "a fair middle-ground solution to most issues" and "[t]he beauty of simply relying on the 'general law,' rather than trying to set out the commercial arrangement in full in a detailed written contract, is that there is no need to negotiate the non-key terms of a deal."

5.   *Expense.* Negotiating detailed written contracts is expensive in terms of management time, lawyer time, and delayed business opportunities.

6.   *Wrong focus.* Detailed written contracts can cause the parties to focus on worst-case scenarios that "can lead to the souring of relationships. . . . [C]ontinuing business relationships are like butterflies. They are subtle and hard to capture. When you do try to nail them down, you can kill them in the process."

The lawyers might have added to this list the concerns that arise when negotiating with individuals from other cultures. For example, in countries such as China, developing a relationship with someone you trust is more important than trying to cover all contingencies in a lengthy contract.

The "wrong focus" problem (#6 above) is illustrated by the IACCM surveys mentioned previously. As noted earlier, the surveys conclude that the *most negotiated* contract provisions relate to risk management. But those most negotiated clauses are not on the latest list of *most important* terms listed here:

1.   Scope and goals

2.   Responsibilities of the parties

3.   Price

4.   Delivery/acceptance

5.   Service levels

In other words, the provisions considered most important for contract creation and enforcement receive less attention from negotiators than do less important clauses oriented toward risk management.

Other ways to achieve business goals. The third and final question the in-house legal team asked is whether negotiators can achieve their business goals without detailed written contracts. The Scottish & Newcastle lawyers answered this question affirmatively by focusing on the concept of "commercial affinity."

Commercial affinity is the force that keeps parties together in "mutually beneficial commercial relationships." Aligning the parties' interests through carefully-constructed incentives, combined with the right of either side to walk away from the deal if it ceases to be attractive economically, incentivizes them to meet the other side's needs and alleviates the need for "a myriad of tactical rights and obligations in a contract."

In summary, the Scottish & Newcastle lawyers realized that a different approach is appropriate "when the parties are in a continuing business relationship, rather than just carrying out a snapshot transaction" that might require a detailed written contract. They do not advocate, however, a complete return to handshake agreements. For example, "exit arrangements (such as obligations to buy dedicated assets from the supplier. . .) do need to be spelled out in the contract." By focusing on the three fundamental questions, they realized that in many other situations leaner contracts were possible.

A lean contract that the company negotiated with a service provider illustrates the company's Pathclearer approach in a continuing business relationship. The two parties initially had a ten-year contract that consumed more than two hundred pages. During contract renegotiations, they used the Pathclearer approach to reduce the size of the contract significantly by giving each party termination rights after twelve months' notice—in essence, a mutual "nuclear button."

> By giving ourselves the ability to terminate at any time, we avoided the need to have to negotiate detailed terms in the contract. . . . This is a much more powerful way of influencing the service provider than a technical debate over whether they were complying with the words set out in the contract.[12]

The following figure illustrates a contract between a US beer company (Coors) and one of its bottle suppliers—twenty-three pages plus eight pages of exhibits.

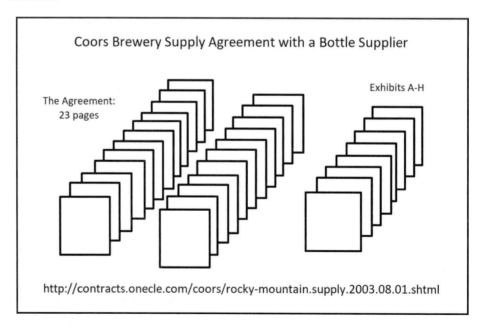

Coors Brewery Supply Agreement with a Bottle Supplier

The Agreement: 23 pages

Exhibits A-H

http://contracts.onecle.com/coors/rocky-mountain.supply.2003.08.01.shtml

Contrast the Coors contract with a Scottish & Newcastle Pathclearer contract with one of its bottle suppliers—one page plus one attachment.

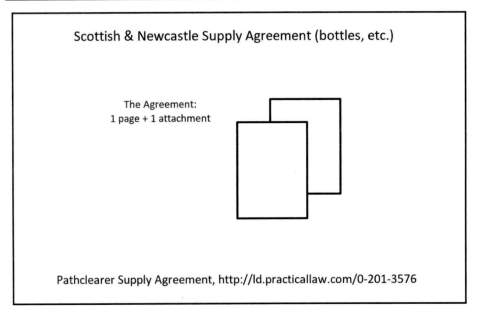

Scottish & Newcastle Supply Agreement (bottles, etc.)

The Agreement:
1 page + 1 attachment

Pathclearer Supply Agreement, http://ld.practicallaw.com/0-201-3576

Use Visualization to Understand Your Negotiations and Contracts

As the above two diagrams illustrate, a picture can be worth a thousand words. Using pictures and other forms of visualization can help you clarify your negotiation decisions and better understand the terms of the contract you are negotiating.

Visualizing negotiation decisions. In making your contracts leaner, you might be able to eliminate or soften certain provisions that cause expensive contract negotiations. Visualization can help you identify these provisions.

For example, an indemnity clause in Microsoft's contracts caused many contract negotiations to last an additional sixty to ninety days, because customers did not want to provide the indemnity Microsoft requested. Microsoft softened the provision after realizing that the benefits of the clause were minimal in contrast to potential costs such as reputational costs (resulting from confrontational negotiations), resource costs (managers' and lawyers' time), and cash flow costs (from delayed sales during the additional two to three months of contract negotiation).

In describing and commenting on these costs, Tim Cummins, CEO of IACCM, concluded that "risk management is about balancing consequence and probability. Here is an example where consequence was managed without regard to probability—and as a result, other risks and exposures [such as reputational and resource costs] became inevitable."[13]

Decision trees are useful in visualizing negotiation decisions that balance risk and probability, like Microsoft faced. Let's assume that the contract clause in question provided Microsoft with $20 million in indemnity, and there is a 1 percent chance that the company will lose $20 million and invoke the clause. (This probability can be estimated on the basis of your company's past experience. In practice, the chance that such a clause would be invoked is probably less than 1 percent.)

Let's also assume that management and lawyer time to negotiate the indemnity and cash flow costs resulting from delayed sales during negotiations total $1 million. In effect, Microsoft would pay $1 million for the equivalent of a $20 million insurance policy. Given these assumptions, should Microsoft pay $1 million for this insurance?

The following decision tree depicts the 1 percent chance that Microsoft will lose $20 million if it drops the indemnification clause demand and the 99 percent chance that it will lose nothing. This results in an expected value of –$200,000 (0.99 × 0 + 0.01 × $20 million). Based on these assumed values and probabilities (and not factoring in its attitude toward risk), Microsoft made a wise decision when it softened its negotiating stance.

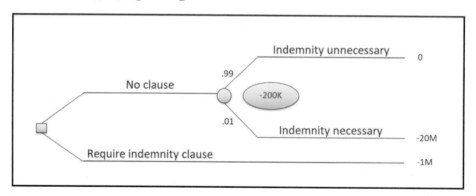

In this case, we assumed that Microsoft's negotiation costs were $1 million. Sometimes the lost opportunities relating to slow negotiations are much higher. For example, a prominent oil and gas attorney told author Siedel that he represented a company that negotiated the sale of property to a buyer for $30 million. Signing the contract was delayed when the buyer's law firm insisted on a clause that immunized the buyer from a low-probability event. As negotiations regarding this clause were in process, another buyer offered to pay more than $100 million for the property. The law firm's desire for a perfect legal contract cost the client more than $70 million!

Visualizing contract provisions
also help you understand the terms
documents. For example, contracts a
following, which challenge the cognitive s

> This Agreement shall be valid for an initial
> the date of signing. Unless either Party give
> least six (6) months before the expiry of the th
> remain in force until further notice, with a notice p
> (3) months. Notice shall be given in writing.[14]

In the following diagram, leaders in the visualization n
Passera and Helena Haapio show how visualization can clarify the
clause.

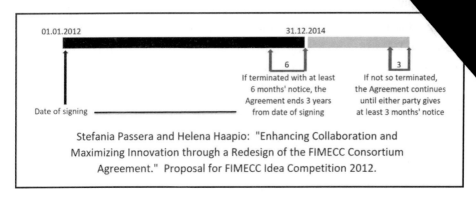

01.01.2012   31.12.2014

6   3

If terminated with at least   If not so terminated,
6 months' notice, the   the Agreement continues
Agreement ends 3 years   until either party gives
Date of signing   from date of signing   at least 3 months' notice

Stefania Passera and Helena Haapio: "Enhancing Collaboration and
Maximizing Innovation through a Redesign of the FIMECC Consortium
Agreement." Proposal for FIMECC Idea Competition 2012.

Another example illustrates the value of using visualization when dealing with other forms of complex legal documents. In 2013, Helena Haapio invited one of the authors (Siedel) to a Legal Design Jam—a design hackathon to visualize the Wikimedia Foundation's trademark policy. She was a facilitator, along with Stefania Passera, Margaret Hagen from Stanford, and Yana Welinder, Legal Counsel for the Foundation. The small group of participants included a mixture of designers and attorneys.

Before the redesign effort, the trademark policy was a typical densely-worded legal document. The end result of the Legal Design Jam was a revised policy that is colorful and clear: http://wikimediafoundation.org/wiki/Trademark_policy.

At this web address, a green checkmark is used to denote situations in which users can freely use marks, such as when they are used to discuss Wikimedia sites in literary works. An orange question mark is used in situations where permission is required (such as when you want "to use the Wikipedia logo in a movie"), and a red "x" indicates uses that are prohibited (for example, when you create a website that mimics a Wikimedia site).

ate Value for Both Sides

257

and other legal documents.** Visualization can

in a contract and in other legally complex

e often filled with clauses such as the

ills of negotiators:

period of three (3) years from

notice of termination at

ree-year period, it shall

riod of at least three

ovement Stefania

meaning of this

o business
ity, creates
e Strategy
pillars you

the
es a

ide
sts,

s.
e
u

and

.... In this Three

......ng a standard contract and reforming it according to

The Coors Brewing Company is a division of the third largest brewing organization in the world, Molson Coors. At the company's website, the brewer details its ideal relationship with vendors and suppliers:

> *Molson Coors Brewing Company wants to build winning relationships with our suppliers, vendors, distributors, and business partners. We are committed to doing business the right way by acting ethically, responsibly, and in compliance with the law. We achieve this by respecting human rights, demanding quality, and embracing diversity and inclusion. We have a responsibility to ourselves, the communities we live in, people we work with, customers we serve, and beer drinkers we seek to delight to always operate with integrity, honesty, and respect.*[16]

In accordance with Coors' interest in creating value through its supplier relationships, access its bottling contract at the following link and change it to a lean contract: https://contracts.onecle.com/coors/rocky-mountain.supply.2003.08.01.shtml.

For reference, consult the Pathclearer process of lean contracting by Scottish & Newcastle, which may be accessed at this link: http://www.clarity-international.net/documents/Pathclearer%20article%20in%20PLC-3.pdf.

VALUE GOAL: To simplify contracts and save company time and money.

STRATEGY: Use lean contracting principles to simplify the Coors contract.

LAW: Review the elements required for an enforceable contract. Does the lean contract you developed include all of the required legal elements?&0

ETHICS: Review the CODEX principles discussed in Chapter 3. Do lean contracting and the concept of "commercial affinity" align with any of the principles outlined there? How does the strategy of lean contracting create value for a company? In your ethics analysis of the lean contract you created, work through these four steps of ethical decision making: (1) describe the ethical dilemma, (2) identify the stakeholders involved, (3) analyze options (including how each group of stakeholders will be affected), and (4) make a decision based on your analysis. After examining ethical issues associated with the strategy, determine whether any modifications should be made.

&0*Check for law research materials in the Appendix: Legal Resources for Business Decisions*

STRATEGY LAW ETHICS	***Three Pillars Decision: Think Food and Morality***

When establishing a relationship through contracting, it is important for both parties to protect themselves in the event of a disagreement over morality. In this disagreement, the provision left out of the contract—a morals clause—is nearly as important as what is included.

In 2015, Chef Jose Andres pulled out of a deal to develop a Spanish restaurant in then-presidential candidate Donald Trump's Washington, DC Old Post Office Building hotel. The plan for Andres' Think Food Group company was to place and operate an upscale restaurant named *Topo Atrio* within the international luxury hotel. The world-famous chef refused to continue with the project after Trump disparaged Mexicans as "rapists" and "drug dealers," saying, "The perception that Mr. Trump's statements were anti-Hispanic made it very difficult to recruit appropriate staff for a Hispanic restaurant, to attract the requisite number of Hispanic food patrons for a profitable enterprise, and to raise capital for what was now an extraordinarily risky Spanish restaurant."[17]

The Trump Organization sued Andres for $10 million for breach of contract, with the chef's company countersuing for $8 million. In 2017, the case was settled, with both parties declining comment on the details. In 2019, the celebrity chef said he "would serve small dishes of faith, immigrants, inclusion and democracy" if he were tasked with creating a menu for President Trump, saying that "what you eat, you become."[18]

VALUE GOAL: To protect contracting parties in a morality-based disagreement.

STRATEGY: Design a strategy that would provide protection in a contract in case of a moral dispute between the contracting parties.

LAW: Research the contract language known as the "morality" or "morals" clause. This type of provision has been used in all types of contracts and is especially common in agreements between athletes or actresses/actors and their employers. After studying the form of this clause, decide if this language has any impact on your strategy. If necessary, refine your strategy to align this option with the law.&

ETHICS: In the abstract, businesses are a synthesis of contracts, internal standard operating procedures, and industry/external rules and regulations. But in their day-to-day concrete practices, companies are often an amalgamation of the beliefs and perceptions of their owners and employees, and this combination directly influences decision making. In your ethics analysis, keep this key factor in mind as you work through these four steps of ethical decision making: (1) describe the ethical dilemma, (2) identify the stakeholders involved, (3) analyze options (including how each group of stakeholders will be affected), and (4) make a decision based on your analysis. After examining ethical issues associated with the strategy, determine whether any modifications should be made.

&*Check for law research materials in the Appendix: Legal Resources for Business Decisions*

STRATEGY	
LAW	***Three Pillars Decision: Contracts in Cyberspace***
ETHICS	

Modern contracting is not limited to new approaches like visualization. New methods, such as negotiating through electronic mail, are also becoming the norm. Some of these methods may not be the most effective in achieving objectives, as the following case demonstrates.

A newly minted Ph.D. philosophy graduate received a tenure-track job offer from a small liberal arts college. She replied by sending this email:

"As you know, I am very enthusiastic about the possibility of coming to your institution. Granting some of the following provisions would make my decision easier: 1) An increase of my

starting salary to $65,000, which is more in line with what assistant professors in philosophy have been getting in the last few years; 2) An official semester of maternity leave; 3) A pre-tenure sabbatical at some point during the bottom half of my tenure clock; 4) No more than three new class preps per year for the first three years; and 5) A start date of academic year 2015 so I can complete my postdoc." She ended the email by saying, *"I know that some of these might be easier to grant than others. Let me know what you think."* The college search committee replied: *"It was determined that on the whole these provisions indicate an interest in teaching at a research university and not at a college, like ours, that is both teaching and student centered."* The email continued: *"Thus, the institution has decided to withdraw its offer of employment to you."*[19]

In an age where communication through electronic means is so popular, contracting through email is becoming commonplace. The exchange above introduces many questions about the strategy of contracting through email, especially with regard to important negotiations. For example, would the college have so quickly withdrawn the offer if the prospective employee had communicated by phone or in person?

A comment at Harvard Law School's Negotiation Blog, notes that, "Email negotiations are . . . fraught with misunderstanding, both because emotion and tone are difficult to convey accurately and because parties neglect to consider the other side's perspective." The comment recounts a study where "individuals were asked to communicate a series of statements with sarcasm, seriousness, anger, or sadness to either a friend or a stranger via email, over phone, or face-to-face. Individuals generally overestimated how accurately their recipients would decode their tone, regardless of whether the other person was a friend or a stranger, but this deficiency was particularly strong with email. As a result, email often decreases information exchange, thereby leading to an impasse and inefficient agreements compared with negotiations conducted in person."[20]

VALUE GOAL: To protect contracting parties and avoid misunderstanding in negotiations conducted via electronic mail, while preserving its efficiency benefits.

STRATEGY: Design a strategy for negotiating and contracting via email. Rewrite the professor's correspondence above to align with your strategy.

LAW: At the following site, research the law related to contracting via email: https://www.legalmatch.com/law-library/article/email-contracts.html. Was it legal for the college search committee to rescind its offer? If necessary, refine your strategy to align within the law.&

ETHICS: Consider the college search committee's response to the candidate's email. Analyze the committee's decision using an ethical framework. Was rescinding the contract ethical? In your ethics analysis, work through these four steps of ethical decision making: (1) describe the ethical dilemma, (2) identify the stakeholders involved, (3) analyze options (including how each group of stakeholders will be affected), and (4) make a decision based on your analysis. After examining ethical issues associated with the strategy, determine whether any modifications should be made.

∞_Check for law research materials in the Appendix: Legal Resources for Business Decisions_

---

[1] Miller, *Fundamentals of Business Law* (2012).

[2] *Leonard v. Pepsico, Inc.*, 88 F.Supp.2d 116 (1999).

[3] Curriden, "Joe Jamail," *ABA Journal*, March 2, 2009.

[4] https://www.sec.gov/Archives/edgar/data/1326801/000119312512046715/d287954dex106.htm.

[5] *Lucy v. Zehmer* (1954).

[6] Adapted from: http://docshare.tips/law-for-business-strategy_574a31e9b6d87f6d218b49d5.html.

[7] https://www.jdsupra.com/legalnews/limitation-of-liability-clauses-61680/.

[8] Stein and Harris, "Bulletproof," http://www.hcc.com/DivisionsProducts/HCCSpecialty/Products/ProfessionalLiability/ArchitectsEngineersContractorsProfLiability/RiskManagementLibrary/RiskManagementLibrary/BulletproofLimitationofLiabilityinDesignPro/tabid/442/Default.aspx.

[9] University of Texas System, "Indemnification Sample Clauses".

[10] *PLC Law Department Quarterly*, October–December, 2005.

[11] Adapted from: http://docshare.tips/law-for-business-strategy_574a31e9b6d87f6d218b49d5.html.

[12] http://www.clarity-international.net/documents/Pathclearer%20article%20in%20PLC-3.pdf.

[13] "Best practices in commercial contracting," in *A Proactive Approach* (2006).

[14] Adapted from Ruuki, *Framework Agreement for Purchasing Services*.

[15] Coors Brewing Company slogan.

[16] http://www.molsoncoors.com/-/media/molson-coors-corporate/policies/supplier-standards.ashx?la=en.

[17] https://www.npr.org/sections/thetwo-way/2017/04/07/523004201/trump-organization-settles-lawsuit-with-chef-jos-andr-s.

[18] https://thehill.com/homenews/administration/445805-what-you-eat-you-become-chef-jose-andres-reveals-what-hed-cook-for.

[19] https://www.insidehighered.com/news/2014/03/13/lost-faculty-job-offer-raises-questions-about-negotiation-strategy.

[20] https://www.pon.harvard.edu/daily/conflict-resolution/email-more-cons-than-pros/.

Use Dispute Resolution Processes for Value Creation

Like the contracting process (Chapter 8), dispute resolution processes—especially litigation—play an important role in business success because they affect all stakeholders. These processes usually are associated with risk management and minimizing liability. However, as we will see in this chapter, these processes also have the potential to create value.

LEGAL BRIEFING ON DISPUTE RESOLUTION

This briefing focuses on alternatives to litigation that are designed to keep you out of court. These alternatives fall under the collective heading of "alternative dispute resolution" (ADR).

Understanding ADR processes is important for at least three reasons. First, during your business negotiations, you must decide whether to include ADR provisions in your contracts. To understand what you are negotiating, you should understand the basics of the two key ADR processes: mediation and arbitration.

Even when your attorney is involved in the negotiations, you might have to take the lead in negotiating ADR clauses. According to one study, around one-third of attorneys "never advised their clients to try mediation or arbitration."[1] This is what legendary litigator Joe Jamail had to say about mediation: "I'm a trial lawyer. . . . There are some lawyers who do nothing but this mediation bull****. Do you know what the root of mediation is? Mediocrity!"[2]

On the other hand, many lawyers are enthusiastic about ADR. Perhaps Gandhi said it best:

> My joy was boundless. I had learned the true practice of law. I had learned to find out the better side of human nature and to enter men's hearts. I realized that the true function of a lawyer was to unite parties. . . . The lesson was so indelibly burnt into me that a large part of

my time during the last 20 years of my practice as a lawyer was occupied in bringing about private compromises of hundreds of cases. I lost nothing thereby—not even money, certainly not my soul.[3]

The second reason why understanding ADR processes is important is that you might participate in these processes if you are involved in a business dispute. If you have agreed to arbitration, for example, you will participate in selecting the arbitrator, you must decide whether you need an attorney, you should understand whether you can appeal the arbitrator's decision, and so on.

Third, in the course of your business life and personal life, you might play the role of a third party as you resolve work disputes or family disputes. At a minimum, you should be able to make an informed decision about whether it is better to act as an arbitrator or whether a mediator role makes more sense.

This section opens by describing a process that is often considered the enemy of business—litigation. "Alternative" in alternative dispute resolution refers to alternatives to litigation, which is viewed as an expensive and time-consuming process. To understand when and how to use ADR, you should first understand litigation. We will then turn to the two key ADR processes—arbitration and mediation.

Litigation

There are fundamental differences between litigation in the United States and other countries. In a global economy, it is especially important for you to understand these differences so that you can make sound decisions regarding litigation strategy and settlement possibilities. Here are five key differences.

1. **Contingency fees.** In the United States, lawyers can be hired on a contingency fee basis, which means that their fees are contingent on the outcome of the case. For example, if a lawyer hired on a 30 percent contingency fee basis wins $10 million, the fee would be $3 million. If the lawyer loses the case, the fee would be 30 percent of zero. In recent years the contingency fee system has spread to several countries beyond the United States.

2. **Punitive damages.** In countries around the world, the purpose of damages is to compensate a party injured by someone else. In certain circumstances, courts in the United States will also award punitive damages designed to punish someone whose actions were intentional, malicious, or reckless.

3.   Discovery. Discovery is the process by which lawyers uncover evidence that is used in litigation. US courts have historically been more liberal than elsewhere in allowing lawyers to search for evidence by rummaging through documents the opposing party holds.

4.   Juries. In the United States, unlike most countries, juries are allowed to decide civil cases.

5.   "American Rule." In the United States, the traditional rule is that each side must pay its own attorney's fees, even the party that wins the case. Other countries have a "Loser Pays" rule (also known as the "Everywhere but America Rule"), where the losing party must pay the winner's legal fees.

In combination, these features of the US system can make litigation an attractive process for plaintiffs. For example, if I hire an attorney on a contingency fee basis to sue you, you would hire your own attorney to defend the case. If the court dismisses the lawsuit, I would owe my attorney nothing because the fee would be contingent on a successful outcome. And under the American Rule, I would not have to cover your attorney fees even though I am the losing party.

A Case Example. To illustrate the US system, let's examine a case decided by the Tennessee Supreme Court in 2008, *Flax v. DaimlerChrysler*. In this case, a grandfather drove a Dodge Caravan with three passengers—a friend who was sitting in the front seat, the driver's daughter in the seat behind her father, and his eight-month-old grandson in the seat behind the passenger. Someone driving a pickup truck well over the speed limit crashed into the rear end of the Caravan, causing the passenger's seatback to collapse onto the baby, who died from his injuries.

Although not discussed in the case, we can assume that negotiations between the car company and the parents over damages were unsuccessful. We can also assume that the parents hired an attorney on a **contingency fee** basis, although this was not discussed in the case.

Cases begin with filing a complaint. In their complaint, the baby's parents alleged that the seats were defective and that the company failed to warn consumers. In answering the complaint, the company denied that the seats were defective.

The next stage after the complaint and answer is **discovery**. In this case, the parents' attorney discovered that the company's Safety Leadership Team had concluded "that the seats were inadequate to protect consumers." The company had ordered the minutes destroyed from a meeting where this issue was discussed, disbanded the team, and fired the team chair.

The next stage is the trial, where a **jury** awarded the parents $5 million in damages for the wrongful death of their baby and another $98 million in **punitive damages**. The trial and appellate courts eventually reduced the punitive damages to $13.4 million, so the damages ultimately totaled $18.4 million. Although not discussed by the court, we can assume that under the **American Rule**, the parents' attorney fees were deducted from this total and were not recoverable from the company.

One feature that the US system unfortunately shares with other legal systems is that the process takes a long time. The accident in this case took place on June 30, 2001; the final decision in the case was reached almost eight years later on May 26, 2009. Inventor Thomas Edison, who was involved in numerous lawsuits during his life and career, wrote in his personal journals that "Litigation is the suicide of time."

Business Damage of Litigation. Attorney David Bates explains why entrepreneurs should avoid litigation: "Consider all the associated costs, the risk of losing the litigation and having to pay damages, potential adverse publicity, damage to your reputation and image and, perhaps most importantly, the arduous and lengthy litigation process that will inevitably distract your management team from focusing on improving your business."[4] Sprinting to court at the onset of a dispute, especially if the disagreement is with a longstanding client or vendor, might damage your company's reputation and adversely influence potential future business prospects.

Bates suggests that businesses work to establish and maintain good relationships with employees, customers, and business partners. These relationships act as a buffer against litigation and encourage friendlier settlement of disputes if they do arise. This prophylactic approach also aligns well with proactive reputational risk management, which, according to the *Harvard Business Review*, is essential "in an economy where 70% to 80% of market value comes from hard-to-assess intangible assets such as brand equity, intellectual capital, and goodwill."[5] As Benjamin Franklin said: "It takes many good deeds to build a good reputation, and only one bad one to lose it."[6]

Psychological Damage of Litigation. In his article "Litigation as Violence," Vincent Cardi notes that being involved in litigation can cause psychological damage that includes symptoms such as "stress, anxiety, depression, irritability, difficulties in concentration, loss of motivation, loss of social involvement, loss of enjoyment and pleasure in life, aches and pains, [and] low self-esteem. . . ."

As if these aren't enough, personal injury litigation such as product liability (see Chapter 4) can produce these additional symptoms:

insomnia, tension, restlessness, dizziness, appetite disturbances, low energy, lowered self-esteem problems, disruptions of attention and concentration, indecisiveness, agitation, feelings of hopelessness and pessimism, disruptions of sexual functioning, distressing dreams, headaches, numerous other physical complaints, and related problems affecting marriage and family life.[7]

Clearly, ADR makes sense in terms of maintaining your health in addition to the potential time and cost savings.

Although these symptoms accentuate the value of alternative processes, the litigation process is not devoid of humor. Here, for a bit of levity, is a list of questions lawyers have asked. They were collected by the editor of the *Massachusetts Bar Association Lawyer's Journal* from unverified newspaper accounts:[8]

- "Now doctor, isn't it true that when a person dies in his sleep he doesn't know about it until the next morning?"

- "Were you present when your picture was taken?"

- "Were you alone or by yourself?"

- "Was it you or your younger brother who was killed in the war?"

- "Did he kill you?"

- "The youngest son, the 20-year-old, how old is he?"

- "How far apart were the vehicles at the time of the collision?"

- "How many times have you committed suicide?"

We now turn to the two primary alternatives to litigation—arbitration and mediation. Like the litigation process (which involves a judge) both processes use so-called third parties: an arbitrator and a mediator.

Arbitration

Agreements to resolve disputes through arbitration permeate our personal lives. If you use a credit card, have automobile insurance, buy stock, use eBay, or use Amazon, you probably have agreed to arbitrate your disputes. For example, your arbitration agreement with Amazon provides:

Any dispute or claim relating in any way to your use of any Amazon Service, or to any products or services sold or distributed by Amazon or through Amazon.com will be resolved by binding arbitration, rather than in court. . . . There is no judge or jury in arbitration, and court review of an arbitration award is limited.[9]

Beyond consumer agreements, arbitration is commonly used to resolve disputes between businesses and is even used to resolve disputes with governments. In 2014, an international arbitration tribunal decided that Russia owes $50 billion to the shareholders of Yukos as compensation for company assets that were seized.[10]

The Arbitration Process. The arbitration process generally follows this sequence, as noted in *A Guide to Mediation and Arbitration for Business People*.[11]

Agreement. In most situations, arbitration is not used unless you first agree to the process. You can agree when you first enter into a contract, as in the Amazon example, or you can agree after a dispute arises.

Selecting an arbitrator. Your agreement might provide that an arbitration service, such as the American Arbitration Association, will provide a list of potential arbitrators from a roster it maintains. If you and the other side cannot agree on an arbitrator from the list, the service can name one for you.

You can also use a more informal approach when selecting an arbitrator. For example, if you are creating a partnership with another person, you could provide in your agreement that if a dispute arises each of you will appoint an arbitrator and these two arbitrators will then select a third arbitrator.

Hearing and award. The arbitration hearing is much like a trial in court, and you must decide whether to be represented by an attorney. The arbitrator has the power to subpoena witnesses if necessary. The hearing will begin with an opening statement, followed by an examination and cross-examination of witnesses, as well as a closing statement.

Unlike litigation, the hearing is private, and the arbitrator will normally use common sense rather than technical rules of court procedure in deciding what evidence is relevant to the case. Following the hearing, the arbitrator will reach a decision. Although not always the case, the arbitrator might make the decision without providing an opinion that explains the rationale for the decision. If the losing party does not comply with the award, the decision can be enforced by a court.

Appeals. Because public policy favors the finality of arbitration awards, the ability to appeal an award using the court system is limited. Although courts might overturn an award when, for example, the arbitrator is engaged in corruption or fraud, they will not usually intervene even when the arbitrator makes a mistake regarding the facts or the law.

This rule of finality was cited in a California case.[12] A City of Palo Alto employee threatened other employees with physical violence and even threatened to shoot them. The employees treated the threats as jokes. The employee also said that he could kill someone while six hundred yards away. He owned eighteen rifles and pistols and had a personalized license plate that read "SHOOOT."

Following a dispute, the employee in question threatened to shoot another employee and that employee's wife and baby. This led to an arrest for making a terrorist threat, and he eventually pled guilty to disturbing the peace. The City also obtained an injunction that prohibited the employee from having any contact with the person he threatened and decided to terminate his employment.

The City's decision then went to an arbitrator as allowed under a union contract. The arbitrator decided, among other things, that the threats were "everyday 'boy talk'" that were tolerated at this workplace and were not genuine. As a result, the arbitrator ordered reinstatement of the employee to his position and awarded him back pay.

On appeal, the court quoted precedent that "judicial review of arbitration awards is extremely narrow" and that "an arbitrator's decision is not generally reviewable for errors of fact or law [even when it] causes substantial injustice to the parties." In an unusual twist in this case, however, the court eventually decided that the employee could not be reinstated because of the earlier injunction.

If you want to use arbitration but are concerned about placing too much power in the hands of an arbitrator whose decision usually will not be reviewed by courts, you can try to negotiate an arbitration agreement that includes an appeals process. For example, the American Arbitration Association has adopted rules permitting an appeal to a panel of arbitrators that can review "errors of law that are material and prejudicial, and determinations of fact that are clearly erroneous."[13]

The Costs of Arbitration. Negotiators often attempt to include arbitration agreements in contracts because of perceived cost savings. But certain aspects of arbitration might be more expensive than litigation. Based on cost estimates from experts in Texas, Florida, and Pennsylvania, the arbitration of a $600,000 construction dispute would cost $25,400 for the filing fee, case service, and compensation for the arbitrator. The comparable litigation cost would total $300 for a filing fee (because the case service, judge, and courtroom are free).

The total litigation costs, however, would be $120,300 compared to $94,500 for arbitration. One reason for this is that legal fees for litigation are much higher than those for arbitration. Legal fees for preparing for and attending the trial alone are $12,000 higher than for attending an arbitration hearing. And an appeal of the court decision would add substantially to the cost differential.[14]

Arbitration agreements, like other contracts, are subject to law-based ethical standards. The following case was mentioned in Chapter 3, when we discussed an arbitration agreement that employees of Hooters restaurants were required to sign. In the case excerpts below, you will understand in more detail why the trial and appellate courts decided that the terms of the contract were unconscionable.

STRATEGY
LAW   *Three Pillars Case: Now Serving Beer, Wings, and ADR*
ETHICS

Citation: *Hooters of America, Inc. v. Phillips*, 173 F.3d 933 (1999)

In this case, the Hooters restaurant group attempted to compel arbitration for a sexual harassment suit filed by one of its employees. Both the district court and the decision recorded here by the Fourth Circuit appellate court concluded that while arbitration is favored in business disputes, Hooters' ADR plan clearly missed the mark.

United States Court of Appeals, Fourth Circuit.

Annette R. Phillips alleges that she was sexually harassed while working at a Hooters restaurant. After quitting her job, Phillips threatened to sue Hooters in court. Alleging that Phillips agreed to arbitrate employment-related disputes, Hooters preemptively filed suit to compel arbitration under the Federal Arbitration Act, 9 U.S.C. § 4. Because Hooters set up a dispute resolution process utterly lacking in the rudiments of even-handedness, we hold that Hooters breached its agreement to arbitrate. Thus, we affirm the district court's refusal to compel arbitration.

Appellee Annette R. Phillips worked as a bartender at a Hooters restaurant [HOMB] in Myrtle Beach, South Carolina.

. . . Phillips alleges that in June 1996, Gerald Brooks, a Hooters official and the brother of HOMB's principal owner, sexually harassed her by grabbing and slapping her buttocks. After appealing to her manager for help and being told to "let it go," she quit her job. Phillips then contacted Hooters through an attorney claiming that the attack and the restaurant's failure to address it violated her Title VII rights. Hooters responded that she was required to submit her claims to arbitration according to a binding agreement to arbitrate between the parties.

This agreement arose in 1994 during the implementation of Hooters' alternative dispute resolution program. As part of that program, the company conditioned eligibility for raises, transfers, and promotions upon an employee signing an "Agreement to arbitrate employment-related disputes." The agreement provides that Hooters and the employee each agree to arbitrate all disputes arising out of employment, including "any claim of discrimination, sexual harassment, retaliation, or wrongful discharge, whether arising under federal or state law."

The benefits of arbitration are widely recognized. Parties agree to arbitrate to secure "streamlined proceedings and expeditious results [that] will best serve their needs." The arbitration of disputes enables parties to avoid the costs associated with pursuing a judicial resolution of their grievances. By one estimate, litigating a typical employment dispute costs at least $50,000 and takes two and one-half years to resolve. Further, the adversarial nature of litigation diminishes the possibility that the parties will be able to salvage their relationship. For these reasons parties agree to arbitrate and trade "the procedures and opportunity for review of the courtroom for the simplicity, informality, and expedition of arbitration."

... In this case, the challenge goes to the validity of the arbitration agreement itself. Hooters materially breached the arbitration agreement by promulgating rules so egregiously unfair as to constitute a complete default of its contractual obligation to draft arbitration rules and to do so in good faith.

The Hooters rules when taken as a whole ... are so one-sided that their only possible purpose is to undermine the neutrality of the proceeding. The rules require the employee to provide the company notice of her claim at the outset, including "the nature of the Claim" and "the specific act(s) or omissions(s) which are the basis of the Claim." Hooters, on the other hand, is not required to file any responsive pleadings or to notice its defenses. Additionally, at the time of filing this notice, the employee must provide the company with a list of all fact witnesses with a brief summary of the facts known to each. The company, however, is not required to reciprocate.

The Hooters rules also provide a mechanism for selecting a panel of three arbitrators that is crafted to ensure a biased decision-maker. The employee and Hooters each select an arbitrator, and the two arbitrators in turn select a third. Good enough, except that the employee's arbitrator and the third arbitrator must be selected from a list of arbitrators created exclusively by Hooters. This gives

Hooters control over the entire panel and places no limits whatsoever on whom Hooters can put on the list.

. . . Nor is fairness to be found once the proceedings are begun. Although Hooters may expand the scope of arbitration to any matter, "whether related or not to the Employee's Claim," the employee cannot raise "any matter not included in the Notice of Claim." Similarly, Hooters is permitted to move for summary dismissal of employee claims before a hearing is held whereas the employee is not permitted to seek summary judgment. Hooters, but not the employee, may record the arbitration hearing "by audio or videotaping or by verbatim transcription." The rules also grant Hooters the right to bring suit in court to vacate or modify an arbitral award when it can show, by a preponderance of the evidence, that the panel exceeded its authority. No such right is granted to the employee.

In addition, the rules provide that upon 30 days notice, Hooters, but not the employee, may cancel the agreement to arbitrate. Moreover, Hooters reserves the right to modify the rules, "in whole or in part," whenever it wishes and "without notice" to the employee. Nothing in the rules even prohibits Hooters from changing the rules in the middle of an arbitration proceeding.

If by odd chance the unfairness of these rules were not apparent on their face, leading arbitration experts have decried their one-sidedness. George Friedman, senior vice president of the American Arbitration Association (AAA), testified that the system established by the Hooters rules so deviated from minimum due process standards that the Association would refuse to arbitrate under those rules. George Nicolau, former president of both the National Academy of Arbitrators and the International Society of Professionals in Dispute Resolution, attested that the Hooters rules "are inconsistent with the concept of fair and impartial arbitration." . . . Finally, Lewis Maltby, member of the Board of Directors of the AAA, testified that "This is without a doubt the most unfair arbitration program I have ever encountered."

. . . The National Academy of Arbitrators stated that the Hooters rules "violate fundamental concepts of fairness and the integrity of the arbitration process." Likewise, the Society of Professionals in Dispute Resolution noted that "[i]t would be hard to imagine a more unfair method of selecting a panel of arbitrators." It characterized the Hooters arbitration system as "deficient to the point of illegitimacy" and "so one sided, it is hard to believe that it was even intended to be fair."

We hold that the promulgation of so many biased rules—especially the scheme whereby one party to the proceeding so controls the arbitral panel—breaches the contract entered into by the parties. The parties agreed to submit their claims to arbitration—a system whereby disputes are fairly resolved by an impartial third party. Hooters by contract took on the obligation of establishing such a system. By creating a sham system unworthy even of the name of arbitration, Hooters completely failed in performing its contractual duty.

… AFFIRMED AND REMANDED.

THREE PILLARS CASE QUESTIONS

(1)   List the elements in Hooters' arbitration agreement cited by the Court in its decision that the agreement was unconscionable. How could each rule be rewritten to create an equitable agreement for both parties in the arbitration?

(2)   Mandatory arbitration agreements, like the contract used by Hooters in this case, are becoming fairly commonplace among employers. The Economic Policy Institute argues that this "trend toward increasing use of arbitration in consumer and employment relationships threatens to undermine decades of achievements in worker and consumer rights."[15] Do you agree with this view? Why?

(3)   The Hooters organization has experienced numerous lawsuits in its thirty-plus years of existence, including lawsuits for sexual harassment; racial, pregnancy, disability and gender discrimination; ADA non-compliance; spam text messaging; wage violations; and many others. The US Supreme Court and Congress have been described as promoting "a liberal federal policy [of] arbitration agreements."[16] While arbitration can be a definite plus for companies to resolve disputes, what strategic steps could a company take to implement arbitration that simultaneously creates value and guards against abuse?

Mediation

Mediation is the second of the two basic ADR processes. In essence, mediation is a negotiation assisted by a third party. Traditionally, the goal of mediation was to solve a specific problem using one of two mediation processes. In the first process, facilitative mediation, the mediator's role is to make it easier for the parties to discuss and resolve their concerns. In the second process, evaluative mediation, the mediator is also asked to evaluate the merits of each side's case without making a decision (unlike arbitration).

In recent years, a third option has developed—transformative mediation. Although transformative mediation might also result in solving a specific problem, the ultimate goal is to improve the relationship between the parties. After the US

Postal Service adopted transformative mediation in the 1990s, it saved millions of dollars in legal costs and productivity improvements.[17]

For example, a letter carrier who had filed a sexual harassment claim against her supervisor. Through transformative mediation, the parties discovered that the real problem was their relationship. The supervisor referred to the letter carrier and other letter carriers by their route numbers, and the postal worker felt that this was dehumanizing. After the relationship was fixed and the supervisor started referring to the letter carrier personally, the complaint was withdrawn.

The Caucus. One especially effective tool many mediators use is the caucus. With a caucus, the mediator meets separately with each side to discuss their interests and positions. The mediator keeps each set of information confidential if the parties so desire. With this confidential information in mind, the mediator can either help the parties reach an agreement or advise them that the mediation is a waste of time.

The case below involved a mediation negotiation between National Football League (NFL) players, their counsel, the NFL, the League's counsel, and a court-appointed mediator. The mediation related to concussion injuries the players received during their careers in the NFL. The mediation was ordered by a US federal judge after more than 4,200 NFL players filed 250 suits against the League for diagnosed brain injuries. US District Judge Anita Brody appointed retired US District Judge Layn Phillips to be the mediator in the case. Judge Phillips used a combination of joint meetings and caucuses to develop his recommendations in support of the Players-League mediation settlement.

STRATEGY LAW ETHICS	*Three Pillars Case: Armchair Quarterback*

Citation: *In Re: National Football League Players' Concussion Injury Litigation,* No. 2:12-md-02323-AB, MDL No. 2323 (2014)

In 2013, Federal Judge Anita Brody sought to avoid a dismissal ruling with the hopes that the injured NFL players at the heart of this action against the National Football League could achieve some relief through the mediation process. The declaration of mediator Layn Phillips below records the result of these negotiations.

DECLARATION OF MEDIATOR AND FORMER UNITED STATES DISTRICT COURT JUDGE LAYN R. PHILLIPS IN SUPPORT OF PRELIMINARY APPROVAL OF SETTLEMENT.

Layn R. Phillips declares as follows:

1. I am the Court-appointed mediator in this action and a former United States District Court Judge. I submit this declaration in support of preliminary approval of the proposed class action settlement between the proposed Plaintiff Class and defendants NFL and NFL Properties LLC (collectively, the "NFL Parties").

2. At the request of the Court, I conducted an extensive mediation over the course of the last five months that produced the proposed settlement now before the Court for preliminary approval. The parties negotiated this settlement under my supervision. The talks were vigorous, at arm's length, and in good faith. . . .

5. Under my supervision, beginning immediately upon my appointment by the Court in July of this year, the parties engaged in arm's-length, hard-fought negotiations. As is my practice, I conducted multiple face-to-face mediation sessions with both sides present, as well as many separate caucus sessions where I met only with one side or the other. . . . In addition, counsel for the parties conducted extensive negotiations outside my presence pursuant to requests and directions that I gave to them. I dedicated more than twelve full days to mediate this matter in addition to the considerable hours I invested in discussions with the parties outside these formal sessions.

6. At all times, the parties aggressively asserted their respective positions on a host of issues. On occasion, the negotiations were contentious (although both sides were always professional). Because of the schedule that the Court imposed and the number and complexity of issues to be resolved, members of my mediation team and I sometimes multi-tracked mediation efforts by separately addressing different sets of issues with various counsel and the parties' experts during in-person mediation sessions in New York City, as well as during the telephonic follow-up process. On almost every day between my appointment as mediator and the announcement of the settlement on August 29, the parties and I discussed issues relating to possible settlement. . . .

9. During the course of the mediation and at my request, the parties submitted various mediation materials to me and made multiple presentations regarding their positions on various factual and legal issues. . . . During the mediation sessions, there were extensive discussions of the strengths and weaknesses of the parties' various positions and of possible settlement structures. 10. As would be expected, the proposed terms of the settlement changed substantially over the course of time. On numerous occasions, although the parties shared a common goal, they proposed very different visions of how to achieve that goal. I worked constructively with counsel to offer possible compromises and solutions.

11. At all times, Plaintiffs' counsel . . . regularly and passionately expressed the need to protect the interests of the retirees and their families and fought hard for the greatest possible benefits in the context of a settlement that the NFL Parties could accept. It was evident throughout the mediation process that Plaintiffs' counsel were prepared to litigate and try these cases, and face the risk of losing with no chance to recover for their labor or their expenses, if they were not able to achieve a fair and reasonable settlement result for the proposed class.

12. At the same time, Plaintiffs' counsel recognized—correctly in my judgment—the significant legal and factual hurdles Plaintiffs faced if they proceeded with the litigation. First and foremost, a litigation of this size and complexity can take many years to litigate. By resolving the litigation at this time, Plaintiffs' counsel, in part, sought to compensate impaired retired NFL players who need money now in order to address their medical conditions. They also ensured that compensation and medical testing will be available for retired NFL players who are not impaired at present, but may become so in the future. Second, Plaintiffs faced the serious risk that the Court would find that their claims were preempted, in whole or in part, by federal labor law and under the various Collective Bargaining Agreements. . . . Third, Plaintiffs also faced significant hurdles in proving causation, i.e., that the players suffered cognizable injuries as a result of concussions and sub-concussive hits they experienced while playing in the NFL. There is little doubt that both general and case-specific causation would be hotly contested if these matters were litigated, and Plaintiffs faced a significant risk that they would not be able to prevail in the end. In particular, Plaintiffs would likely be faced with having to prove that their alleged injuries were caused by their NFL careers rather than by some cause unrelated to football or by prior football experience in middle school, high school and college. Many members of the proposed class had short NFL careers and played substantially more football before joining the NFL, which made this burden all the more challenging. There are also many members of the proposed class who developed their symptoms later in life and may therefore have had difficulty proving that their alleged injuries are not a result of the normal aging process. More broadly, the science regarding concussions and sub concussive hits and cognitive impairment is still evolving, which makes it more difficult to prove negligence or fraud the earlier a player played. The research is often contradictory, thereby creating additional hurdles for a successful prosecution of Plaintiffs' claims. . . .

15. Plaintiffs faced other legal hurdles as well, including, but not limited to, various statute of limitations arguments and the assertion of the "assumption of risk" defense based on the argument that the retired NFL players knew at the time

they played that football could be a dangerous activity and that the players assumed that risk when they chose to play.

16.   Like Plaintiffs, the NFL Parties also faced great risks if they chose to litigate these cases. There was a significant risk that the Court would not accept, in whole or in part, the NFL Parties' preemption defense, which in turn would leave much of the case intact. The same was true of the NFL Parties' other legal defenses of statute of limitations and assumption of risk. If the NFL Parties did not succeed on dismissing all of these cases as a matter of law, they faced years of very expensive discovery and potentially hundreds of trials in state and federal courts around the country. Among Plaintiffs' many claims and allegations, the NFL Parties faced the risks of litigating issues relating to helmet safety standards and rules of football play. Each potential lawsuit carried with it the risk of a significant damage verdict and a negative precedent that could affect all cases that followed.

17.   In short, both sides faced substantial risks if they chose to litigate these matters and tremendous benefits if they could fairly resolve their differences. . . .

20.   I believe that the $760 million paid by the NFL Parties for the settlement is fair and reasonable and will be sufficient to fund the benefits to which the parties have agreed. . . .

21.   I should note that the NFL Parties also have agreed not to object to an award of attorneys' fees and reasonable costs of up to $112.5 million in addition to the $760 million settlement. This is another significant benefit that Plaintiffs' counsel obtained for the proposed class, as compared to the vast majority of other class settlements where the attorneys' fee and reasonable cost component is deducted from the common fund. Ultimately, the total settlement, with attorneys' fees and reasonable costs, will approach $900 million. This, in my judgment, is an outstanding result for the class members.

Executed this 3rd day of January 2014.

Layn R. Phillips

THREE PILLARS CASE QUESTIONS

(1)   Why do you think Judge Anita Brody suggested mediation rather than ruling directly on the NFL's motion to dismiss the case?

(2)   What reasons did mediator Phillips provide that suggested that mediation was the best process for resolving this dispute?

(3)   Mediators often seek common ground between the parties to help them design a solution to their dispute. Despite the sometimes contentious nature of the mediation described above, what shared interests would the parties have in this case?

(4)   The mediator mentions the "assumption of the risk" defense against the players' allegations of injury. The NFL argued that the players knew the game was dangerous yet engaged in playing football anyway. Is this a fair argument? If you represented the players, how would you refute this defense?

(5)   Analysts and commentators have suggested that players' health has been endangered by a conflict of interest with teams' medical staff, as the doctors and athletic trainers have a responsibility to both players (their patients) and the club (their employers). How could this conflict of interest be resolved ethically to create value for all stakeholders?

Be Creative in Using ADR Processes

The two basic models of dispute resolution—arbitration and mediation—provide many opportunities for creativity and innovation. In one case at the outer limits of creativity, a judge, apparently fed up with the parties' relying on the federal courts, decided to "fashion a new form of alternative dispute resolution, to wit: at 4:00 p.m. on Friday, June 30, 2006, counsel shall convene at a neutral site. . . [and] shall engage in one game of 'rock, paper, scissors' to determine who wins a motion."[18]

The mini-trial and rent-a-judge are two prominent examples of mediation and arbitration variations.

Mini-Trial. The mini-trial is a variation of the mediation model. The prototypical mini-trial involved a $6 million intellectual property lawsuit filed by Telecredit against TRW. This lawsuit began much like any other. The parties spent around $500,000 and exchanged one hundred thousand documents, with no resolution in sight. Given the slow pace of the litigation, executives from the two companies created a structured process that came to be known as a mini-trial.

The process essentially involved five parties: one attorney and one executive from each side and a neutral expert on intellectual property. The attorneys each had a half a day to explain their respective versions of the case and to answer questions from the executives. The executives then met briefly and resolved the case.

The estimated savings in legal fees was around $1 million. Through this process, the executives were able to hear the case as presented by the other side's attorney (which might have been quite different from what they heard up to that point from their own attorneys). They were also able to resolve the case in a way that made business sense, as opposed to a typical court decision that produces a zero-sum result (in this case, with one side winning and the other side losing $6 million).

Rent-a-Judge. Rent-a-judge, a variation of the arbitration model, uses retired judges as arbitrators. Although the hearing is similar to a trial, rent-a-judge offers the same benefits as other forms of arbitration. When Brad Pitt and Jennifer Aniston used rent-a-judge to handle their divorce in 2005, they were able to select their own judge (presumably a judge who was familiar with divorce proceedings). They were also able to conclude the divorce proceeding quickly and maintain their privacy because the press was not allowed to attend the hearing.[19]

THE LAW PILLAR: DISPUTE RESOLUTION AND RISK MANAGEMENT

Risk management begins with understanding the two key third-party processes—arbitration and mediation—that are alternatives to litigation. To use them effectively, however, four key ADR tools are recommended for managing risks relating to business disputes: a corporate pledge, screens, contract clauses, and online resources.

Corporate Pledge

The International Institute for Conflict Prevention & Resolution (CPR) was a pioneer in developing a pledge that companies can adopt as a statement of their corporate policy. The key sentence in the pledge states:

> In the event of a business dispute between our company and another company, which has made or will then make a similar statement, we are prepared to explore with that other party resolution of the dispute through negotiation or ADR techniques before pursuing full-scale litigation.

More than four thousand operating companies have adopted this policy.[20]

Suitability Screens

Suitability screens are a series of questions designed to help parties select a binding or non-binding form of dispute resolution. Binding processes are arbitration and litigation; non-binding processes are mediation and negotiation.

CPR publishes an especially useful *ADR Suitability Guide* that features a mediation screen. In helping the disputing parties decide whether to use mediation, the screen asks questions that focus on the following factors, among others:

- The parties' relationship
- Importance of control over the process and decision
- Importance of discovery
- Chances for success in court
- Cost of litigation
- Importance of speed and privacy
- Relative power of both sides

Contract Clauses

Parties can enter into an ADR contract as part of the initial business negotiation before a dispute arises or they can wait until after a dispute develops. Post-dispute agreements are often difficult to negotiate because the relationship of the parties has soured. Here is an example of a pre-dispute agreement, which is part of Oracle's letter offering Mark Hurd the position of president:

> You and Oracle understand and agree that any existing or future dispute or claim arising out of or related to your Oracle employment, or the termination of that employment, will be resolved by final and binding arbitration and that no other forum for dispute resolution will be available to either party, except as to those claims identified below. The decision of the arbitrator shall be final and binding on both you and Oracle and it shall be enforceable by any court having proper jurisdiction.[21]

ADR contract clauses might provide for only one process, such as Mark Hurd's arbitration clause, or the processes can be linked. For example, the parties might agree to use negotiation and/or mediation before turning to arbitration.

Online Dispute Resolution

In recent years, advances in technology have enabled ADR to become online dispute resolution (ODR). Online systems allow parties to use negotiation, mediation, and arbitration to resolve business and personal disputes.

Your decision to use online dispute resolution involves a cost-benefit analysis. On the one hand, online processes save travel costs and are convenient. On the other hand, there is evidence that they are less effective—especially because it is difficult to build a relationship with the opposing side. One way to surmount this problem is to combine face-to-face negotiation with online ODR by scheduling face time at the outset of the negotiation before moving to the online phase.

ALIGN STRATEGY AND LAW: USE ADR TO CREATE VALUE

Linking dispute resolution to value creation is especially difficult for many business leaders who view litigation and other processes as a waste of time and money. Because of this difficulty, those who can bridge the gap between the Strategy Pillar and Law Pillar have an opportunity to create *sustainable* competitive advantage. This section reviews three value-creating opportunities: dispute prevention, using ADR for deal making, and using litigation to create value.

Dispute Prevention

Often overlooked by business leaders and lawyers intent on developing alternatives to litigation is the simple fact that disputes that never arise do not have to be resolved. Dispute prevention focuses on predicting what people will do rather than on what courts might decide.[22] One rationale for this principle was painfully stated by the French philosopher Voltaire: "I was never ruined but twice: once when I lost a lawsuit and once when I won one."

Author Siedel had firsthand experience with dispute prevention several years ago after spending a night at a Marriott hotel in Texas. He was scheduled to give a legal briefing to a group of corporate executives the following morning and asked the front desk for a wake-up call. The call never came.

When checking out, he mentioned the missing call when completing a card that provided feedback to the hotel. A couple of weeks later, the President of Marriott, Bill Marriott, sent a personal note in which he apologized for the missed call and mentioned that he had asked the hotel general manager to investigate the matter.

Another hotel adopted a different approach following a well-publicized, tragic incident. An intruder raped international recording star Connie Francis when she was staying at a Howard Johnson Motor Lodge. Her reaction: "I never received so much as a note from Mr. Howard B. Johnson saying 'We're sorry it happened.' After being shocked, I was very angry."[23] After becoming angry, she sued the hotel and eventually won $2.5 million.

We can only speculate why the hotel never communicated with Connie Francis. Probably the company leaders followed the traditional approach by asking their lawyers whether a court might hold them liable—focusing on what a court might do. The attorneys might have responded that the hotel should not be held liable for the acts of an independent third party (the rapist), and they might have gone further by advising company management not to contact the singer or do anything else that might indicate that it was liable. This was the traditional approach, which is in sharp contrast to the Marriott apology.

The two examples illustrate situations where hotels did (Marriott) and did not (Howard Johnson) use a dispute prevention approach *after* a problem occurred. You can also incorporate a preventive approach into your contracts before incidents arise. For example, a process called "partnering" is used in the construction industry. While there are many variations, this is the usual format, as described in *The Construction Industry's Guide to Dispute Avoidance and Resolution* published by the American Arbitration Association:[24]

> [R]epresentatives of the project's stakeholders attend pre-construction workshops in order to get to know each other and share concerns. Neutral facilitators guide discussions about the project, specific individual goals and agendas. It is during these meetings that participants develop ways to recognize risks that may create obstacles to the success of the project. They develop methods to avoid, control or cope with potential sources of conflict. The eventual outcome is a joint agreement signed by the workshop participants that sets forth their goals and expresses their commitment to the project.

As the hotel examples illustrate, an apology is a powerful tool for preventing and resolving disputes while creating value for a business in the form of customer retention. But the value-creation aspects of an apology can also influence operations. For example, the University of Michigan Health System developed a claims management model that includes apologies (combined with compensation) to patients who receive unreasonable care.

By openly acknowledging errors, the health system is able to use patient experiences to improve processes. This model has resulted in a significant drop in lawsuits coupled with a reduction in new claims as processes have improved. As noted by the director of the Michigan model, "the real goal is to improve patient safety."[25]

Use ADR for Deal-Making

Historically, processes like arbitration and mediation have been used as alternatives to litigation for resolving disputes. In recent years, however, these processes have also been increasingly used to negotiate value-creating deals. Mediation is especially promising because the use of a caucus enables mediators to prepare a negotiation analysis that takes into account confidential information from each side.

According to one study, close to 40 percent of the mediators surveyed had used mediation for deals ranging from $100,000 to $26 million. Examples of the deals included negotiations involving angel investments, physician partnerships, the sale of cable television rights, and a software joint venture.[26]

Arbitration is also a possibility for resolving difficult issues during negotiations. Baseball arbitration is a highly-publicized example that is used when players are involved in salary disputes with their teams. The unique feature of baseball arbitration is that each side submits a final figure to the arbitrator, who then must select one of the two figures.

For example, assume that a deadlock arises during negotiations in which Pitcher demands a salary of $20 million and Team offers $10 million. If they use the baseball form of arbitration, Pitcher and Team would privately submit salary figures to the arbitrator, who must select one of the two numbers. Wanting the arbitrator to select their number, each side is likely to be more reasonable than when making the original demands. While commonly used to facilitate baseball negotiations, this form of arbitration could be used in any type of deal-making negotiation.

In addition to using dispute resolution processes to make a deal, you can use a dispute resolution mindset to convert a dispute into a deal that creates value for both sides. For example, author Siedel gives students a real-world scenario involving a dispute between a company that developed a statistical software package and its licensee. The company learned that the licensee was working on an adaptation of the software, which the licensee planned to market to other companies in violation of the licensing agreement. The company sued the licensee for several million dollars.

Students are given a role as leader in the company, and they must decide whether to accept a settlement offer from the licensee. Most students become adversarial and recommend against settling the lawsuit. But a few students recognize that both sides might benefit by working together to form a joint venture. Rather than letting a court determine who wins and who loses, which is a zero-sum game, both sides have a chance to win through a strategic marketing plan that increases total profits that exceed the sum of their separate profits.

Use Litigation for Value Creation

Despite the risk of psychological injury discussed earlier in this chapter, litigation has value-creating opportunities for both plaintiffs and defendants. From the plaintiff's perspective, companies use so-called "plaintiff's recovery" lawsuits to turn their law departments into a source of revenue. For example, Ford Motor Company has expanded its "Affirmative Recovery" program from the United States to Europe and Asia. And Switzerland-based Tyco has started an "Asset Recovery" program that focuses on recovering debts from suppliers and others. In short, in the words of a *Wall Street Journal* article, "Companies are warming to a new way of generating revenue: suing for it."[27]

From a defendant's perspective, the litigation process can generate information that is difficult for an organization to obtain elsewhere. This information comes in the form of complaints filed by plaintiffs, documents unearthed during discovery, depositions of company personnel, expert witness reports, and so on. In her article "Introspection through Litigation," Joanna Schwartz notes that "This information, placed in the hands of an organization's leaders as the result of litigation, can be used to improve systems and personnel." She uses the example of hospitals that "analyze information from every stage of litigation to help understand weaknesses and improve the quality of care."[28]

Even an adverse conclusion to the litigation process can produce positive benefits. For example, after Home Depot settled a sex discrimination class action, the company "used the lesson of the lawsuit settlement as a springboard to develop an automated personnel hiring information system. The legally-motivated system uncovered significant underutilization of employee talent and increased employee diversity, retention, and morale."[29]

KEY TAKEAWAYS

Dispute resolution processes are important to business success because they touch all stakeholders. Using these processes provides an opportunity to preserve business relationships and create value. To succeed at this form of value creation, you must:

1.   **Become legally savvy about the menu of dispute resolution processes.** The key third-party processes are litigation, arbitration, and mediation.

2.   **Use risk management tools when resolving disputes.** These tools are: a corporate pledge, suitability screens, contract clauses, and online resources.

3.   **Create value while resolving disputes.** Value-creating opportunities arise from preventing disputes, using ADR for deal making, and analyzing litigation for insights about how to improve your business.

STRATEGY
LAW   *Three Pillars Decision: ADR Home Runs*
ETHICS

Although Alternate Dispute Resolution is a tremendously helpful process in resolving impasses, care must be taken in selecting the best practice for the circumstances.

"Baseball Arbitration" is a process that assists players and management to resolve disagreements related to salary and contract negotiations. Introduced in 1974, the practice involves submitting salary/compensation packages to an arbitration board; the arbitrators then select either the player's or the team's package, and both sides have no recourse other than to accept the board's choice. It is believed that the baseball procedures are quick, relatively inexpensive, and uncomplicated.

Due to these aspects, the process is becoming increasingly popular in other industries, such as real estate and construction. However, the issues in these other contract disputes are often quite different and do not always lend themselves well to traditional baseball arbitration tactics. Real estate deals are frequently complex, with substantial financial consequences for both sides. The clauses in real property contracts rarely have the flexibility required for the baseball arbitration process. Drawbacks in construction claims include the fact that there are usually other parties of interest, such as subcontractors, who might not be directly involved in the arbitration, but who will have the decision "passed through" to them—meaning that they are not a party to the dispute but might be affected by the court decision—when the dispute is resolved.[30]

VALUE GOAL: To apply an efficient arbitration method to settling real estate and construction disputes.

STRATEGY: Design a strategy that would effectively apply "Baseball Arbitration" to disputes in real estate and/or construction contracts.

LAW: Examine the rules for construction and real estate arbitration at the following link: https://www.adr.org/construction. Also consult the issues raised in the following articles: (1) on "Baseball Arbitration" in real estate, at http://www.lawjournalnewsletters.com/2019/05/01/risks-of-baseball-arbitration-in-resolving-real-estate-disputes/ and (2) in construction, at https://www.americanbar.org/groups/construction_industry/publications/under_construction/2019/spring2019/resolving_dispute_baseball/. ℘

ETHICS: As mentioned above, there is some criticism of applying the baseball process to construction contracts where some parties might be excluded. Examine the ethics of extrapolating Baseball Arbitration to construction and/or real estate contracts by working through these four steps of ethical decision making: (1) describe the ethical dilemma, (2) identify the stakeholders involved, (3) analyze options (including how each group of stakeholders will be affected), and (4) make a decision based on your analysis. After examining ethical issues associated with the strategy, determine whether any modifications should be made.

℘*Check for law research materials in the Appendix: Legal Resources for Business Decisions*

STRATEGY	
LAW	***Three Pillars Decision: ADR in Cyberspace***
ETHICS	

Many would agree that social media now influences nearly every aspect of personal and business interactions. Facebook is one company trying to bring the value of alternative dispute resolution to the online space.

The social network Facebook has been designing a strategy to bring dispute resolution techniques online. According to CNNMoney, the company has especially been focusing on settling disputes between Facebook users over "offensive or upsetting posts, including insults and photos."[31] At the Harvard Negotiation Blog, author Katie Shonk reports that "Facebook created message templates that allow users to explain what they object to about a particular post. For example, they can select options such as 'It's embarrassing' or 'It's a bad photo of me.' Users are also asked to state how the offensive post makes them feel—such as angry, sad, or afraid—and how strongly they experience the emotions they report."[32] Although Facebook believes the process is convenient and may be an efficient way to resolve differences, some have been critical of the online procedure. What happens if the dispute escalates rather than trends toward resolution? Without moderation by a trained mediator, the situation may intensify and get worse, and Facebook users may lack the skills to bring about an effective resolution.

VALUE GOAL: To provide for effective online dispute resolution.

STRATEGY: Design a strategy that would improve Facebook's online social media dispute resolution program. Then decide whether a similar strategy could be used to mediate business disputes.

LAW: Examine the mediation techniques posted by the International Institute for Conflict Prevention & Resolution at https://www.cpradr.org/resource-center/rules/mediation/cpr-mediation-procedure. How do these rules affect your strategy?ℙ

ETHICS: Examine the ethics of Facebook's dispute resolution program by working through these four steps of ethical decision making: (1) describe the ethical dilemma, (2) identify the stakeholders involved, (3) analyze options (including how each group of stakeholders will be affected), and (4) make a decision based on your analysis. After examining ethical issues associated with the strategy, determine whether any modifications should be made.

ℙ*Check for law research materials in the Appendix: Legal Resources for Business Decisions*

STRATEGY	
LAW	***Three Pillars Decision: Making Twitter Waves***
ETHICS	

As we have seen in this chapter, litigation might have serious psychological, emotional, and financial repercussions for a business and its owners and managers. We now examine a recently-evolving dispute resolution technique that uses social media to add "muscle" to small business efforts to avoid litigation.

According to author and professor David Orozco, using the technique of crowdsourcing (also called "lawsourcing") to settle business disputes is a defensive strategy that is especially beneficial to small companies seeking to avoid litigation. The business universe is replete with stories about small companies being bullied into meeting legal demands by large companies with extensive resources. Orozco suggests that social media and technology platforms may provide a method by which these smaller companies can potentially fight back.

One example is the use of lawsourcing by Vermont artist Bo Mueller-Moore when he was challenged for selling T-shirts with the slogan "Eat More Kale." Chick-fil-A Inc. claimed the Kale phrase infringed its trademark "Eat Mor Chikin," and it insisted that Mueller-Moore cease and desist using his slogan. Instead, the artist reached out to the public and garnered tremendous support for his Kale campaign. Between the media coverage and his persistence, Mueller-Moore was able to trademark his slogan in 2014.[33] An upwelling of public support—including going "viral" on an issue such as the Kale-Chikin battle—has become the latest cyberspace-supported method of dispute resolution, moving the fight from the courtroom to the pages of Twitter, Facebook, and other social media-fueled venues.

VALUE GOAL: To provide for an effective online dispute resolution campaign.

STRATEGY: Design a social media strategy that would support a small business in a battle against larger adversaries.

LAW: Examine the crowdsourcing online dispute resolution techniques and discussion of Internet law posted in the following article: David Dimov, *Crowdsourced Online Dispute Resolution* https://papers.ssrn.com/sol3/papers.cfm?abstract_id=3003815. How do these rules affect your strategy?৪০

ETHICS: Examine the ethics of dispute resolution by social media crowdsourcing. Is this a viable ethical method to resolve disputes? Use these four steps of ethical decision making in your analysis: (1) describe the ethical dilemma, (2) identify the stakeholders involved, (3) analyze options (including how each group of stakeholders will be affected), and (4) make a decision based on your analysis. After examining ethical issues associated with the strategy, determine whether any modifications should be made.

৪০*Check for law research materials in the Appendix: Legal Resources for Business Decisions*

---

1   "Attorneys' Use of ADR is Crucial to Their Willingness to Recommend It to Clients," *Dispute Resolution Magazine*, Winter 2000.

2   "Lions of the Trial Bar," *ABA Journal*, March 2009.

3   Gandhi, *An Autobiography: The Story of My Experiments With Truth* (1927).

4   https://www.bizjournals.com/bizjournals/how-to/growth-strategies/2014/08/heres-how-entrepreneurs-can-avoid-litigation.html.

5   https://hbr.org/2007/02/reputation-and-its-risks.

6   *Id.*

7   *Wake Forest Law Review*, 2014, quoted in Lande, "Litigation as Violence," *Mediate.com*.

8   Jacobs, "'Were You Alone or by Yourself?' And Other Courtroom Gaffes," *Wall Street Journal*, June 15, 1998.

9   https://www.amazon.com/gp/help/customer/display.html?nodeId=508088.

10   "Now Try Collecting," *The Economist*, August 2, 2014.

11   AAA (2008).

12   *Palo Alto v. Service Employees International Union* (1999).

13   AAA, *Optional Appellate Arbitration Rules*.

14   Zuckerman, "Comparing Costs in Construction Arbitration & Litigation," *Dispute Resolution Journal*, May/July 2007.

15   https://www.epi.org/publication/the-arbitration-epidemic/.

16   Moses H. Cone Mem'l Hosp. v. Mercury Constr. Corp., 460 U.S. 1, 24, 103 S.Ct. 927, 74 L.Ed.2d 765 (1983).

17   "Companies Adopting Postal Service Grievance Process," *The New York Times*, September 6, 2000.

18   *Avista Management v. Wausau Underwriters* (2006).

19   For further information, see http://www.npr.org/templates/story/story.php?storyId=4812658.

20   "Corporate Pledge," https://www.cpradr.org/resource-center/adr-pledges/corporate-policy-statement.

21   "Sample Business Contracts," http://contracts.onecle.com/.

22   CPR, *Corporate Dispute Management* (1982).

23   Seigel, "Jury Awards Connie Francis 42.5 Million in Westbury Rape," *The New York Times*, July 2, 1976.

24   AAA (2009).

25   Block, "UMHS Malpractice Approach Wins Praise," *The Michigan Daily*, January 10, 2013.

26   "Why Mediation is Important," http://www.pon.harvard.edu/daily/mediation/mediation-in-transactional-negotiation-2/.

27   O'Connell, "Company Lawyers Sniff Out Revenue," May 13, 2011.

28   *Notre Dame Law Review*, 2015.

29   "Rediscovering the Power of Law in Business Education," http://www.aacsb.edu/blog/2016/february/rediscovering-the-power-of-law-in-business-education.

30   http://www.lawjournalnewsletters.com/2019/05/01/risks-of-baseball-arbitration-in-resolving-real-estate-disputes/.

31   https://www.pon.harvard.edu/daily/dispute-resolution/on-facebook-dispute-resolution-goes-live/.

32   *Id.*

33   https://sloanreview.mit.edu/article/using-social-media-in-business-disputes/.

Legal Resources for Business Decisions

Chapter 1: Meet the Three Pillar Model (Strategy, Law, Ethics)

Three Pillars Decision: Last Trip to Disney World

    › For a summary of rules in Florida for scattering cremation ashes: https://legalbeagle.com/6163401-rules-florida-scattering-cremation-ashes.html.

    › For a discussion of scattering ashes at Disney parks: https://www.disboards.com/threads/people-scattering-ashes-at-parks.3713695/.

    › For a news story at the site *Above the Law* about Disney parks and scattering cremains: https://abovethelaw.com/2018/10/disney-disapproves-of-the-disposition-of-your-remains-the-happiest-place-on-earth-has-become-a-receptacle-for-cremains/.

    › For more about Florida laws on scattering cremains: https://www.nolo.com/legal-encyclopedia/burial-cremation-laws-florida.html.

    › For the Florida edition of The Living Urn's guide to scattering human cremains: https://www.thelivingurn.com/blogs/news/2019-state-guide-to-scattering-ashes-florida-edition.

Three Pillars Decision: Reservations of the Heart

    › For a guide from the National Conference of State Legislatures on "State Laws on Cardiac Arrest and Defibrillators": http://www.ncsl.org/research/health/laws-on-cardiac-arrest-and-defibrillators-aeds.aspx.

    › For an interactive listing of AED laws by state: https://www.aeduniverse.com/AED_Laws_by_State_s/97.htm.

⁚ For a risk management discussion of AEDs in hotels: http://www. ultrariskadvisors.com/wp-content/uploads/2012/07/MHR_Defibrillators. pdf.

Three Pillars Decision: "Fair and Square" Strategy

⁚ For the Federal Trade Commission's Advertising Guide: https://www. ftc.gov/tips-advice/business-center/guidance/advertising-faqs-guide-small-business.

Three Pillars Decision: "Nor Any Drop to Drink. . ."

⁚ For information about high risk businesses operations: https://smallbusiness.findlaw.com/starting-a-business/high-risk-business. html.

⁚ For information about Boulder Outdoor Survival School: https://www. boss-inc.com/.

⁚ For information about risk management for recreation service companies: https://www.sagamorepub.com/sites/default/files/2018-07/pages-riskmgmt-6th.pdf.

⁚ For information about liability waivers: https://www.liabilitywaiver.org/.

⁚ For general information about negligence laws: https://en.wikipedia.org/ wiki/Negligence.

Chapter 2. The Key Chasm: Closing the Gap Between Strategy and Law

Three Pillars Decision: "You've got a fast car . . . ."

⁚ For a guide from the National Conference of State Legislatures on car-sharing state laws: http://www.ncsl.org/research/transportation/car-sharing-state-laws-and-legislation.aspx.

⁚ For information on the Turo car-sharing service: https://support.turo. com/hc/en-us/articles/203991850-Is-it-legal-for-me-to-share-my-car-Is-it-okay-with-my-personal-insurer-.

⁚ For additional information on car-sharing legislation: https://support. turo.com/hc/en-us/articles/203991840-Does-the-car-sharing-legislation-in-California-Washington-and-Oregon-affect-me.

Three Pillars Decision: McFacts v. McFiction

⁚ For information about coffee temperatures in the restaurant and hospitality industry: https://www.coffeedetective.com/what-is-the-correct-temperature-for-serving-coffee.html.

⡪ For additional information about the McDonald's hot coffee case: https://corporate.findlaw.com/litigation-disputes/products-liability-law-explaining-the-mcdonald-s-coffee-case.html.

⡪ For information about the case of *Liebeck v. McDonald's*: https://www.tortmuseum.org/liebeck-v-mcdonalds/.

⡪ For additional information about *Liebeck v. McDonald's*: https://en.wikipedia.org/wiki/Liebeck_v._McDonald%27s_Restaurants.

⡪ For more information on coffee serving temperatures and coffee serving operations: https://www.coffeeenterprises.com/2014/07/thoughts-on-coffee-drive-thrus-and-safety-for-handling-hot-coffee/.

⡪ For materials from the National Coffee Association: http://www.ncausa.org/.

⡪ For a consumer study of preferred coffee drinking temperatures: https://www.researchgate.net/publication/230106152_At_What_Temperatures_Do_Consumers_Like_to_Drink_Coffee_Mixing_Methods.

Three Pillars Decision: TripAdvising in Jamaica

⡪ For information about Section 230 of the Communications Decency Act: https://en.wikipedia.org/wiki/Section_230_of_the_Communications_Decency_Act.

⡪ For the actual text of the law: https://www.law.cornell.edu/uscode/text/47/230.

Chapter 3. Ethics: Icing on the Strategy-Law Pillar Cake

Three Pillars Decision: All Hands on Deck

⡪ For the text of H.R.3142—Cruise Passenger Protection Act at Congress.gov: https://www.congress.gov/bill/114th-congress/house-bill/3142.

⡪ For text of proposed amendments to H.R.3142: https://www.congress.gov/111/plaws/publ207/PLAW-111publ207.pdf.

⡪ For information on passenger safety from the US Department of Transportation: https://www.transportation.gov/mission/safety/passenger-cruise-ship-information.

⡪ For information from Carnival Cruise lines' website on the Cruise Passenger Protection Act: https://help.carnival.com/app/answers/detail/a_id/1186/~/cruise-vessel-security-and-safety-act-of-2010.

Three Pillars Decision: Redefining "Haute" Cuisine

    ❧ An article from *Missouri Medicine* on "Hemp & Cannabidiol: What is a Medicine?": https://www.ncbi.nlm.nih.gov/pmc/articles/PMC6140266/.

    ❧ Information from the Colorado Department of Public Health & Environment: https://www.colorado.gov/pacific/cdphe/cottage-foods-ingredients.

    ❧ Additional information from the Colorado Department of Public Health & Environment: https://www.colorado.gov/pacific/cdphe/industrial-hemp-food.

    ❧ A *USA Today* article about restaurants adding cannabis extracts to menus: https://www.usatoday.com/story/news/2019/01/10/chefs-cannabis-food-drinks-2019-s-hottest-dining-trend/2520890002/.

    ❧ A California Department of Public Health primer on Industrial hemp and CBD in food products: https://hempsupporter.com/wp-content/uploads/2018/07/Web-template-for-FSS-Rounded-Final.pdf.

    ❧ An article about banning CBD in food and drink: https://cannabidiolcbd.org/another-state-bans-cbd-in-food-and-drinks-citing-fda-stance-the-takeout/.

    ❧ Maine legislation related to hemp-derived food additives and food products: http://www.mainelegislature.org/legis/bills/bills_129th/billtexts/HP045901.asp.

    ❧ Additional Maine legislation on the hemp issue: http://www.mainelegislature.org/legis/bills/getPDF.asp?paper=HP0459&item=2&snum=129.

    ❧ Guidance from the FDA on cannabis in food: https://www.fda.gov/news-events/public-health-focus/fda-regulation-cannabis-and-cannabis-derived-products-including-cannabidiol-cbd.

Three Pillars Decision: Droning for Drugs

    ❧ Information about the FAA rules on commercial drone use: https://www.dartdrones.com/faa-drone-regulations-commercial-drone-use/.

    ❧ More information on drone use from the Federal Aviation Administration: https://www.faa.gov/uas/.

❧ For a guide from the National Conference of State Legislatures on drone operations by state: http://www.ncsl.org/research/transportation/current-unmanned-aircraft-state-law-landscape.aspx.

❧ An article on drone delivery methods: https://www.dronezon.com/drones-for-good/drone-parcel-pizza-delivery-service/.

❧ A Wikipedia entry on drone use: https://en.wikipedia.org/wiki/Delivery_Drone#Drug_smuggling.

Three Pillars Decision: Lighter than Air

❧ For the Virginia law on wide-scale balloon releases: https://law.lis.virginia.gov/vacode/title29.1/chapter5/section29.1-556.1/.

❧ For information on other state laws related to balloon releases: http://www.longwood.edu/cleanva/balloonlaws.htm.

❧ Information about considerations for placing a ban on large scale balloon releases: https://patch.com/new-york/easthampton/intentional-balloon-release-ban-weighed-lawmakers.

❧ Information about a ban for balloon releases in North Carolina: https://www.change.org/p/north-carolina-state-senate-ban-mass-balloon-releases.

❧ An article that discusses alternatives to balloon releases: http://balloonsblow.org/environmentally-friendly-alternatives/.

Three Pillars Decision: Flying the Friendly Skies

❧ Site with information on the US Department of Transportation's consumer rights: https://www.transportation.gov/airconsumer/fly-rights.

❧ Video of United passenger who was removed from an overbooked flight: https://www.bing.com/videos/search?q=video+of+dr.+david+dao+taken+off+plane&&view=detail&mid=93F98E1BA30929658A6793F98E1BA30929658A67&&FORM=VRDGAR.

❧ A site with information about overbooking issues: https://www.bustle.com/p/if-your-flight-is-overbooked-here-are-your-rights-as-a-passenger-18808992.

❧ Information about why airlines overbook flights: https://www.cnbc.com/2017/04/11/three-charts-that-show-why-airlines-overbook-flights.html.

Chapter 4. Transform Product Liability into Product Innovation

Three Pillars Decision: Pulling Some Strings

    ໝ Information on the use of drawstrings in children's' clothing from the US Consumer Product Safety Commission: https://www.cpsc.gov/Business--Manufacturing/Business-Education/Business-Guidance/Drawstrings-in-Childrens-Upper-Outerwear/.

    ໝ Access to the US Consumer Safety Commission's "Regulatory Robot" where you can determine what safety regulations apply to your product: https://www.cpsc.gov/Business--Manufacturing/Regulatory-Robot/Safer-Products-Start-Here/.

Three Pillars Decision: Lunch at the Laundromat

    ໝ Article about a Tide POD lawsuit: https://www.bizjournals.com/cincinnati/news/2018/03/16/p-g-challenge-to-tide-pods-lawsuit-rejected.html.

    ໝ Journal article about chemical burns from laundry pods: https://www.ncbi.nlm.nih.gov/pmc/articles/PMC4141917/.

    ໝ Additional information about Tide POD lawsuits: http://www.consumerjusticefoundation.com/products/tide-laundry-pod-suit/.

    ໝ For the American Association of Poison Control Centers website: http://www.aapcc.org/press/83/.

    ໝ For the U.S. Consumer Product Safety Commission website: https://cpsc.gov/s3fs-public/390%20Laundry%20Packets.pdf.

    ໝ Additional information about Tide POD lawsuits: https://www.truthinadvertising.org/wp-content/uploads/2015/07/Guargilia-v-Procter-Gamble-complaint.pdf.

    ໝ Journal article about pediatric exposure to laundry pods: https://www.ncbi.nlm.nih.gov/pubmed/25384489.

Three Pillars Decision: Golfing with Gizmo

    ໝ *Hauter v. Zogarts*, 534 P. 2d 377 (1975) at https://scocal.stanford.edu/opinion/hauter-v-zogarts-27822.

    ໝ Photograph of the Gizmo Golf operator's manual: https://lawprofessors.typepad.com/tortsprof/files/Gizmo0001.PDF.

Chapter 5. Use Employment Law to Attract and Retain the Best Business Talent

Three Pillars Decision: Frozen in 9-to-5 Time

    ⁖ Journal article about oocyte cryopreservation: https://repository.uchastings.edu/cgi/viewcontent.cgi?article=1379&context=hwlj.

    ⁖ A report from the Ethics Committee of the American Society for Reproductive Medicine: https://www.asrm.org/globalassets/asrm/asrm-content/news-and-publications/ethics-committee-opinions/planned_oocyte_cryopreservation_for_women_seeking_to_preserve-pdfmembers.pdf.

    ⁖ Guidance on oocyte cryopreservation from the American College of Obstetricians and Gynecologists: https://www.acog.org/Clinical-Guidance-and-Publications/CommitteeOpinions/Committee-on-Gynecologic-Practice/Oocyte-Cryopreservation.

    ⁖ More on the issue from Wikipedia: https://en.wikipedia.org/wiki/Oocyte_cryopreservation.

Three Pillars Decision: Good Samaritan—"You're Fired!"

    ⁖ A listing of good Samaritan laws by state at: https://recreation-law.com/2014/05/28/good-samaritan-laws-by-state/.

    ⁖ An article on the origin of good Samaritan laws: https://www.ncbi.nlm.nih.gov/books/NBK542176/.

    ⁖ Wikipedia entry on good Samaritan laws: https://en.wikipedia.org/wiki/Good_Samaritan_law#cite_note-25.

Three Pillars Decision: Controlling the Demon

    ⁖Illinois General Assembly law on artificial intelligence in hiring: http://www.ilga.gov/legislation/publicacts/fulltext.asp?Name=101-0260.

    ⁖ Article on ways that AI is being used in employment situations: https://www.cio.com/article/3219857/how-ai-is-revolutionizing-recruiting-and-hiring.html.

Three Pillars Decision: Hopping Around the Issue

    ⁖ US Equal Employment Opportunity Commission Guidelines on workplace harassment: https://www.eeoc.gov/eeoc/newsroom/wysk/harassed_at_work.cfm.

℞ Findlaw's guide on sexual harassment: https://employment.findlaw.com/ employment-discrimination/sexual-harassment-at-work.html.

Chapter 6. Use Government Regulation to Develop New Business Models

Three Pillars Decision: Muzzle on the Mills

℞ For Maryland legislation related to the sale of pets by retails establishments: http://mgaleg.maryland.gov/2018RS/bills/hb/hb1662f. pdf.

℞ For California legislation related to the sale of pets by retails establishments: https://leginfo.legislature.ca.gov/faces/billNavClient. xhtml?bill_id=201720180AB485.

Three Pillars Decision: In Pursuit of Food Justice

℞ Journal article on the impact of the toy ordinance on restaurants: https:// www.ncbi.nlm.nih.gov/pmc/articles/PMC4110247/.

℞ Notice/ordinance from the San Francisco Department of Public Health: https://www.sfdph.org/dph/hc/HCCommPublHlth/Agendas/ CPHC092110/healthy%20meal%20ordinance.pdf.

Three Pillars Decision: Climbing Conundrum

℞ Information on climbing rules at: https://www.tripnepal.com/nepal/ expedition-in-nepal/equipments-and-mountaineering-rules-regulations.

℞ Additional information on climbing rules: https://adventureblog.net/ 2019/02/more-details-on-chinas-new-climbing-rules-for-everest.html.

Three Pillars Decision: Don't Tread on My Hemp

℞ For a guide from the National Conference of State Legislatures on state hemp laws: http://www.ncsl.org/research/agriculture-and-rural-development/state-industrial-hemp-statutes.aspx.

℞ Virginia law on growing hemp: https://law.lis.virginia.gov/vacode/title3. 2/chapter41.1/section3.2-4112/.

℞ Massachusetts law on growing hemp: https://malegislature.gov/Laws/ GeneralLaws/PartI/TitleXIX/Chapter128/Section116.

℞ Connecticut law on growing hemp: https://www.lawserver.com/law/ state/connecticut/ct-laws/connecticut_statutes_21a-240.

℞ More on Connecticut law on growing hemp: https://www.cga.ct.gov/ 2019/ACT/pa/pdf/2019PA-00003-R00SB-00893-PA.pdf.

Three Pillars Decision: Home Turf Brewing

 ∞ Information from the New York State Brewer's Association: https://newyorkcraftbeer.com/about/legislation/.

 ∞ Information about what is required to sell alcohol on premises in New York: https://www.businessexpress.ny.gov/app/answers/cms/a_id/3737/kw/on%20premises.

Chapter 7. Use Your Intellectual Property to Create Shareholder Value

Three Pillars Decision: Secrets of Steamboat Willie

 ∞ Information about intellectual property protection: https://www.law.cornell.edu/wex/intellectual_property.

 ∞ Additional information about intellectual property protection https://www.upcounsel.com/intellectual-property-law.

Three Pillars Decision: "Betcha Can't Eat Just One"

 ∞ Information on the Indian Protection of Plant Varieties and Farmers' Rights Act, 2001: https://en.wikipedia.org/wiki/Protection_of_Plant_Varieties_and_Farmers%27_Rights_Act,_2001.

 ∞ Additional Information on the Indian Protection of Plant Varieties and Farmers' Rights Act, 2001: http://nbaindia.org/uploaded/Biodiversityindia/Legal/30.%20PPVFR%20Act%202001.pdf.

Three Pillars Decision: FaceTime with Trolls

 ∞ Massachusetts legislation at: https://malegislature.gov/Bills/191/H229.

 ∞ More information about Massachusetts legislation at: https://www.gandb.com/2019/05/legislative-update-massachusetts-proposes-patent-troll-act/.

Three Pillars Decision: Mutiny in Cyberspace

 ∞ Information about how to protect your company's domain name by Gigalaw: https://giga.law/blog/2015/06/02/8-easy-ways-to-protect-your-domain-name.

 ∞ Information about how to protect your company's domain name by GoDaddy: https://www.godaddy.com/garage/how-to-protect-your-domain-name/.

Chapter 8. Develop Contracts That Create Value for Both Sides

Three Pillars Decision: The King of Beers

⁜ Pathclearer article on lean contracting: http://www.clarity-international.net/documents/Pathclearer%20article%20in%20PLC-3.pdf.

⁜ Contract to "lean"-up: https://contracts.onecle.com/coors/rocky-mountain.supply.2003.08.01.shtml.

⁜ Elements of a legally binding contract: https://www.upcounsel.com/5-elements-of-a-legally-binding-contract.

Three Pillars Decision: Think Food and Morality

⁜ Wikipedia entry about the morals clause in contracts: https://en.wikipedia.org/wiki/Morals_clause.

⁜ More information about the morals clause: https://definitions.uslegal.com/m/morals-clause/.

⁜ Journal article about the use of morals clauses: http://www.nmmlaw.com/pdf/FMP%20-%20Morals%20-%20Seton%20Hall%20-%20Nov.%202009.pdf.

Three Pillars Decision: Contracts in Cyberspace

⁜ Information about e-mail contracts: https://www.legalmatch.com/law-library/article/email-contracts.html.

⁜ Information about the enforceability of electronic mail contracts: https://www.forbes.com/sites/oliverherzfeld/2013/12/09/are-your-emails-enforceable-contracts/#7d206f5b4f8a.

⁜ Information about disadvantages of email contracting: https://newmedialaw.proskauer.com/2015/06/09/meeting-of-the-minds-at-the-inbox-some-pitfalls-of-contracting-via-email/.

Chapter 9. Use Dispute Resolution Processes for Value Creation

Three Pillars Decision: ADR Home Runs

⁜ Information about Construction ADR at the American Arbitration Association: https://www.adr.org/construction.

⁜ Information about using baseball arbitration in real estate disputes: http://www.lawjournalnewsletters.com/2019/05/01/risks-of-baseball-arbitration-in-resolving-real-estate-disputes/.

ℰꙩ More information about baseball ADR: https://www.americanbar.org/ groups/construction_industry/publications/under_construction/2019/ spring2019/resolving_dispute_baseball/.

Three Pillars Decision: ADR in Cyberspace

ℰꙩ International Institute for Conflict Prevention & Resolution Mediation Procedure: https://www.cpradr.org/resource center/rules/mediation/cpr-mediation-procedure.

ℰꙩ Information on Facebook ADR: https://www.pon.harvard.edu/daily/ dispute-resolution/on-facebook-dispute-resolution-goes-live/.

Three Pillars Decision: Making Twitter Waves

ℰꙩ *Crowdsourced Online Dispute Resolution* located at: https://papers.ssrn.com/ sol3/papers.cfm?abstract_id=3003815.

ℰꙩ *The Use of Legal Crowdsourcing ('Lawsourcing') as a Means to Achieve Legal, Regulatory and Policy Objectives* located at: https://papers.ssrn.com/sol3/ papers.cfm?abstract_id=2520515.

Index